The Art of Gardening
through the Ages

Tassilo Wengel

The Art of Gardening through the Ages

Edition Leipzig

Illustration on the half-title:
Wrought-iron garden gate at Grossedlitz

Translated from the German by Leonard Goldman

© 1987 Edition Leipzig
Drawings: Britta Matthies
Design: Traudl Schneehagen
Printed by Druckwerkstätten Stollberg VOB
Binding: VOB Kunst- und Verlagsbuchbinderei, Leipzig
Lic.-No.: 600/106/86
Order No.: 594 425 9

ISBN: 3-361-00050-5

Manufactured in the German Democratic Republic

Contents

A passion for chinoiseries and grottoes and a predilection
for ruins · The Würzburg palace garden ·
Veitshöchheim — a typical Rococo garden · Apollo Temple
and bath-house at Schwetzingen

Clumps and lakes · Pagodas and pavilions in Chinese style,
flower gardens · The "natural" garden in France ·
Rousseau's ideas · One more theory of garden design ·
German gardens in the age of sensibility · Famous
landscape gardeners of the time · Lenné and Sanssouci ·
The classical landscape garden at Muskau · Arkadia, Wilanow
and other imitations of the English garden · The demand
for public parks · Effect of the American example ·
Frederic Law Olmstedt · Municipal parks in Europe ·
The combination of formal and informal elements ·
Villa gardens augment the public parks

Foreword

Written documents and illustrations that have been handed down to us from past centuries, excavations of temple gardens, palaces and garden remains help us to realize that the human striving to shape our natural surroundings and to change them to satisfy our aesthetic feelings, began long before the Christian era. The first evidence of the gardener's art is to be found in the ancient world.

Right up to the present day, constantly changing forms of artistically designed gardens have appeared, in harmony with the architecture and the pictorial arts of the time, closely related to and conditioned by social, material and technical developments. Periods when wonderful gardens flourished have alternated with periods of stagnation. Whenever peace and tranquility have ruled the land, there has been a new desire to get closer to nature and there have been great advances in gardening.

All this gardening construction would not have been possible without the ideas and the creative abilities of the garden designers, working together with untold numbers from other professions and trades, who translated their ideas into practical reality and devoted themselves to the care and maintenance of the gardens.

One other fundamental difference between gardening and other arts and crafts is that the gardener hardly ever sees the completion of his work; this adds great significance to his visionary planning and the working out of his fantasies, so that he may gain the spatial experience he seeks. It is also important to have an exact knowledge of the characteristics of the plants in their seasonal rhythms — especially of the species of trees and bushes — in order to obtain the future effects desired.

The individuality of the plants was less important in formal gardens than it was in parks with lawns and wooded areas. While, in gardens laid out in a geometric pattern, the natural growth of the plants was even partly suppressed, in parks it was precisely the exploitation of the individuality of the wooded areas in the designing of the whole that was especially stressed.

The present work attempts to give an overview of the development of gardening as an art. If it still seems simple to present the evidence of earlier periods — as far as they are known — in their general outline, the abundance of material on gardens of the Renaissance and Baroque periods and on landscaped parks, compels a very careful choice.

This extensive study would not have been possible without the help of a whole number of institutions and individuals. My special thanks go to Dr. Harri Günther, Director of Gardens in the administration of "Staatliche Schlösser und Gärten" at Potsdam-Sanssouci, for his helpful guidance. I also thank Dr. Detlef Karg for his advice as well as the colleagues of the State Museums in Berlin, who were always ready to help and advise, and the Publishers.

Tassilo Wengel

Gardening
in Ancient Times

Today we stand in awe before the works of art of a period which still breathes of splendour and riches, of an epoch that the Egyptians, themselves, later described as the Golden Age. There is a great deal of evidence handed down to us which shows that, some 5,000 years ago, there was already a highly developed gardening tradition. Presumably, the long periods of security and peace, with no enemy attacks, were the main preconditions which enabled gardening to develop.

Due to the annual flooding of the Nile, gardens, with their large tree plantations, were only constructed on the edges of the valley or on heights above it. Water from the river could not find its way there by natural means; it had to be brought to these places with the help of canals, dams and drainage systems and by human labour. Even today, we still find the shaduf in use in Egypt; this is a kind of see-saw mechanism for raising water. At one end it has a heavy stone attached to it, at the other end a bucket or scoop.

The Egyptian wanted his garden to provide him with edible fruits and shade-giving trees. There were also certain religious cults which required the construction of gardens. The temple garden of Queen Hatshepsut, for example, in Deir-el-Bahri (*c.* 1480 B.C.) was created in honour of the Sun God Amon-Re.

The life of the people was circumscribed by a deep religious awareness. The "right" to create gardens was thought to stem from the grace of Amon-Re and was a concession only granted to the rich. Indeed, gardens were only attainable by the wealthy upper strata, and their size was dependent upon the social standing of the owner. The Pharaonic gardens were big and wide, if only to denote strength and power. The gardens of the governors and commanders-in-chief were, therefore, somewhat smaller, in accordance with their status.

Ground plan of an Ancient Egyptian villa with garden at Thebes. In the centre is a vine arbour.

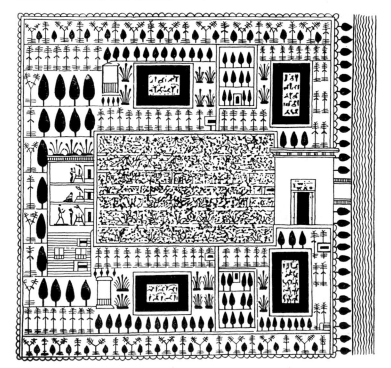

9

If we can say that, in the Old Kingdom (*c.* 2950–2450 B.C.), mainly orchards, vineyards and vegetable gardens were widespread, as also in the Middle Kingdom (2150 to 1780 B.C.), we are also able to establish that in the New Kingdom (1580–945 B.C.) there was more systematic arrangement and grouping of different plants. The earliest pictures frequently show gardeners at work, the planting of trees and the utilization of their wood, harvesting and so on.

What we learn from tomb walls of the Egyptian pyramids

We find the first description of a garden in the tomb of Methen, a viceroy of King Sneferu (*c.* 2600–2576 B.C.), the first king of the Fourth Dynasty. The story of his life is written on the tomb walls. From this we learn that he possessed a garden 200 ells wide and 200 ells long (Cowell). This garden, which included a house, had a

The holy tamarisk symbolizes the Ancient Egyptian deity Osiris. Representation of the tomb of Osiris, who at a later time was worshipped as God of the Dead.

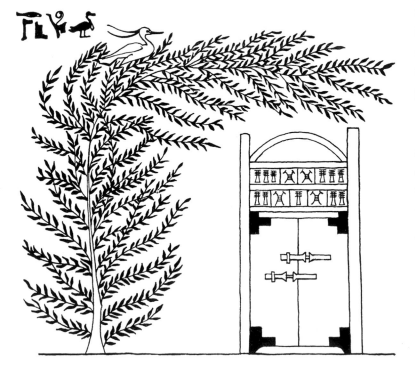

lake in its centre and was well provided with fig and other types of trees.

Cults of the dead and tomb art played a great role in the Egyptian way of life. As they believed that, after death, one would need all earthly requirements, we find tomb deposits reflecting every aspect of life.

In the tombs of several kings, flowers were provided for the after life, arranged in many different shapes. The best known tomb is that of Tutankhamen (reigned 1347 to 1338 B.C.), in which floral wreaths in remarkably good condition were found. They were composed of olive and willow leaves, lotos and cornflowers, wild celery, berries of the nightshade or bittersweet nightshade and devil's apples.

Little gardens for the dead were laid out in front of the tombs so that "the soul can lower itself onto a tree" when it emerged from the tomb. So we usually find palms or, as before the tomb of Osiris, a holy tamarisk.

Literary works and writings found in the tombs make further allusions to Egyptian gardens. And, not least in importance, we have the sand to thank for preserving foundations and pictorial records, and thus making it possible for archaeologists to reconstruct and describe these gardens. Considered as a whole, we are today in the happy position of having absolutely exact knowledge of gardening in this part of the world. It is unlikely that there have been any great changes there in methods of planting or design.

The temple gardens, already mentioned, constructed for Queen Hatshepsut in honour of the Sun God, consisted of three broad terraces with pillared halls, connected by steps with ramps. A long double line of sphinxes, which were perhaps flanked by trees on both sides, let the visitor through a mighty pylon gateway into the temple gardens. A steadily rising path was laid out from the lower to the upper terrace through gaps in the walls. It is assumed that the trees were date palm and doum palm. To plant the trees, holes were dug through the rocky lower levels of the ground and filled with fertile mud from the Nile. As these holes were connected with each other by trenches, the trees could be constantly watered.

It was in the pillared halls that the queen had her deeds immortalized. The side towards the garden is decorated with reliefs in which various plants are depicted — among them, frankincense trees.

Queen Hatshepsut's plant expedition

At the command of the God Amon-Re, who had ordered her to plant a garden of frankincense trees or, as it was written: "… to make a 'Punt' in his house …" (Gothein) she organized an expedition to the fabulous land of Punt. It is assumed that this was situated deep in southern Africa, on the coast of modern Somaliland.

It would seem that commercial interests must have played just as great a role in this expedition, for olibanum was precious and dear. It was used in religious worship, for preparing mummies and also as a medicament and, from time immemorial, was procured in the coastal area of Hadhramaut in southern Arabia.

The reliefs at Deir-el-Bahri show what they were loading onto the ships on the shores of Punt. And, the inscription adds, "… with all the lovely plants from the god's country and heaps of myrrh resin and myrrh trees, with ebony and genuine ivory, with red gold from the land of Amy, with fragrant woods, with olibanum and eye cosmetics" (Ismail).

This expedition gives us the first clear evidence, in ancient times, of an attempt to acclimatize foreign trees to their new biotope. We shall later establish that — especially in Europe — use was constantly being made of foreign plants to enrich native parks and gardens, to beautify them with new plants, sometimes with exotic effect. The beauty of flowers was as greatly appreciated in Ancient Egypt as it was in later times.

It was not only Queen Hatshepsut who fitted out expeditions to foreign countries. Thutmose III (*c.* 1490 to 1436 B.C.), joint ruler and successor to the very energetic queen, brought back from his third campaign against Palestine and Syria "all the growing plants, all the flowers that bloom in God's world" (Cowell).

In the festal temple of Karnak he had illustrations made of a whole number of plants and animals that the

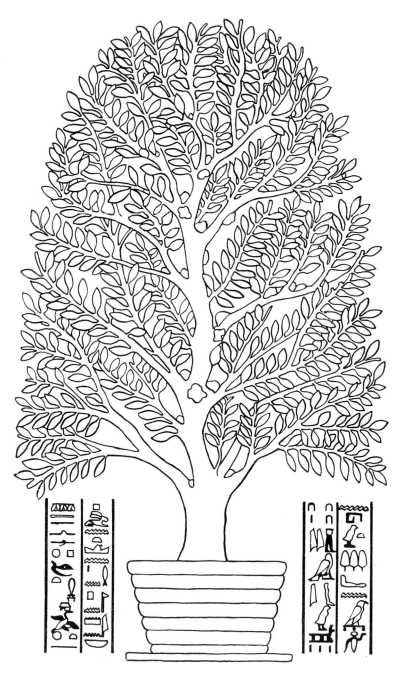

Representation of a frankincense pine in the burial temple of Queen Hatshepsut. Actually frankincense refers to the fuel product, but is also used for the resin, which should correctly be called olibanum

travellers had either brought with them or seen during their foreign travels. Some 300 years later, Pharaoh Ramesses III (*c.* 1198–1166 B.C.) repeated the difficult experiment of introducing trees and plants from the above-mentioned land of Punt, for transplanting in Egypt.

The depictions of house and garden plants which have been handed down to us cannot be taken entirely at their face value. The artists wanted to depict as many views as possible, so we get front elevation, ground plan and other aspects all crammed in close to each other. From this we can see that the positions of the individual parts are not recorded realistically.

From a painting in the Theban tomb of one of the army leaders of Amenophis III (*c.* 1405–1370 B.C.), we can recognize his garden. It is a remarkable picture and from it we can see that these gardens represent the beginnings of real gardening in Egypt and, apart from a very few deviations, may be seen as the basic pattern of the Egyptian garden.

Egyptian gardens had either a square or a rectangular lay-out, surrounded by walls of differing heights. These were made up of processed stone, clay bricks or mud, according to the wealth of the owner. The erection of such a wall afforded protection against animals but also against other members of the populace; they meant privacy and security. The entrance was through a portal whose size and appearance expressed the status of the owner; in larger gardens there were additional smaller doors.

The height of the wall is difficult to guess. One assumes that the outer protective walls were three to five metres high. As far as the size of the individual gardens is concerned, we have very few clues. The garden of a high priest of the Fourth Dynasty, for example, was said to have sides of 105 metres, i.e., to have an area of 11,025 square metres. Buildings had a central place in Egyptian gardens.

The danger of flooding in the Nile valley compelled the Egyptians to raise both the gardens and the buildings in them, so gradually rising paths led from the landing stages on the river to the living quarters and the temples. Two flights of stairs with a large ramp in the middle led from the river to the entrance building of the garden belonging to the army leader already mentioned.

Representation of the plant expedition to Punt from which, among other trees, thirty-one frankincense pines were brought back.

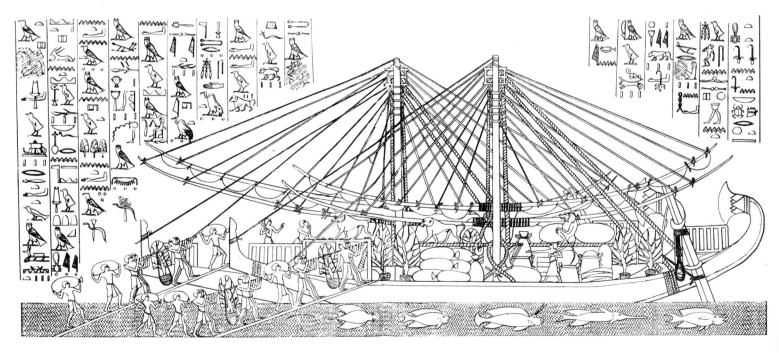

A good example has been handed down to us of a terraced garden of some considerable size, in the temple we mentioned earlier — of Queen Hatshepsut in Deir-el-Bahri. As far as we know, this is the first example in history of three broad terraces, laid out one above the other, with the hill side of each wall enhanced by pillared halls.

The paths in Egyptian gardens were always straight. A curve was unthinkable, either at the time of the Old, the Middle or the New Kingdom. If, for example, the living quarters could not be reached by a straight path from the portal, then another path would be built from it at a right angle.

There has been less enquiry into the question of what kinds of statuary were put up in Egyptian gardens. Excavations have, for example, brought to light figures of gods, lions and sphinxes. Although we may only be able to say with certainty that such works of art were put up in temples — such as those at Deir-el-Bahri or along the two-kilometre "Processional way" between the temples of Karnak and Luxor — it can be assumed that such objects were also to be found in gardens.

The pond could either be situated in the middle of the garden or else somewhere on the perimeter. There was no set place for it and larger gardens usually had several ponds. Their shape varies, too; as well as the rectangular form, we find many that were built in the form of a "T", the vertical arm of which offered the possibility of a small feeder-canal linking it with the river. We know little about the size or depth of these ponds.

Ancient Egyptian representation of the sycamore, which is widely spread in East and Northeast Africa. Its edible fruit has the appearance of a fig.

Gardens of the Pharaohs

Amenophis IV (reigned *c.* 1361–1340 B.C.), son of Amenophis III of Thebes, continued his father's method of garden construction. It seems clear that gardens and flowers held a great attraction for him. This can be seen from the way he decked out his palace. His bedroom is decorated throughout with painted flowers. Most of the little court-gardens contain ponds with beautiful flowers growing around them. Excavations have brought to light a floor of this Pharaonic palace in Tell el-Amarna, which

shows beautifully how these ponds were adorned with flower-beds, from which the pillars of the building arise like the stems of flowers.

As already noted, shade-providing trees played a role in determining the form of these gardens. The harvesting of fruit and wood was also a significant element right from the start. Trees stood around the outer wall to protect privacy or, in the area of the ponds, as a garden in themselves; they were also planted in avenues.

Date palm frequently alternated with doum palm within each row. The Egyptians also often planted fig

The doum palm is frequently depicted on reliefs of Tell el-Amarna and Deir-el-Bahri. It is native to Upper Egypt. The middle section of the seed vessel is edible and tastes like gingerbread. From time immemorial the fruit measuring about 10 cm by 2 cm has been in great demand.

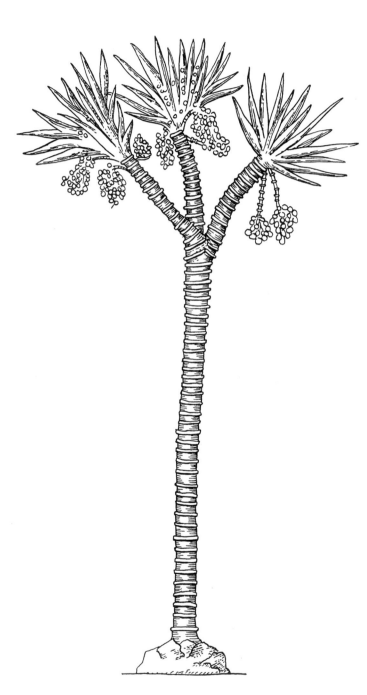

trees, black mulberry trees, sycamore, persea, acacia, tamarisk and various others.

Much evidence has come to light which clearly indicates that trees were objects of reverence for religious cults. The sycamore was the most revered; it was a tree that was among the very earliest to appear in Egyptian gardens and in ancient texts was even a generalization for tree. For life after death, too, the shade of this tree is of great significance. According to Lajard, a tomb inscription reads: "That I may issue forth every day without end to the banks of my ponds, so that my soul may rest on the branches of the tree which I have planted and that I may refresh myself in the shade of my sycamore."

The ben-nut tree was also very attractive and valuable to the Egyptians and reputedly provided the food of the gods. "Bakhu" was obtained from it; this was an oil used as perfume, as an ointment for embalming corpses and as a medicament. The nature of the fruit-tree, "ishid", is not easy to determine; on its leaves — so they said — the gods wrote down the names of the kings and their heroic deeds.

The olive tree, too, had already been known for a very long time. A painting of one of them was found in the pyramid of King "Titi" of the Sixth Dynasty. Wreaths were made of their leaves and placed round the head of the mummy. In these death-wreaths of mummies, we have found cornflowers, field poppies, mallows, saffron, thistles and roses.

Many flowers also had religious and ritual significance. The Egyptian sacred or blue-flowered lotos is the most important of them and was the symbol for Upper Egypt, while the papyrus was characteristic for Lower Egypt. Its blossom was frequently pictured on beakers and other ornamental pieces. People thought of the lotos as source and beginning. They imagined the world as a wide black sea upon whose surface the lotos suddenly appears and the Sun God Amon-Re arising from its calyx. The rhythm of its life meant that it disappeared in winter, to re-appear in all its fresh beauty in spring; for the Egyptians, this symbolized resurrection after death. The whole palace garden became transformed, at times, into a sea of white and blue-flowered lotos — the occasion for sumptuous festivals.

Many representations show a further glorification of this flower. Kings represented them to their wives as love tokens, slaves and prisoners handed lotos blossoms to their masters which were of greater significance than even ivory, jewellery, grapes or poultry. Guests, too, were greeted with flowers and the tables were adorned with them on festive occasions.

Next to flowers and trees, there were also vegetable patches, intensively cultivated. In the main, only a certain part of the garden was given over to vegetables; onions, garlic, white cabbage, beans, lettuce and cucumber were grown. Utility was the order of the day and kitchen gardens were of the simplest kind.

We read the following about garden life in Ismail: "In summer, when it got hotter, the Ancient Egyptians were not keen to leave their estates; they preferred to rest in the shade of the trees during these months, to enjoy the cool and perfume-laden air and to feast their eyes on the ponds, which were covered with water-flowers like papyrus and lotos waving in the wind, and enlivened by water-fowl and shoals of lively fish. Then they spent their time in pleasant discussion, music and song, or watched their slave-girls dancing. They couldn't have enough of the beauty of nature. The father of a family felt happy when he saw his children playing or swimming and when his wife brought him all that the heart may desire: love, food, drink and sweet-smelling flowers."

In Mesopotamia

The Bible speaks of the original home of mankind, the Garden of Eden, abundantly watered by the rivers of Paradise. We read of four rivers, two of which were called the Euphrates and the Tigris. These two rivers linked the Armenian Highlands with the Persian Gulf and were the borders of an area in the Near East known as Mesopotamia, the Land of the Two Rivers.

The people living there, the Sumerians, the Babylonians and the Assyrians, had to live in walled townships to protect themselves against predatory neighbours from

Already in 2500 B.C., the papyrus was utilized for manufacturing purposes in Egypt. For this reason it was of great economical importance.

the hills. This was how the cities of Ashur, Nineveh and Babylon arose as royal residences.

Destabilizing events like floods and wars, as well as the instability of their brick constructions, have left little of the highly developed Assyrian and Babylonian cultures to future generations. So it has transpired that, in the history of the ancient world, there is nothing to equal the high level of gardening we find in Egypt.

Only fragments have remained to us of the *Gilgamesh Epic,* a heroic saga describing the deeds and the fate of King Gilgamesh of Uruk. But, in these fragments, we can find the earliest clues to the history of gardening.

The homes of mighty conquerors lay mainly in the middle of forests. This epic speaks of one such forest stronghold in the cedar mountains of the north. According to it, King Gilgamesh sallies forth with his friend Enkidu to slay Humbaba. They search him out in his home on a high mountain, "... pause and observe the forest, look at the height of the cedars, look at where he will enter the forest with long strides. The paths are straight and well

The date palm was the dominating tree in Assyrian tree groves. As they were of great value to their owners, the felling of them by enemies was regarded as an especially vengeful act.

made. They see the cedar mountain, seat of the gods, sanctuary of the Irnini. In front of the mountain rise the cedars in all their luxuriant abundance; their shade is pure joy, where thorn-bushes, dark gorse and fragrant plants nestle under the cedars" (Jensen).

Sacral veneration of certain types of trees is also to be found here. The cedar woods were sacred and were regarded as the seat of the gods even if, in this particular case, King Gilgamesh disregarded their special status.

Vineyards

In addition to these so-called arboreta — the expression appears again when dealing with the Persians — one can assume that viticulture had already developed and that other useful plants were being cultivated. We learn this from the report of a war between Egypt and Asia around 2500 B.C. It reads: "The army returned to Egypt, safe and sound, after they had chopped down their [the enemy's; the Author] fig trees and vines" (Ungnad, Ranke and Gressmann). Later pictorial evidence confirms this assumption. A little later, about 2340 B.C., the Sumerian king Gudea just as proudly boasts of his vine groves. And allusions are also made to it in the First Babylonian Dynasty (1830–1583 B.C.).

4   Stylized representation of palms with genii and
human figures with birds' heads from the palace of
Ashurnasirpal II in Kalchu, 9th century B.C.
Staatliche Museen zu Berlin, Vorderasiatisches Museum.

5   Photograph of the excavations at Babylon showing the
"hanging gardens", one of the Seven Wonders of the World.
The lowest terrace is credited with a length of 40 metres.

6   The Assyrian king Ashurbanipal with his wife partaking
of a festive meal in a vine arbour. Relief on an
alabaster orthostat from the upper rooms of the North Palace
of Nineveh, about 660 B.C. British Museum, London.

7 This Caucasian carpet shows the pattern of a garden lay-out
of Antiquity. The garden is surrounded by patterns of trees
and flowers, and cut through by four rivers. About 1800.
Staatliche Museen zu Berlin, formerly Cassirer Collection.

8 This garden carpet displays a constantly recurring
regularity: watercourses in which fish are swimming and
whose crossing points are decorated with flowering bushes.
Staatliche Museen Preussischer Kulturbesitz Berlin (West),
Museum für Islamische Kunst.

Page 24:
9 Stylized palms on a relief from the outer façade of the
throne room in the palace of Nebuchadnezzar II.
Staatliche Museen zu Berlin, Vorderasiatisches Museum.

The period from 1200–900 B.C. is regarded as the prelude to the great empires of the Assyrians, Babylonians and Persians. In successful military campaigns, the Assyrian king Tiglath-Pileser I (reigned *c.* 1116–1090 B.C.) was able to extend the Assyrian Empire and in this way to establish it as a great power. On the upper reaches of the Tigris, in Ashur, parklands were its greatest adornment; they contained extensive hunting reserves. Tiglath-Pileser I not only collected and brought back plants from foreign territories he had conquered but he also introduced undomesticated animals.

Hanging gardens and arboreta

Textual documentation is still very scarce as is also pictorial representation. The first reliefs with landscape backgrounds that we have found were in the palaces of Sargon II (reigned 721–705 B.C.) and his son Sennacherib (704–681 B.C.).

The mighty King Sargon II dethroned Merodach-Baladan II (*c.* 721 B.C.), ruler of Babylonia, conquered his empire and founded (710 B.C.) a town above Nineveh, surrounded it with a wall and constructed a park there. The inscription repeatedly compares the beauty of the park and its grounds with the Amanus Mountains in the land of the Hittites, which lies on the furthest northeast coast of the Black Sea. Assyrian parks were of formal design and the trees were planted in rows.

There were few Assyrian kings who could avoid wars long enough to enjoy the kind of security which was also a requirement for the peaceful art of gardening. Sennacherib tells in detail of how he built a palace on gigantic terrace foundations. He also constructed a park around this palace and, like his father, compared it with the Amanus Mountains.

This description indicates the first terrace garden that one could also describe as a "hanging garden". A small relief from Kuyunjik, stemming from Sennacherib's time, sheds light on its outlook. Sennacherib was especially proud of the irrigation canals whose complex network promoted plant growth. This creator of blooming gardens reported: "To dam up the flow of water I made a

At the time of King Sennacherib, the Assyrians planted their vineyards in hilly areas because of the better climatic conditions.

pond and planted reeds in it ... At the command of the gods, the gardens with their vines, fruit, sirdu wood and spices waxed prodigiously. The cypresses, palms and all other trees grew magnificently and budded richly" (Meissner, Rost).

Excavations have uncovered remains of a festive hall with circular planting holes in several rows close to each other. From a canal, they were all connected by irrigation channels built in stone, so that the plants grew abundantly and surrounded the whole building with dense greenery. The pools between the planting holes may have been surrounded by reeds and stocked with fish.

After Babylon was able, briefly, to free itself from the Assyrian yoke (699–689 B.C.), it was again conquered and this was when the town was completely destroyed. There is evidence of a rapid rise of the Assyrian Empire between 625 and 621 B.C. In 614, the Medes destroyed the old capital, Ashur, and in 612 the Medes and Babylonians together razed Nineveh to the ground. This meant that the parks were completely obliterated. Although Ashur-uballit II was able to flee from Nineveh and to found a new Assyrian empire in Harran, Assyria was liquidated for ever when, in 610 B.C., the Medes and Persians conquered Harran.

Temple and "hanging gardens" at Kuyunjik from the time of King Sennacherib. On the right, next to the temple, is a wall planted with trees, which is supported by arches. An artery of water flows across the hill.

The Babylonian Empire, on the contrary, experienced a new golden age under Nebuchadnezzar. In Babel and other towns, numerous imposing buildings arose and gardening also got an impetus again. The outstanding example for this epoch are the "hanging gardens" of Babylon, one of the so-called Seven Wonders of the ancient world.

Nebuchadnezzar II had them constructed for his young wife from the mountains so that she would feel at home in that arid area. These gardens have been falsely attributed to the legendary Assyrian queen Semiramis. The only fragmentary references to these gardens come from the Greek writers Diodorus and Strabo who, however, never saw the gardens themselves. Nevertheless, their descriptions are quite illuminating. And thus we can today well imagine what these gardens were like.

The famous archaeologist Robert Koldewey (1855 to 1925) excavated ruins which he construed as remains of these gardens, as they corresponded to the description of them in ancient writings. A reconstruction which he produced gives us an impression. We have never been able

to discover the method of planting, the choice of flowers etc. in any of the detailed reports. Every assertion about gardening in Mesopotamia must be viewed with great caution, because very few archaeological finds enable us to draw accurate conclusions. There is no authentic picture permitting us a clear view of the art of gardening in Assyria and Babylonia, with their terraced gardens; all modern portrayals are but attempts at reconstruction.

Persian "paradises" and artistic garden-carpets

First the Medes and then the Persians were, in succession, heritors of the Babylonian Empire. In 539 B.C., the Babylonian hosts were defeated and utterly destroyed at Opis by the Persian king Cyrus II (died 529 B.C.); thus Babylonia finally lost its independence and was incor-

This is an attempt by the archaeologist Robert Koldewey to reconstruct the "hanging gardens" of Babylon. Cross-section through the eastern part of the central chamber. Artificial irrigation was essential for the growing of plants in these gardens.

porated into the area under Persian control. The gardens, which began to develop in this region, deserve more attention than has usually been accorded them; the point is that they spread out from here to other areas and later reached western Europe. There are both social and political reasons why this garden construction influenced such a wide area of the world.

Shortly after the death of King Khosrau II (reigned 590–628) of the Sassanid Dynasty, Islam, the religion of the conquerors, was established. Within a few years, the Arabs had also conquered Syria, Egypt, large sections of Asia Minor (today's Turkey), the North African coast and parts of Spain. If the political coherence of this mighty empire did not prove very durable, the Mohammedan belief remained as a binding element in those regions.

The Persian Garden is the origin of the Islamic garden, so, with the spread of Islam, the characteristics of Persian gardens were transmitted to all corners of the Islamic world. We still find evidence today of this dispersion, in the Moorish gardens of Spain, among others.

The Greek historian Xenophon (430–354 B.C.) writes in his work *Oikonomikos* about the gardens of Prince Cyrus the Younger of Great Persia (died 401 B.C.), who showed them with pride to the Greek envoy, Lysander. Mention is made of the beauty of the trees, which grew at regular intervals and in straight lines, and of the multiplicity of sweet perfumes.

When the Greeks conquered Persia, they still found wonderful parks whose size and beauty filled them with wonderment — the great park in the valley of Bagistana, for example, or the park in Chaucon. The actual living quarters, that is to say the palace, was a mere accessory swallowed up by the park; it was these grounds which alone conferred dignity and were worth looking at. We have to thank Xenophon for the knowledge of its completely geometric design.

King Darius is depicted on a rhinestone, hunting in a palm grove. From this as well as from various reports, we can deduce that these "paradise" gardens were similar to hunting reserves of the Babylonians and the Assyrians. On the other hand, the Persians also hunted in the open countryside.

This engraving by F. X. Habermann makes the symmetrical lay-out of the Persian gardens evident. Main *allée* in a magnificent garden at Ispahan.

Most valuable information about Persian gardens is given by the so-called garden-carpets. Unfortunately, no pre-17th century carpets have been unearthed. There are, however, earlier miniature paintings in which such carpets are depicted. The earliest description comes from the time of Khosrau I (reigned 531–579). This piece of craftsmanship must have been about 137 metres long and 27.5 metres wide; it was woven from precious materials and was an illustration of the king's spring garden.

A scoop-wheel for watering Persian gardens.

The symbolical quartering of the formal garden

Many examples of these garden portrayals show a constantly recurring regularity in their lay-out. In the middle of every Persian garden a reservoir was to be found from which canals or rivers proceeded in four directions. The symbolic quartering of the gardens by running water was a direct reference to Paradise, the Garden of Eden, from which, supposedly, four rivers flowed. Paths were layed out around the reservoir and between these paths there were flower-beds at regular intervals.

Also characteristic of the Islamic garden are pavilions and covered seating, which were either placed around the reservoir or most picturesquely on a small island at their centre. In a later period, they were sometimes richly ornamented.

As far as the plant life in the Persian gardens is concerned, trees were again exceptionally important both because of the shade they provided and also because the splendour of their blossoms and fruit was highly prized. Specifically to provide shade but also partly as decoration, they planted plane and poplar, also elm, ash, maple, oak, willow, cypress and pine. The many fruit trees like al-mond, cherry, apricot, peach, fig, orange and lemon, quince, pomegranate and pistachio produced wonderful blossoms and luscious fruit.

There were numerous flowering shrubs and herbaceous plants. In descriptions of journeys, in the 16th century, most frequent mention is made of roses, already in those days the queen of flowers, next to carnation, tulip, narcissus, lily, iris and jasmine. The Persian poet Sadi (1213 to 1292) paid homage to the rose even earlier, in his main work *Gulistan* (The Rose Garden).

Burial groves

For the Persians, burial groves had a great significance. The grave of Cyrus at Pasargadae was surrounded by a grove. His successors, the Achaemenidan kings, arranged for their burial in huge rock graves near their residence in Persepolis.

The first real idea of what these burial groves were like has been handed down to us by modern Persia. The graves of the two greatest Persian poets of the Middle Ages, Sadi and Hafiz, are to be found at Shiraz, surrounded by cypress, poplar and flowering shrubs.

Greek and Roman Gardens

On the outside periphery of a mountain chain, stretching from Greece through the Aegean Sea to Asia Minor, lies the Island of Crete. Its geographical position was a favourable precondition for the emergence of a high level of culture. An impressive fleet plus the remarkable craft skills of its inhabitants contributed to Crete's commercial and artistic reputation. The remarkable level of Cretan-Minoan art also gave Greek cultural development important stimuli.

In spring and autumn, the Greek countryside is submerged in a sea of flowers, and beautiful crocuses, lilies, iris, water lilies, cistus, oleander and lotos flowers captivated the visitor. There is no evidence of a garden culture in Crete. But what was uncovered at the excavation of the palace of King Minos of Knossos, by the English archaeologist Arthur Evans (1851–1941), has enabled us to make deductions about the Cretans' attitude to nature.

Flowers and trees were depicted in the fresco-decorated rooms. The wall paintings showed youths walking across meadows, picking slender-calyxed crocuses or maidens striding through fields of lilies. The frescoes in the throne room represented complete landscapes, which are taken by some authors to indicate the existence of a garden architecture. Whether there really were gardens in this climatically favourable area, must remain an open question. When Arthur Evans came across large vessels with holes at the bottom during his excavations at Knossos, he deduced that potted plants were part of the Minoan culture and that these were used to decorate the palace courtyards.

The ornamental garden, as we know it, was not to be found in Ancient Greece, either. The development of a luxuriant natural growth, because of their favourable climatic conditions, enveloped the people in a rich world of flowers, as indeed it still does today. So it was usually only wooded groves that were actually constructed for religious worship, or so-called fruit groves (i.e. orchards). In these fruit groves, in addition to fruit trees, there were also scattered vegetable patches and vineyards, so that we can assume that they were used as kitchen gardens.

Literary evidence of gardening

The richest source of written evidence is to be found in the Homeric epic the *Odyssey* (8th century B.C.). There we read of a conversation between Odysseus and his old father, Laertes, in the garden after his return from Troy.

"And his illustrious son came up to him and said: Old man, you have everything so tidy here that I can see that there is little about gardening that you do not know. There is nothing, not a green thing in the whole enclosure, not a fig, olive, vine, pear or seed-bed that does not show signs of your care." (Book XXIV)

And, in another place, Odysseus says to his father:

"Then, again, I can tell you all the trees you gave me one day in this very plot that shows your care. I was only a little boy at the time following you through the orchard, begging for one tree and then another, and as we wound our way through these very trees you told me all their names. You gave me thirteen pear trees, ten apple trees und forty fig trees, and at the same time you pointed out the fifty rows of vines that were to be mine. Each ripened at a different time, so that the bunches on them were at various stages, when the branches felt their weight as the seasons of Zeus shed down their influences from above." (Book XXIV)

Homer gives a further description of another garden that was apparently larger and in which flower-beds are also mentioned. It lies in the city of Scheria and belongs to Alcinoüs, the king of the Phaeacians (who, according to the Greek saga, were a carefree, seafaring people on the island of Scherid). Here it is remarked that the garden is the source of an inexhaustible supply of fruit, and the description makes it clear that ceaseless growth and creation are specially stressed.

"Outside the courtyard but stretching close up to the gates and with a hedge running down on either side, lies a large orchard, where trees hang their greenery on high, the pear and the pomegranate, the apple with its glossy burden, the sweet fig and the luxuriant olive. The fruit never fails nor runs short, winter and summer alike. It comes at all seasons of the year, and there is never a time when the West Wind's breath is not assisting, here the bud, and there the ripening fruit; so that pear after pear, apple after apple, cluster on cluster of grapes, and fig upon fig are always coming to perfection. In the same enclosure there is a fruitful vineyard, in one part of which there is a warm patch of level ground, where some of the grapes are drying in the sun, while others are gathered or being trodden, and on the foremost rows hang unripe bunches that have just cast their blossoms or show the first faint tinge of purple. Trim plots of various kinds of herbs are neatly laid out beyond the farthest row and make a smiling patch of never failing green. The garden is served by two springs, one led in rills to all parts of the enclosure, while its fellow opposite, after providing a watering place for the townsfolk, runs under the courtyard gate towards the great house itself. Such were the beauties with which the gods had adorned Alcinoüs' estate." (Book VII)

The fruit gardens were also watered, so that, in the long dry periods, yields would be improved. In Homer's *Iliad* a supervisor of irrigation is mentioned, who directed the waters of the springs over the planted areas and gardens, presumably by means of reservoirs in which the water remained dammed up until it was required.

The *Iliad* and the *Odyssey* speak far more often of sacred groves than of gardens. Homer describes wooded groves as places where heroes were honoured and as part of the grounds surrounding temples and altars. The altar is always in the midst of trees providing shade and a spring is also usually mentioned.

Near Alcinoüs' estate lies the grove of Athene. There, in a meadow, stands an altar shaded by poplars. The spring is also there. Charmingly described is the shrine of the nymphs on Ithaca through which Odysseus passed on his way home with the swineherd.

"Beside the rocky path which they followed down, and not far from the city, there was a public watering-

The crocus was the favourite decorative motif used on ceramic vessels and also on clothing.

place, where a clear spring ran into a *bassin* of stone that Ithacus, Neritus and Polyctor had made for the townsfolk. A grove of poplars, flourishing on the moisture, encircled the spot. The cool stream came tumbling down from the rock overhead, and an altar had been erected up above to the nymphs, where all travellers paid their dues." (Book XVII)

This grove consists not only of the natural landscape but has also been partly created by the hand of man, as "made for the townsfolk" makes clear, while in other places we find descriptions of nymphaea in whose construction man had played no part. In Book V of the *Odyssey,* Odysseus is held prisoner on Ogygia, the island of the nymph Calypso. Her cavern lies in the middle of a copse of poplars, willows, alders and cypresses. Mention is made of a garden vine that "ran riot with great bunches of ripe grapes" and trailed round the mouth of the cavern. Also mentioned are four springs "with four crystal rivulets, trained to run this way and that". Irrespective of whether these grounds were artificial or natural, it can be assumed that here is the first description of a nymphaeum which are also significant for the art of gardening in ancient times.

Holy groves, nymphaea and gymnasia

In the sacred groves in which, in Homer's time, the sole building was an altar, temples of various sizes served as places of worship. In Delphi, the Greeks put up a laurel grove dedicated to the God Apollo. They also built a shrine in Delphi to Dionysus, the God of Wine. Just as in Mycenaean times, portrayals of sacred groves are to be found on Greek vases of the 5th and 6th centuries B.C. This motif also appears even more frequently and in greater detail still on reliefs of the Hellenistic age.

In later times games and competitions took place in the groves. With the increasing significance of these games, in Greece more durable training establishments were created: the gymnasia. It was especially during the reign of Cimon (died 449 B.C.) that the gymnasium became a much admired installation. The centre was made up of a spacious court surrounded by pillared halls, exercise halls and baths.

It was only later when, after the Peloponnesian War (431–404 B.C.), general conscription gave way to a professional army, that physical training for war service lost its importance. It was now that the gymnasium mainly came to serve the needs of high-school education; even philosophers gave lectures there.

In Athens, all four large gymnasia lay outside the city and were richly enhanced by tree plantations. At the time of Plato (427–347 B.C.), they were so much a part of the park grounds that the philosopher insisted that gymnasia should only be set up "in areas richly endowed with water und favoured by nature". The Roman Vitruvius described with detailed clarity the kind of gymnasium he envisaged; he called it a palaestra. "In palaestras, square or rectangular pillared halls must be laid out so that the length right round them is two stadia [*c.* 380 metres; the Author]. This is what the Greeks call diaulos. Of these pillared halls, three should be simple but the fourth, which should face towards the south, should be a double one so that when there are rain storms, the rain cannot penetrate inside. In the three pillared halls, however, ample exedra [semi-circular niches; the Author] with seats should be erected ..."

Excavations have revealed gymnasia of various periods and of varying design and size. The gymnasium at Pergamon, capital of King Attalus' kingdom from 283 to 133 B.C., is certainly one of the most imposing in the ancient world because of its enormous size. The ground rises majestically in three mighty terraces, each with an elevation of about 15 metres. The earth is held up by gigantic wall supports that were apparently embellished with statues. The middle terrace seems to have been especially suitable for accommodating larger gardens. On the top one there was a mighty peristyle whose inner area seems to have been decked out like a garden; on nearly every pillar there was a sacred statue. The whole place was surrounded by extensive tree plantations.

In Corinth the old gymnasium was situated close to the theatre; around a spring, pillared halls and seats were arranged, the whole being framed in a setting of trees and plants.

Page 33:
10 The circular Temple of Sibyl in Tivoli was often copied
by garden designers and painters.

11 The Egyptian Goddess of Fertility, Isis, had many
followers in the Roman Empire. In Pompeii,
too, there is a temple to Isis with palms. This painting from
Herculaneum represents a cult scene. Museo nazionale, Naples.

12 One of the oldest and most beautiful examples
of architectural garden design
at Pompeii is the Casa del Fauno.

13 The sea lily is native to the Mediterranean area
and was widespread throughout Crete.

14 View of the inner courtyard, enclosed by a peristyle,
of the Casa dei Vettii at Pompeii.

15 The villa of Telesforus in Herculaneum.

16 The Farnesian gardens in Rome were laid-out in terraces
on the orders of Pope Paul III. The gardens which already
existed on the Palatine were re-designed by Barozzi da Vignola.

17 Reconstruction of the Laurentium near Rome.
Ashmolean Museum, Oxford.

18 Temple to Apollo. Corinth, 6th century B.C.

19/20 Wall paintings in Roman villas depicted
garden landscapes. Fresco in the Villa Livia near Primaporta,
about 30 B.C., section. Museo delle Terme, Rome.

21 Casa detta del Torello di Bronze – house of the bronze bull – in Pompeii. It links a three-sided portico with a nymphaeum.

22 Casa di Loreio Tibortino, Pompeii. View of the garden.

Page 44:
23 Representation of the olive harvest on an amphora from Toscanella, about 510 B.C. Staatliche Museen zu Berlin, Antikensammlung.

Greek philosophers' gardens

Very soon the well-bred were not satisfied with public gymnasia. They erected gymnasia and baths of their own. Foremost among these were the philosophers, who justified this practice by asserting that public places were too noisy for their gatherings and too exposed to the press of the multitude. Philosophers' gardens appeared.

Especially worthy of mention is the garden of Theophrastus (372–287 B.C.). He speaks a lot about his garden in his last will but does not describe it. However, his botanical writings, most importantly *The History of the Plant World*, in 10 volumes, are most detailed. He writes very extensively about the olive, whose cultivation — as evidenced by pre-historic finds on the island of Thera — dates right back to the Stone Age.

Vines play an important role in Theophrastus' garden. Just as in Egypt and Assyria, these plants have been of great significance in Greece from time immemorial. Already in Theophrastus' time, there were various cultivated sorts. There are, he writes, "as many cultivated sorts as there are soils". This shows that he obviously knew the requirements of vines from long observation.

He also described the fig, a fruit that originated in the Mediterranean area. He gives a very exact description of the cultivation of myrtle, and mentions fruit trees like apple, pear, plum and cherry (Capelle), all of which are still widely spread in central Europe.

With the exception of the philosophers' gardens, there were no gardens to private houses in the cities. The democratic principles underlying Greek government precluded any such luxurious houses with gardens or grounds. The first description by the Greek historian Xenophon (*c.* 430 to 354 B.C.) of the Persian parks that he called "paradises", aroused interest in the idea of enhancing with flowers what had, until then, been simply utilitarian gardens without aesthetic characteristics.

Elegant parks and gardens

Oriental influences were strengthened in the times of Alexander the Great (356–323 B.C.). Tamarisks, oleander bushes, roses, violets and hyacinths appeared in the

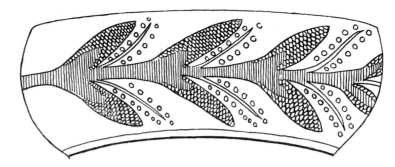

The olive tree is frequently portrayed in Cretan art, either as a tree or a twig, on beakers, vases and frescoes.

gardens and parks. People no longer contented themselves with carrying wreathes of flowers at festivals and celebrations; there was downright wastefulness. Alexander founded many new towns and had green areas laid out in them. It is said that public and royal parks in Alexandria covered a quarter of the whole space of the city. The museum garden — mainly the haunt of learned men —, the great gymnasium and the grove of Dicasterion were all connected with one another and so formed a regular green belt around the city. And the panorama of Alexandria could be admired from the Paneion, an artificial hill with ascending spiral paths.

Antioch — capital of the Seleucid Empire — was even more famous than Alexandria for its beautiful gardens. While one side of the city's main street was made up of houses, the gardens on the other stretched right up to the foot of the mountains. There were garden houses, baths and fountains there. The gardens also stretched out in the direction of the river Orontes. The path to the famous Daphne pleasure gardens, which lay only a few kilometres away from Antioch, wound through vineyards and rose-beds. This shady park contained a large number of springs.

Villa gardens in the Roman Empire

If so far we had to confine ourselves, in the main, to assumptions and the evidence from excavations (with the exception of a few written documents), when dealing with Minoan-Mycenaean culture and the Hellenistic era, when we come to investigate gardening in Roman times we are, so to speak, on firmer soil. From the works of numerous Roman writers we not only have fairly exact information about the existence and composition of Roman gardens but also descriptions that go right into the smallest details.

The wealth that flowed from the Roman provinces into the capital made it possible for the upper strata to enjoy greater luxury. The Roman commander Lucullus (*c.* 117 to *c.* 57 B.C.) may serve as a typical example of an extravagant life-style in wonderful villas with gardens. We know of the huge grounds that surrounded his palace which was situated above the present Spanish Steps in Rome. Lucullus was also known as a gourmet and we have to thank him for the introduction of the sweet cherry into Europe.

Drawing of the Borghesian vase from the garden of Sallust. It is of white marble.

The Greek philosopher Cicero (106–43 B.C.), who lived in Rome, gave detailed accounts in his writings of the way of life in those days and of the changes which were brought about under Greek influence. While, in his grandfather's day, the family villa at Arpinum was a small house in the "style of our forefathers" (Gothein), thanks to his father's interest in developing the building it was turned into a comfortable, bright house.

Cicero revealed that in the Roman villa garden, which had completely divorced itself from the kitchen garden of the rustic villa, we are dealing with the Roman adaptation of Greek-style gymnasium grounds. The villas consisted of living accommodation, with many wings, and an entrance hall that had a rectangular opening in its roof and a basin *(impluvium)* to catch the rain-water. Beyond that lay an open, rectangular courtyard, surrounded by pillars — the peristyle. There was a pillared hall along the front of the building, known as the porticus.

In country areas, the whole complex was always surrounded by tree plantations. At first the Greek philosophers had, to a great extent, taken over the form of the gymnasium grounds in their private gardens. Cicero's circle of Roman philosophers simply followed this fashion. We also learn something about the way these gardens were decorated. Statues were set up, following the Greek model, and Cicero writes, enthralled, after receiving a bust of Athene, that it was so effectively placed that the whole gymnasium seemed only to exist to show it off.

Nymphaea, too, frequently mentioned in Hellenistic gardens, were not lacking in Roman villa gardens. The Amaltheion, which Cicero had copied from a model, was also a nymphaeum. Presumably it was a grotto with springs trickling through it. The inside of such grottoes was covered with pumice-stone, tufa or mussel-shells; the ground around the pool was covered in moss.

One result of the long period of peace and prosperity — Italy was not attacked by enemies for four hundred years — was that the Romans gave increasing encouragement to the construction of gardens. Not only in Rome, but also in other Italian cities and in the Roman provinces on the Rhine and Moselle, in southern France, Spain and northern Africa, traces of the gardens of those days are still to be found. One way of informing oneself about their type, spread and architecture in the Roman Empire, is to visit the two little country towns of Pompeii and Herculaneum, south of Rome.

The mighty eruption of Vesuvius in A.D. 79, which buried both little towns in lava and ashes, means that some of the villas were preserved for posterity. Carefully excavated, they now enable us to take a peep into the time just after the beginning of the Christian era. The lay-out of houses and gardens have come to light along with statues, water *bassins,* frescoes etc., giving an insight into the gardens and the way of life of the people of those days.

One of the most beautiful and, at the same time, oldest examples in Pompeii is the garden of the Casa del Fauno. This house has two peristyles. Apart from the pillared hall which surrounds the whole, a further architectural ornament is the decorative late-Hellenistic fountain in the middle of the front garden. The peristyle in the house of the Vettii gives us the picture of a house garden in ancient times, around the middle of the first century A.D.

"The open space has eighteen white pillars, standing all round it, with colourful capitals and only measures 18 by 10 metres. Twelve statuettes placed around the verge gush water into eight *bassins;* there are two fountains with another two *bassins* attached in the middle of the garden. Marble tables and bowls and small pillars, supporting busts, complete the plastic decoration" (Gothein).

Pictures of gardens as wall decoration

Mural painting was widely in evidence. Landscape paintings decorated the walls as views, seen through painted portrayals of architecture, or as the background to smaller gardens, to make the room seem larger. But the owners were not even satisfied with that; the walls themselves were to appear as gardens.

The most beautiful garden room was in the Villa Livia, at Primaporta in Rome. All four windowless walls are painted as blooming green gardens. First, there is an openwork wooden fence, that divides a broad green path from the room. On the other side of the path the garden is en-

hanced by another fence, more splendid and variegated, in three different designs. There are niches at regular intervals; in each of these stands a tree — some deciduous, some conifers; acanthus grows round the trunk or, in a few cases, ivy winds its way upwards round the trunk.

Gazing across the borders of this picturesque little place, we can see a mass of trees in the neighbouring garden; first, there are fairly regularly planted trees and bushes, lemons with blossoms and fruit and, between them a gorgeous flower-bed in glowing colours can be seen above the fence. Further back are palms and cypresses amongst other deciduous trees. This wall picture and many others enable us to make assumptions about the kind of plants which grew in the gardens in those far off days, and how they were utilized.

Popular plants and regular tree-clipping

Far larger and more impressive than the small gardens of Pompeii were the mansions and country houses of Roman citizens which lay well away from the imperial city. We get descriptions of these from Pliny the Younger (*c.* A.D. 61–114) and from his uncle, Pliny the Elder (A.D. 23 to 79), whose famous book *Naturalis Historia* combined traditional teachings with his own experiences of trees, flowers, plants and fruits together with information on their use. Regular tree-clipping played an important role, too. With this type of clipping, known as topiary *(opus topiarius),* the art of gardening achieved further prominence in later epochs.

Pliny the Elder had a considerable quantity of plants, himself, arranged scientifically. Of greatest interest is the yellow onion, which he — like Homer before him — prized greatly. Also of note were the primrose and the peony. He also grew medicinal and food-flavouring herbs as well as vegetables.

Pliny the Younger, in about A.D. 100, distinguished clearly between the beauty of nature and the art (or artificiality) of gardening. In the description of both his villas, which he gave in two letters, all the details are brought together to give one vivid picture.

One of these villas lies in Tuscany and so he calls it Villa Tusci or Tusculum. It was built "in a gigantic amphitheatre, which only nature can create". A whole number of water courses fed the fountains and waterworks. In the middle of "a small courtyard, shaded by four plane trees", fountains bubbled; "a fountain plays in a marble *bassin* and sprinkles the plane trees around it and the earth beneath them with a fine rain of spray".

And Pliny the Younger tells us, likewise, of a garden shaped like a *hippodromus*. "At its head, a circular seat of white marble is shaded by a vine which is supported by four caryatids ... opposite, a fountain spouts water and gathers it up again as, shot upwards, the stream returns

once more to its source and is sucked up through adjacent openings and tossed skywards. Directly opposite the circular seat, a little summer-house reflects back to the seat the charming picture that it received from it.

Its marble shimmers; its French windows open outwards and lead us forward into the verdure; ... a luxuriant grape-vine reaches over the whole building and climbs to the very top. ... A natural spring rises by a little house and is immediately lost again under the earth.

In several places, there are marble seats which gladden the hearts of those tired by walking, just as the little house itself does. Beside the seats are little fountains; everywhere, little streamlets splash across the riding-ground, directed there in little pipes, and follow wherever the hand may lead them; it is these little brooklets that

Ground-plan of the Tusculum.

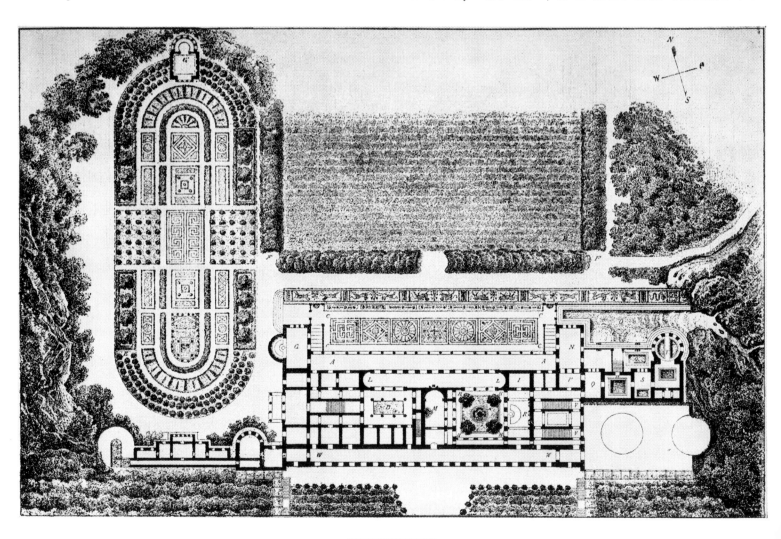

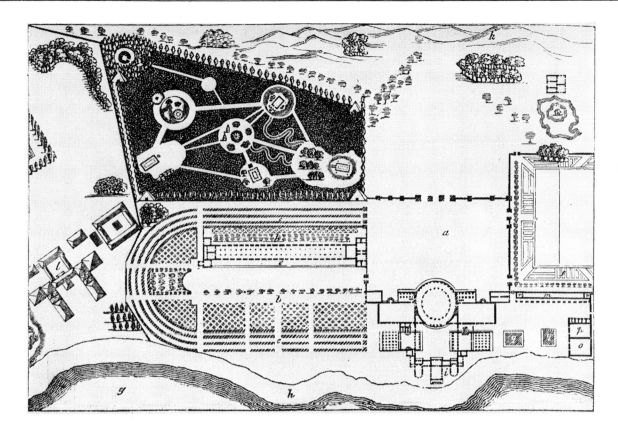

Plan of the Laurentium: a) *atrium* or seat of honour; b) *hortus* or pleasure garden; c) *gestatio* or riding ground; d) *vinea* or vineyard; e) *xystus* or terrace; f) *hortus pinguis rusticus* or kitchen garden and orchard; g) *mare*, the sea; h) *littus*, the beach; i)*gymnasium* or exercise ground; k) *sylvae et montes*, distant woods and hills; l) *villa vicina*, neighbouring villa; m) *equilia*, horse stables; n) *texta vehiculis*, carriage house; o) *lignarium*, woodyard; p) *foenile*, place for storing hay; q) *piscina dux*, two fish ponds; r) *cellae cervorum*, cattle pen.

sprinkle the lawn — now here, now there — until the whole area is watered" (Thacker).

The art of topiary, as mentioned by Pliny the Elder, was also practised by Pliny the Younger. He writes, for example, of a stunted plane that "was produced by a special method of planting and clipping". There are even clipped groves *(nemora tonsilia)*, at the Villa Tusci.

If we observe the front of this typical Roman villa, we see a broad portico with two protruding wings; in one there is the living room and in the other the dining room. In the middle of the portico, the courtyard extends to the rear through a double row of pillars outside the building. There are three apartments, of which one is described as a particularly attractive garden room. The ornamental garden *(xystus)* extends in front of the triple façade. Attached to the western end of the portico are the bathing facilities from whence steps lead to a higher terrace with three small pavilions, used as living quarters.

The second villa, the Laurentium, is clearly different from the first one. It lies by the sea, in the vicinity of Rome and has neither a large park nor a richly ornamental garden.

There is a garden terrace and a portico situated on the seaward side. Box-tree borders are to be found only in a few places like, for instance, at the entrance or along the paths of the orchard. Where box was too greatly exposed to the saline spray of the sea-water, they were replaced by rosemary. The orchard mainly comprises fig and mulberry trees.

In his letters, Pliny praises most highly the charming surroundings and the healthy climate. "A covered walk extends outwards from this building complex ... In front of this walk is a terrace pervaded by the perfume of violets. The walk reflects and so increases the warmth of the sunbeams that fall on it, and just as it catches the sun so it restricts and drives out ... the north wind; it is as fresh at the back as it is warm in the front. In the same way, it sets up a barrier in the south-west, and breaks and abates the winds from opposing directions ..." (Thacker).

Byzantium takes over elements of the Roman garden

The fall of the Roman Empire also brought with it the end of a glorious artistic epoch. The unrest at the time of the Great Migration, protracted neglect, plundering and conflagrations led to the decay of the splendid Roman palaces and gardens. Only in a few places the advanced culture of the Romans still held out into the 6th century. In Italy, southern France and Spain, a few elements of ancient culture could still, falteringly, endure. Byzantium, too, maintained the tradition of villa and garden, for a while yet.

When Emperor Constantine (*c.* A.D. 280–337) announced in 326 that Byzantium was to be the new capital and named it Constantinople, it was a small, flowering city on the European threshold of Asia. In ancient times, already, Byzantium had been a holy city, with temples and other places of worship.

Next to the temple of the god Poseidon stadiums and gymnasiums were erected and running tracks were laidout; in a word, the picture was one of Greek-Hellenistic domination. It was here that Emperor Constantine, in the year 330, laid the foundation stone for an imperial palace which, in the subsequent eight hundred years, developed mighty dimensions by several additional buildings. Hardly anything is known of gardens, however.

A later palace, built in the first half of the 9th century by Emperor Theophilus (829–842) in its basic outlines is reminiscent of Hadrian's villa at Tivoli. As we can tell from its name, "Trikonchos", we are here dealing with a hall, tri-conchoid in shape, containing three great niches decorated with mussel-shells. The courtyard was a peristyle with a fountain at its centre crowned by a golden pine cone. The emperor had five gardens constructed around the palace.

Emperor Basil I created the most memorable garden. On the east side of the palace, porticoes surrounded a square on two sides which was planted with trees and flowers and irrigated by running water. In Byzantine gardens oriental influences are most in evidence in the artistic construction of fountains which were mainly made of precious stones and brightly-coloured marble and whose water spouts were often fashioned in the shape of pine cones.

The Mediaeval Garden

With the fall of the Western Roman Empire in the year 476, the development of gardening suffered a reverse, even though there was not a complete break with the cultural past of Rome. In the Eastern Roman Empire, Roman culture was maintained until the Turkish conquest in 1453. In North Africa the destructive Vandals succeeded the Moors with their cultural traditions.

The conquering Ostrogoths established their kingdom in Italy in 493 and occupied the Roman palaces and villas. Theodoric the Great (died 526) had the old Roman gardens at Ravenna reconstructed magnificently and Totila, nephew of Witigis and king of the Ostrogoths (fell in 552), lived in Hadrian's villa at Tivoli.

These are, however, only individual examples. Centuries were to elapse before the art of gardening experienced a new upswing in Europe.

Murmuring fountains in Moorish gardens

Here we must see Spain as an exception. As the Arabs spread out in the Mediterranean area in the 7th century, the architectural traditions they brought with them — stamped with Islamic and oriental influences — introduced a breath of the old Persian garden culture with its fountain traditions. Together with the Moors from North Africa, the Arabs ruled parts of Spain for nearly eight hundred years. During this period, they created artistic garden establishments which still remain living proof of a high and original culture, to this very day.

In a short time, Córdova achieved an unparallelled flowering. The founder of the Umayyad Emirate in Córdova, Abd-ar Rahman I (731–788), decorated his residence in Córdova in oriental style in 756. He built a villa which was a copy of a similar one in Damascus and introduced Syrian plants into his garden, above all palms, which were not to be found there before in such quantities. The following poem expresses his love of these trees — but also his longing:

> "You, o palm, are a stranger
> Just like me, in this land;
> Are a stranger here in the West,
> Far from your homeland shores." (Gothein)

A comparatively long period of peace allowed Córdova and the whole of southern Spain to blossom. Its glory was only to be compared with that of Baghdad, at that time at the height of its fame. Persian influence in garden planning as well as in their furnishing with fountains, coloured glazed tiles and summer houses was evidence of a garden construction which was also typical of the old Persian "paradise" gardens.

That the gardens were terraced was especially conducive to the abundant use of water — just as necessary to the people of the Orient as it was to the Romans. It rushed through halls and courts, poured in cascades over each terrace and surrounded the whole garden. Little pavilions, rising from the surface of the water, were an indispensable ornamentation of Arab gardens. Together with other buildings, they played an important role both in Córdova and in Zahira as well as in Almanzor's (940–1002) pleasure seat and in the Sicilian villas Al-Azira and Favora.

For some three hundred years the Moors, Jews and Christians lived together in Spain. Gradually, however, the power of the Caliphate of Córdova weakened and when, in 1034, Christian knights from the North occupied Córdova, they took one town after another from the Moors. In the end, apart from one mosque, nothing of the splendour survived. Of the fifty thousand blooming gardens that were once supposed to have existed there, not a trace remains.

A fertile valley, not far from Granada, is part of an enchanting landscape; it is largely cut off from the outside world by the mountains which surround it. It was there that the Moslem realm with its Islamic culture was able to resist its complete breakdown for some time (Emirate of Granada, 1246–1492). After the Moors had been removed from many Moslem areas, refugees came to Granada and this allowed oriental splendour to flourish once again in that small area, until the Arabs were finally driven out of Spain.

A precious legacy of Arab culture is preserved in the Alhambra and in the Moorish summer palace Géneralife on the Alhambra hill as well as in the Alcázar at Seville. Unfortunately, destruction, re-building and neglect have changed the whole picture of Arabic palace gardens.

The Alhambra foundations were laid down by Muhammed Abu-il Harras in 1231 and completed in 1274 by Yusuf Abernedyedi. It is the most famous Moorish royal castle, though its gardens and fountains are surpassed by those of the Géneralife. The Alhambra is composed of several courts. In the Court of the Myrtles (Patio de la Alberca, sometimes called Patio de los Arragnes) the original lay-out is clearly discernible. The whole length of this court is divided in two by a rectangular *bassin*. Sheltering under the shade of a fantastically adorned colonnade, there are flat bowls with fountains. According to Thacker, the Court of the Lions (Patio de los Leones) is the most purely Islamic of all the Moorish gardens in

Spain. It is a rectangle sub-divided by four canals and containing garden beds. In its narrow canals, the water flows past slim pillars which border the garden. Previously, the beds lay some 60 centimetres deeper but today we find them on the same level as the paths. The alabaster bowl of the central fountain is borne by twelve lions. Fountains and ponds are characteristic features of the Alhambra. They are fed by a canal directed there from the surrounding Duero Mountains. The quietly rippling liquid and the fountains, from which gentle streams of water rise upwards, pervade the air with a pleasant coolness under the scorching Spanish sun.

Above the royal castle lies the pleasure seat Géneralife that still shows some of its former glory. It is a complex of gardens constructed in the course of several centuries. While the lowest terraces were of Moorish origin, the highest stem from the nineteenth century. Excavations that took place after a fire in 1958, as part of the re-building work, uncovered remains of the original Arab garden in the inner court (Patio de la Acequia). This most famous part of the palace shows the significant features of an Arab garden, although — in Thacker's opinion — it must have previously been more markedly Islamic than it appears today. The basic cruciform design, with its quartering of the garden area, is just as typical of the Islamic garden as the superfluity of water and shade.

The excavations also disclosed that the garden beds previously must have lain much deeper, as has already been mentioned in the case of the Alhambra. The heads of the flowers grew approximately to the level of the path and are again reminiscent of the famous Persian carpet of flowers, between green-and-white glazed tiles along the path. A description of this pleasure seat is to be found in the writings of the Venetian ambassador Bernardo Navagero in his book *Navagera Opera* of 1530, at a time when a golden age of gardening was at its height.

"One leaves the surrounding walls of the Alhambra and steps into the very beautiful garden of a pleasure seat lying at a higher level. Though not very large, this is a really superb construction with wonderful gardens and waterworks; the finest that I have seen in Spain. It has several patios, all richly provided with water, but especially one with a flowing canal in the middle and full of lovely oranges and myrtle.

A loggia permits of a view outwards, and the myrtle rises to such a height that it nearly reaches the balcony. The water flows through the whole area and, when desired, even through the rooms of which some are suitable for a marvellous summer sojourn.

There is also a noteworthy, though not too large court which is so thickly trailed around with luxuriant ivy that one can't see the doors at all; it stands on a rock and has several balconies, from which one can look down into the depths through which the river Dorro flows — a fascinating and enchanting view. In the middle of this court is a beautiful fountain with an enormous basin. The pipe in the middle shoots up jets more than ten fathoms high; the profusion of water is astounding.

In a garden at the highest level of the grounds a lovely broad stairway goes up to a small terrace and, from this latter, the whole mass of water flows out of a rock and then flows in all directions. The water is controlled by many valves, so that one can turn it on at any time, in any direction and in any desired quantity. The stairway is built in such a way that some steps are invariably followed by broader ones with a hollowing in the middle where water can collect.

Even the stone bannisters on either side of the stairway have grooved channels along the top. And above, there are valves for each of these sections, so that one can direct the water as one wishes either into the channels on the bannister, into the hollows in the broad steps or into both at the same time.

One can also, if one wishes, allow the water to well up so that it spills over from these gutterings and floods over all the steps, wetting everyone who happens to be on them at the time; there are a thousand more of such tricks that the water can be used for" (Gollwitzer).

In the Alcázar in Seville, too, excavations have brought to light part of a garden, set out with flower-beds and painted stucco decor. The Spanish conquered Seville in 1248 when many gardens were destroyed. Pedro I (1334

to 1367), though, had parts of the Alcázar rebuilt by Moorish craftsmen between 1364 and 1366. However today, there is a great park with a labyrinth, waterworks and ornate boxwood hedges on the site of the old Moorish gardens. The tiled fountains in the inner part of the Alcázar, the *bassin* with its sexagonal tiles and a canal, lined on both sides with cypresses, are the only features reminding us of its past.

On the basis of old Arabic manuscripts, Dickie has listed the plants most commonly cultivated in this garden. Jasmine, violets, narcissi, red roses, white lilies, blue iris, mallows, water-lilies, marguerites, poppies, lavender and lupins were the most favoured because of their colour and perfume. The aromas of thyme and mint, arising from their ethereal oils, seem to have been equally in demand.

The pine cone is a constantly recurring motif in fountain design.

Oleander was planted in tubs, enchanting people with its blossoms. Also myrtle and laurel were often planted in tubs as decoration and cut into spherical or pillar shapes. Pears, plums, apples, mulberries, medlar, quince, figs, cherries and grapes must have been important elements in the Islamic garden not only because they bore delicious fruits but also because of the shade they provided. Cypresses formed an enchanting scenic background to these gardens.

Contrary to widely held views, it seems that the tradition of none of these Moorish gardens was maintained. After on site inspection, Dickie reported in 1968 "that the gardens of the Partal in the Alhambra were not older than forty years". Also the gardens in the Alcázar in Seville were neither Arabic nor Moorish but "represent the typical Italian garden, introduced into Spain at the time of the Renaissance" (Cowell).

Planted cloisters and kitchen gardens in monasteries

Before the Moors came to Europe from North Africa, the ancient Christian culture had found a refuge in Ireland where, because of its insular position, it could be protected from the storms of the Great Migration and thus preserved. Wandering Irish monks spread these cultural influences over the whole of western and central Europe; the Irish monk Gallus, for example, founded the St. Gall Abbey.

It was not long before the monasteries were regarded as the main bearers of a newly developing cultural phase which was beginning to crystallize after the Great Migration between the 4th and the 6th centuries. The existence of monasteries also had a favourable influence on the development of gardening after the decline of the Western Roman Empire.

Saint Augustine said: "In a garden ... I gathered brothers together, who shared my benevolent feelings ..." (Gothein). If we look further back into history, we learn that the philosophers Plato, Epicurus and Theophrastus spent some time in gardens and used them as a venue for conversation and intellectual exercise.

As Christian monastic life developed in the Mediterranean area, a similarity between the architecture of the monastery gardens and antique methods of construction can be clearly noticed. The actual living quarters were grouped around the garden court (peristyle). Despite a great variety of design, monasteries all hark back to an original type.

Just as the Roman portico garden during the Byzantine era had adopted the name "paradise" from the hunting parks of the Persians, so the open pillared court in front of the Christian basilicas was called paradise. In the same way the Roman term *atrium* was applied to the open courts.

These open pillared courts were frequently paved, like, for example, the atrium in the old St. Peter's Basilica in Rome, previously adorned with the pine fountain. Fountains served, above all, sacral purposes but, in addition, it was a delight to the eye to include water as an enlivening element in the design of the pillared courts. They were constructed according to the oriental models. As already mentioned, we meet with the pine cone as a popular form of gargoyle already in Byzantium.

The pillared courts also contained plants, especially in early times, as did the "paradises" laid out in front of them and the cloisters which formed the courts at the centre of the monasteries.

The Monastery of San Paolo in Rome had such a planted cloister which Pope Hadrian had "most beautifully reconstructed" (Gothein) in the 8th century. In the Mediterranean area, the earliest cloisters were already luxuriantly planted, and still today many of them are resplendent in a profusion of flowers.

The monastery grounds from their early beginnings were not limited to cloisters and "paradises". The herb garden was an inseparable constituent of the 8th-century monastery. The founder of the Benedictine Order, Saint Benedict of Nursia (480–547), through whom monastic life in Europe experienced an upward swing, ruled that "everything necessary" (Gothein) should be available within the walls. This applied first of all to the water and the gardens.

In the library of St. Gall is a 9th-century plan concerning the construction, design and utilization of a monastery garden with farm buildings at St. Gall.

Four gardens are recognizable, of which the fourth lies inside the quadrangle of the cloister, which occupies a central position in the plan. This cloister — it could also be termed an arcade — encloses the inner surface like an ancient peristyle; a regularly shaped rectangle divided by paths.

Ground-plan of the St. Gall Abbey (cloister with inner courtyard, medical herb garden, vegetable garden, orchard and graveyard).

As the monasteries were the only centres of medical attention in the country at that time, the growing of medical plants played a very important role. The medical-herb garden *(herbularis)* was right next to the infirmary. On the sixteen narrow seed-beds the names of flowers and herbs are listed. Foremost among these are the rose and the lily; gladioli, rosemary, sage, rue and mint are also recorded. So besides providing plants for the production of medicaments and health-promoting juices, the medicinal-plant gardens presented an attractive appearance.

In the vegetable garden which was similar to the medicinal-plant garden, "the vegetables grow beautifully

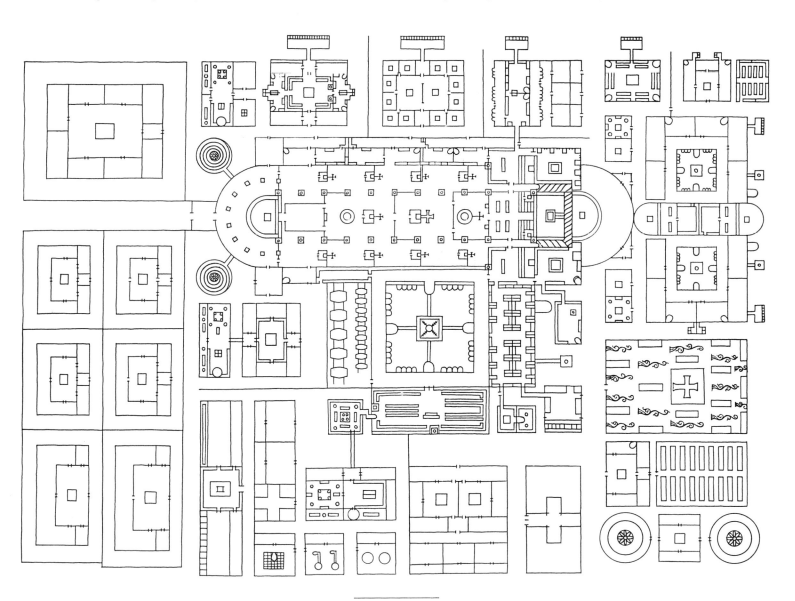

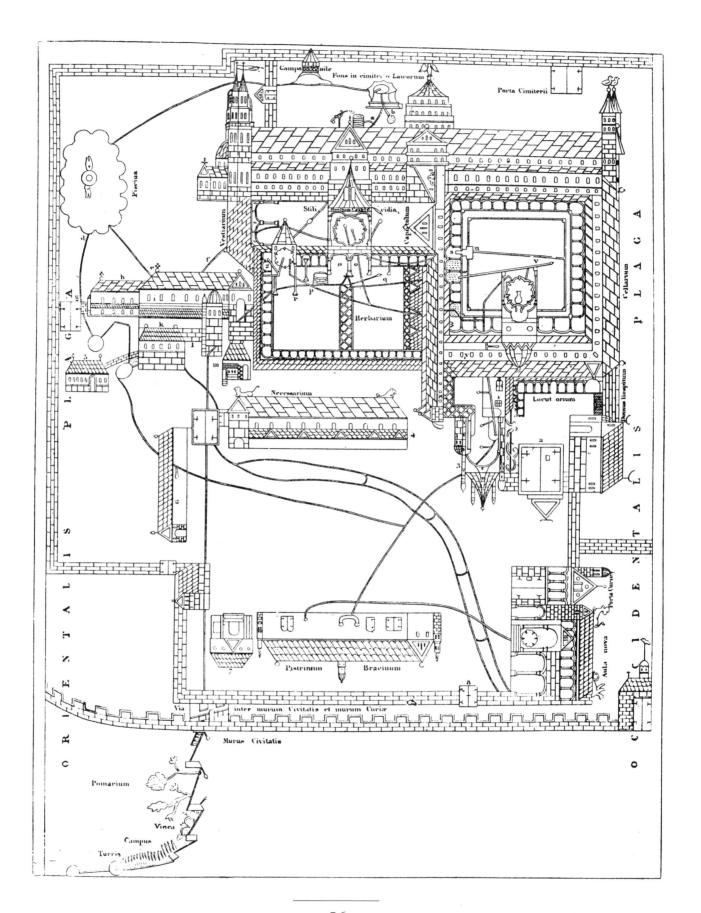

green" (Gothein) on eighteen regularly-shaped beds set out in a rectangle. The monastery plan gives details of types of vegetables which are also largely to be found in an ordinance of Charlemagne (742–814), *Capitulare de villis vel curtis imperii,* which will be referred to later — like onions, leek, celery, coriander, dill, poppy, radish, mangold beet, garlic, shallots, savory, parsley, chervil, lettuce, cabbage and carrots.

Right next to the vegetable garden lay the graveyard which doubled as an orchard, the practical monks planting fruit trees there in orderly rows. We are referring, here, to apple, pear, plum, medlar, laurel, sweet chestnut, pine, mountain ash, fig, quince, peach, hazelnut, almond, mulberry, walnut trees, all mentioned in the *Capitulare.* The graves of the monks are to be found between the trees.

As can be seen from the very detailed plan of the St. Gall Abbey, there is, on the whole, little room for gardens. As the monastery's superior usually had a garden, it is hard to imagine that the abbots of St. Gall, garden lovers themselves, would have done without them. Despite certain doubts, the plan can be seen as an extremely valuable document of garden history that gives us a good idea of how they envisaged the design of a monastery garden.

As the monks constantly extended their cultivation of fruit — and above all with especial intensity of the vine — the areas available within the confines of the monastery walls were soon insufficient. So the orchards, including the vineyards, lay outside the monastery at St. Gall, just as they did at Canterbury in England. This latter intelligence we get from a plan of the Canterbury Monastery dating back to 1165. According to Lenoir, we can clearly recognize the herb garden *(herbarium)* from this plan; it is enclosed by a cloister and divided into two halves by a kind of pergola in the centre.

An interesting feature of this plan is the position of the irrigation ditches or pipes. This water supply leads out

The plan of the Canterbury Monastery shows the vineyard lying outside the monastery gardens.

from a fish-breeding pond — called *piscina* — and flows mainly under the cloisters and gardens to whose plants it brings a plentiful supply of water. The lay brothers' graveyard and the herb garden had an additional well.

The "Hortulus" of Walahfrid Strabo

A lively insight into an early mediaeval monastery garden and its plants is given in the poem "Liber de cultura hortorum". Known as the "Hortulus" or little garden, it was written by the young abbot Walahfrid Strabo (809–849). He lived in the Reichenau Monastery on the island of the same name, on Lake Constance. He helped to give his monastery a widespread reputation for learning, way beyond his country's borders.

Lauenstein interprets this poem as follows: "Strabo is a great garden enthusiast who does not scorn to make his hands calloused by grasping hold of a spade with a will, or to get them brown (in the sun) ... The garden lies on the east side of his house, right outside the door. It is partly covered by the roof of the vestibule, so that neither rain nor wind can penetrate there. On the south side there is a high wall that stands in the way of the sun's beams. At the beginning of spring, the little garden is covered with nettles. After those plants with poisonous pricks on their leaves are rooted out the mole-hills are destroyed and the earth-worms are brought to light. When the earth has been dried by the sun and the wind, beds are prepared by propping up the heaped earth with wooden boards. Now the earth is broken up with the hoe and rich dung is brought in baskets so that the land becomes fertile.

So the soil is prepared and now the various kinds of seeds can be planted or those that have wintered can be transplanted. When the tender seed has now risen and the thin stalks peep out of the earth, then Walahfrid goes and brings fresh water in great containers and carefully waters the tiny little stalks; he does this with his cupped hand, so that the individual seeds are not displaced by a too violent gush of water."

Strabo also describes the appearance and use of the plants he has cultivated. Sierp has examined the description of the plants from the standpoint of a botanist, while

Fischer has given his own version of these plant descriptions as follows:

"We start off with the following medical plants and kitchen herbs cultivated in the little garden: 1st, sage (*Salvia officinalis* L.), then follows 2nd, rue (*Ruta graveolens*) whose habit is superbly delineated with no waste of words, as is also the case with those that follow, 3rd, southern wood (*Artemisia abrotanum* L.), 4th, gourd (*Cucurbita lagenaria*) which is extolled in a poem in such an exalted form and with such minute observation of its nature that hardly any other plant can have been so lauded in song. 5th, the melon (*Cucumis melo*), shaped like a bubble, is so clearly identifiable by the rich streams of juice and multiplicity of seeds which escape when it is cut, that there can be no doubt that this southern fruit, too, was successfully cultivated at that time, in the warm climate in the island Reichenau. 6th, wormwood (*Artemisia absinthium*) that outwardly resembles the mother of all herbs, the common mugwort (*Artemisia vulgaris*), and 7th, horehound *(Marrubium vulgare)* popular because of its healing powers, the same as 8th, fennel (*Feoniculum vulgare),* 9th, gladioli which are always an iris species in the Middle Ages, whereas the mediaeval hyacinth is our modern *Gladiolus vulgaris.* This is also how we are to understand the names given to them by Walahfrid, witness the reported use made of the iris root in curing diseases of the bladder. 10th, lovage (*Levisticum officinale);* 11th, garden chervil *(Anthriscus cerefolium)* are described as *lybisticum* and *cerefolium*; in the poem 12th, the lily (*Lilium candidum*) is eulogized with special enthusiasm by Walahfrid; 13th, papaver, the poppy, gets a special mention, not only for its medicinal use but also because of the unfolding of its buds and its fructification; 14th, sclarega (clary) probably indicates *Salvia sclarea.* The *costus* referred to in the same poem is, of course, not *Costus speciosus* but probably cost mary *(Tanacetum balsamita).* 15th, mentha; like the late mediaeval botanist, Walahfrid already knew an abundance of menthaceous species, of which he especially picks out two—*Mentha aquatica* and *Mentha piperita.* 16th, *pulegium* is *Mentha pulegium;* 17th, *apium,* the celery (*Apium graveolens*); 18th, *vettonica,* then as now growing everywhere which we call betony (*Betonica officinalis*); 19th, *agrimonia,* the agrimony (*Agrimonia eupatoria*).

The second name given in the text, *sarcocolla,* was taken by Walahfrid from *Dioscorides,* where it is used as a synonym for *agremone* (not *agrimonia!*). 20th, ambrosia is a plant which the poet, on his own admission, cannot identify from literature. Fischer Benzon holds it to be a garden variety of tansy (*Tanacetum vulgare*). 21st, *nepeta,* the cat-mint (*Nepeta cataria*) is again as well delineated as 22nd, *raphanus,* the radish (*Raphanus sativus*); 23rd, in a final poetic crescendo Walahfrid closes his poem with the rose."

His enumeration corresponds very well with the actual plants and trees given in the plan in the St. Gall Abbey. And these, again, correspond with the list in the already mentioned ordinance of the Frankish king. If Walahfrid also enumerates some plants, like the lily and the rose, which today are exclusively ornamental, then we must understand that in those days, these plants had a culinary or medicinal value and their inclusion in the kind of small garden we are talking about was justified.

The foundation of the Carthusian monasteries considerably advanced the care and maintenance of gardens. The communal side of the monks' life was limited; true, the central cloister retained its significance as a garden common to all, but around it the individual cells were grouped, each having a little garden attached to it destined

Monks pruning the vines. Painted faience tile of an oven in the summer refectory of Salem Abbey. Baden, 1733.

for the recreation of the inmate. A plan of the Clermont Monastery in France is a typical example of such Carthusian garden areas.

The garden plan of Albertus Magnus

A certain picture of the transition from monastery garden to castle garden — which latter could also be described as the pleasure garden of knightly society — is portrayed by the plan of garden grounds produced by Albertus Magnus (1193–1280), a Dominican monk and famous naturalist of the Middle Ages, in his work *De vegetabilis*.

Meadowlands, an enclosed spring with a water *bassin* in the middle of the garden and a brook are examples of garden components that were going to be the accepted elements for a long time to come. A passage from his famous writings presents us with an impression of how he went about things, in detail, and what ideas about garden construction were being developed.

"There are certain places that are less valuable for their use or their great fruitfulness but more for the enjoyment they afford and are rather neglected for purposes of cultivation and therefore cannot be related to any specific type of crop. These are referred to as 'little green pleasure gardens'. Because they serve, in the main, to delight two of our senses, namely our sight and smell, they do not undergo the treatment that is usual for the cultivation of plants. The eye is not delighted quite so much by anything as by fine grass of moderate height. But that can only be grown on meagre but firm soil. Thus, it is necessary, when preparing the ground for a pleasure garden, first of all to clear old roots. This is hardly possible unless you dig out the roots, level the ground as smoothly as possible and pour boiling water vigorously over the whole area. You must ensure in this way that the remaining roots and seeds, still hidden in the earth, are burnt and are unable to germinate anywhere... The lawn must be laid out on such a scale that all kinds of aromatic herbs, like rue, sage or basil can be planted behind on a square patch, as well as all kinds of flowers, like violets, columbines, lilies, roses, fleur-de-lis and other similar flowers. Between the herb beds and the lawn a raised piece of lawn should be laid-out grown with

Albertus Magnus, Dominican monk, whose lay name was Albert Count of Bollstädt.

beautiful flowers and, about in the centre, an area suitable for sitting on, where people can relax and mentally recuperate.

Trees are to be planted and vines trained on the sunny side of the lawn; their leaves will protect the lawn and provide it with refreshing shade. You expect more shade from such trees than fruit and so do not take much care cultivating or fertilizing them which would greatly harm the lawn. To prevent this you must be very careful that the trees are not too close to each other, as this would prevent the fresh air getting to them and could affect their health. ...

Examples of the symbolical plant representations in the *Hortus sanitatis*: the paradise tree and Narcissus.

The pleasure garden should remain open to the North and East because the winds that blow in from those directions bring health und purity. But in the opposite wind direction, i.e., to the South and West, it must be closed off because the stormy nature and impurity of those winds have a weakening effect. The north wind may hinder the growth of fruit, but it wonderfully preserves the health of man. One demands enjoyment from a pleasure garden — not fruit."

The "paradise garden", plant symbolism and illustrated botanical works

"The Paradise Garden", a painting by a master from the Upper Rhineland from about 1410 is an impressive illustration of Albertus Magnus' description of a garden plan. We can distinguish the boxed-in beds with rose campion, wallflower, stock, fleur-de-lis and hollyhock. Also to be seen is the somewhat raised lawn with seating facilities and a spring with a soakaway. Paths are missing. Where the three male figures are seated, white lilies, cowslips, columbines, periwinkles, violets and spring snowflakes are growing. In the foreground of the picture a peony and

lilies-of-the-valley grow, while there are speedwell and sage on the wall. Thus partly the same plants are mentioned as in the *Hortulus* of Walahfrid Strabo. Lottliese Behling takes the portrayal of this earthly garden "as a symbol and glorification of the creation and especially of Mary, mother of God". Many of the flowers in the picture are intended to indicate Mary's beauty and purity. The rose was to be taken as the symbol of death, the lily embodies purity. In a poem by Sedulius Scottus (*c*. 820) the two flowers quarrel about their order of rank:

"Rose: ... Purple lendeth fame's glory and power to the king/ Kings esteem white but little — the pale colour/ The pallid countenance grows thin, white and miserable/ But the purple colour is honoured throughout the world.

Lily: Apollo loves me, golden-haired ornament of the earth/ And the beauty of my face is clothed in snowey white/ Why do you give yourself airs, with your shamelessly painted face/ Can't you see how you're drooping? Isn't it shame that has brought a blush to your cheeks? ..."

Alcuin made a different point in a poem that he dedicated to a son of Charlemagne. In this poetical work, the rose signifies honour, the lily wisdom, the violet righteousness and the crocus modesty. Here we have four flowers, brought together, that were, throughout the whole Middle Ages, and still are man's favourites. So this is how plants of the paradise garden picture are interpreted both from the Christian as well as the secular viewpoint. Periwinkle also has a symbolical significance; according to Wolffhardt, the Evil Spirit is bedded on the periwinkle lawn beside the three male figures for, according to ancient herbal books, magic can be worked through periwinkle. Plant symbolism of a secular kind is expressed in manifold ways during the Middle Ages — the minnesingers sang of it; we find it in plant representations of pictures, as for example in the portrait of the young Dürer with an eryngo and in folk songs.

The herbal books with their plant illustrations give a wealth of information. The oldest drawing of a plant, according to H. Fischer, is the symbolical depiction of the mandrake. It is contained in a copy of the herb book *Herbarium Apolei Platonici nomina*.

24 "The Paradise Garden". Painting by an Upper Rhenish master,
about 1410. Städelsches Kunstinstitut, Frankfurt/Main.

25 View of the monastery garden at Osek in Czechoslovakia.
In the foreground a raised parterre.

26   In the monastery garden, burial places for the monks
were prepared in suitable spots, usually between trees.
Miniature from *The Book of Hours of Louis of Orléans*,
Saltykov Shchedrin Library, Leningrad.

27   The Garden of Paradise was permeated with
paradise rivers which sprang from the Well of Life. Miniature
from *The Book of Hours of Louis of Orléans*,
Saltykov Shchedrin Library, Leningrad.

Pages 64/65:
28   Similar to the narrow castle gardens of the Middle Ages,
we have here gardens on the slopes outside the town walls at Bari in
Apulia, whose fortifications were erected in 1233 as coastal defence.

29   View of the gardens of the Alhambra at Granada.

30   In the Alcázar in Seville, Islamic, Spanish and Renaissance
elements are interwoven, giving the gardens their special stamp.

31 Rose hedge at a moated castle. Miniature from the
Roman de la Rose by Guillaume de Lorris.
British Library, London.

32 Folio of the *Capitulare de villis vel curtis imperii,*
the famous regulation of the royal estates
by Charlemagne. Herzog August Bibliothek, Wolfenbüttel.

33 Representation of a garden. Miniature from the
Roman de la Rose whose main theme is the ideal garden.
British Library, London.

34 "Castle Garden in Springtime". Painting by Hans Bol, 1586.
Staatliche Kunstsammlungen Dresden,
Gemäldegalerie "Alte Meister".

One of the uniquely illuminated picture manuscripts is the *Dioscorides,* a Greek work already translated from Greek into Latin in Antiquity and known today as the *Langobardian Dioscorides* of Marcellus Virgilius. The earliest extant illustrated adaption of this manuscript dates from the 9th century and was written, according to Stadler, in the famous Italian monastery of Monte Cassino. It is thought that the pictures were originally produced around 540. Spurge, lilies, violets, camomile, christmas roses and the miracle-tree were depicted here.

Another illustrated botanical work coming down to the Middle Ages from Antiquity is the pseudo-Apuleius, *De herbarum virtutibus.*

With increasing trade, the strengthening of the middle classes and the development of the art of book printing, there was also a flourishing of folk medicine. During this time, too, a whole number of herb books appeared which, on the one hand, pictured medicinal plants but also, on the other, included symbolical plant pictures.

A standard work of mediaeval botany is the *Gart der Gesuntheit* (Garden of Health) from 1485, with its series of woodcuts. 382 plants are listed altogether, partly native but also foreign ones. One interesting plant picture is by an artist who depicts the mandrake root. The mandrake is depicted in another illustration, too. Here we find the representation of a male figure in addition to the female figure in the above-mentioned illustration. Both are in the corners of the picture, in which a mediaeval herb garden is shown and people busying themselves with the harvest. A more extensive work, appearing in 1491, is the *Hortus sanitatis* with its description of 530 plants. This work, too, includes examples of how symbolic and purely decorative plant pictures may be incorporated in herbal books.

In general, these illustrations intend to stress the medical significance of the herb concerned, and this is why they frequently portray the plant symbolically. In this way, mediaeval man was "to be educated to observe the realities of natural phenomena" (Fischer). If, for example, a plant is bracketed by a snake, then it is to be used as an antidote to snake-bite.

Title page of the *New Kreüterbuch* — the new herbal book, Basle, 1543.

We often find the castle garden to be identical to the paradise garden, so that the conceptions of Albertus Magnus and the commentary on the painting "The Paradise Garden" may be taken as giving an impression of the castle garden, too. There was little room for extensive garden grounds in castles.

Apart from one or two exceptions, like the famous rose gardens in the palace of Ultrogote, the wife of the Gallic king Childebert I (died 558), or the garden at the old royal château at Saint Germain, famed far and wide, luxuriant gardens were hardly in evidence. The unrest and insecurity of the times compelled the knights and the nobility to contract their castle enclosures and to build walls and towers. These fortresses were constructed on almost unapproachable mountain crests with little space, or they were surrounded by broad moats. So only small gardens grew up which became favourite places for social intercourse in mediaeval castles.

In spring, after the cold winter months when dusk set in early, the inmates were delighted to escape from the inhospitable castle living quarters and found their contentment within the limited space available. The areas originally constructed as herb gardens soon incorporated fruit bushes and vegetable patches. Although it was not yet possible to have ornamental flower gardens, they did start growing sweet-smelling flowers like roses, lilies, primula, violets, cornflowers and pansies both for sacral purposes as well as for table decoration.

Girls and women were partial to wearing flowers in their hair, and wreaths were worn on the head. The perfumes of some flowers were prized and some were used to add delicacy to food. Primula, hawthorn, violets and rose petals were cooked together with honey and sugar. Violets were used in salads, as garnishing and as a spice.

In about 1000 Notker for the first time speaks of a flower garden with roses and violets. From then on orchards are mentioned frequently. Though they contained — first and foremost — fruit-bearing trees, also ornamental and shade-providing trees were planted.

The Latin animal fable of the 10th century, *Ecbasis Captivi,* portrays a royal garden with an oak which is surrounded by herbs and flowers; the oak welcomes the sick king under its shade; a clear spring trickles through the garden. And what about the linden in Central Europe? Specimens of this tree dating from earliest times still decorate many castle courtyards to this very day, often beside a well.

Mandrake (or mandragora) was regarded as a talisman and there was a very profitable trade in these plants. There was faith in their ability to cure illnesses, they were thought to help women's fertility and to ease their confinement; they were also supposed to bring luck to litigants. Symbolical depiction of the mandrake root from the *Gart der Gesuntheit,* the garden of health.

Lorris' "Roman de la Rose"

A new impetus was given to the description of gardens in France in the first half of the 13th century. Most of the elements of mediaeval gardens are reflected in the *belle lettres* of the time and in their illustrations. Between 1220 and 1230, Guillaume de Lorris wrote his *Roman de la Rose* (Romance of the rose). In this poem, the storyteller relates how, in a dream, he arrives at a great garden surrounded by a wall with battlements. He is ushered in through "a wycket small" (a tiny door) by Dame Idleness. Wearing a chaplet "of fyne or froys" (of finest braid) and, over that, a "rose garlande", she leads him through the garden. At first the path runs past fragrant herbs — "myntes full and fennel green".

Sir Mirth, who is the owner of the garden, is rollicking on "the green grasse" with his friends, dancing with seven maidens — some are wearing wreaths and some garlands of roses. The trees are native to the "land of Alexandria", and the garden appears just "like an earthly paradise".

Gart der Gesuntheit, one of the numerous herbal books published in the second half of the 15th century. In the right and left front corners representations of the mandrake root.

Lorris describes the ideal garden with its many trees, such as pomegranate, date, fig, and almond — that is fruits from warm and distant lands —, in detail. Ginger, cardamon, cloves and cinnamon are also mentioned, and exotic spices thrive in this place, too, products of the author's phantasy.

Lorris also enumerates native fruit trees and, in addition, cypresses, pine, olive and laurel. Some of the trees are planted equidistant from each other and intertwined to form arches. Many animals like roebucks, stags, rabbits, squirrels and birds enliven the scenery; water gushes forth from a clear, pure spring.

The first illustrations of this poem originated in about 1300. They have been kept very simple. A woodcut from 1481 shows the garden with a wattle fence around it, later a fence of pales replaces it, to be followed by an

ugly wall. The high battlements mentioned in the poem only appear in later representations.

A Flemish painter who, at a later date, illustrated the famous Harlei Manuscript (Harleian MS in the British Museum) renders an overall view of the garden, full of fantasy. Within a framework of flowers, birds and butterflies surrounded by climbers, the painter portrays three interconnected garden scenes.

In addition to many details mentioned in the text, the artist also painted raised beds, a pruned bush, a raised lawn seat and, the most outstanding feature, a fountain with a nonagonal base and nine gargoyles gushing water out into a circular basin from which the surplus water flows into a stone channel.

This spring does not appear in the poem; Lorris merely writes of water springs, little gurgling and murmuring brooks which are directed through channels. In addition there was the "fontaine d'Amors", whose water mirrors Narcissus and his lover.

Another illustration of the Harlei Manuscript shows, for example, a moated castle surrounded by a double battlement with a tower on each corner of the outer wall. Wonderfully blooming rose-bushes are laid-out between the two walls. They have grown so profusely that the

blooms reach right up to the battlements. The scene is framed by graceful tendrils of flowers, butterflies and fruit-bearing strawberry plants. A rose bower is portrayed on the other side. Bowers or arbours were a centre-piece of mediaeval gardens and formed a protection against the sun or inquisitive observers. Often a pergola served the same purpose, covered with trailing roses or honeysuckle.

Thanks to the miniatures of the *Roman de la Rose* and its later renderings we obtain a vivid impression of the gardens of this period. When we coordinate the fragmentary information to be gleaned from these many individual portrayals, we are able, in the end, to sketch out a clear picture of the mediaeval garden, which is characterized by specific elements.

The garden area was square or rectangular and surrounded by walls, thorn-hedges or ditches. Entrances were constructed with solid wooden gates with ornamental fittings and partly covered by a shingle-roof. They also put up gates between two parts of the garden, only made of light-weight pales.

The areas surrounded by walls were, in the same way, divided into rectangular or square parts, sometimes separated by paths. Trees, flowers and lawns — with springs or fountains — are recognizable features of the mediaeval "pleasure garden".

The most favoured trees were linden, nut trees and all kinds of fruit trees. In warmer areas one could add fig, olive and cedar. The spice garden contained cooking and medicinal herbs as well as what we should today regard as flowers. The habit of putting up trelliswork bowers, wooden pergolas and similar constructions goes back to Ancient Roman traditions and is frequently referred to in writings of the 14th and 15th centuries. It is fairly certain that the plants selected were vines.

The garden culture of western Europe during the Middle Ages could not compete with its highly developed counterpart of Antiquity, even though, already at the time of the Merovingians (*c.* A.D. 500) and the Carolingians (751–911), fruit trees cultivated by grafting were planted in the gardens.

Cultivating the soil in a mediaeval garden. Taken from a Lower German translation of Aesop. Cologne, 1489.

Charlemagne's "Capitulare"

Monks of the 8th and 9th centuries were the first to introduce systematic garden construction into western and central Europe. As already mentioned, gardening experienced a significant impetus from Charlemagne. He encouraged every cultivation in his domain including many new plants, above all in kitchen gardens. The influence on gardening and agriculture of the "Regulations of the royal estates in the empire of Charlemagne" (*Capitulare de villis vel curtis imperii*) of about 795 cannot be ignored. This so-called "Estates Order" included 73 different plant species to be cultivated.

There were several reasons why the *Capitulare* gained such a great significance. Firstly, Charlemagne encouraged the extension of the monasteries in a most generous way, so that building enthusiasm was greatly strengthened. Secondly, the monks busied themselves more and more intensively with the maintenance of gardens which, a great joy to them, was also of practical value. According to investigations by Dopsch, a copy of the *Capitulare* was apparently brought to the island of Reichenau by Abbot Tatto, teacher of Walahfrid Strabo. In this way, the *Capitulare* became not merely a guiding rule for Charlemagne's own estates but also the authentic basis for monastic plant cultivation.

Plants imported from abroad were cultivated mainly in monasteries and convents, for example in Germany in Cologne, Mainz, St. Gall, Ettal, Würzburg, in the island of Reichenau, in Fulda and Hersfeld. The lasting influence of the *Capitulare* continued to have its effect on the plants grown in peasant gardens which have remained fairly constant for centuries.

In Chapter 70 of the *Capitulare*, the following plants are named: "Lilies, roses, costmary, sage, rue, southernwood, cucumbers, melons, bottle gourds *(cucurbitas!)*, runner beans *(fasiolum*; means here a species of *Dolichos)*, carroway seed *(ciminum)*, rosemary, carroway, chickpeas, sea-onions, fleur-de-lis, dragon wort *(Arum dracunculus* [?] or *Artemisia dracunculus* according to Kerner), anise, colocynth, chicory, bishop weed, laser wort, lettuce *(lactucas)*, black carroway seed, hedge mustard, cress, burdock, pennyroyal, alexanders *(olisatrum* or *Smyrnium olusatrum)*, parsley, celery, lovage, juniper, dill, fennel, endives, dittany, mustard, savory, water mint, wild mint, tansy, cat mint, fever few, poppy, silver beet, hazel wort, marshmallow, mallows, carrots, turnips, mountain spinach, amaranth *(blidas* or *Amaranthus blitum)*, kohlrabi, cabbage, summer onions *(uniones)*, chives, leak, radish, shallots and onions, garlic, madder *(warentiam)*, artichokes (or teasels) *(cardones!)*, broad beans *(Vicia faba)*, field peas *(Piros mauriscos)*, coriander, chervil, spring greens *(lacterides* or *Euphorbia lathyris)* and muscatel sage. The gardener should also have house-leek in his home. As far as trees are concerned, we want people to have apple trees of all kinds, pear trees of all kinds, plum trees of all kinds, mountain ash *(sorbarios)*, medlar, sweet chestnuts, peach trees of all kinds, quince trees, hazelnut bushes, almond, mulberry, laurel, pine, fig, nut and cherry trees of all kinds. Names of the apples: Gozmaring, Gerolding, Cravedell, Spirauk, sweet, sour, all durable apples as well as those that have to be eaten quickly because they ripen early."

In the late Middle Ages, craftsmen and traders brought a great economic prosperity to the towns, as well as to the individual citizens. Green belts arose around the periphery of the towns, with meadow areas shaded by trees; the name given to these meadows came from the Latin, *pratum commune*. In Madrid this became "Prado", whereas in Vienna it was called "Prater".

Botanical gardens

Apart from small gardens attached to houses, there were also larger and lavishly stocked gardens which were partly for purposes of status. But they also represented the newly awakened interest in the natural sciences, for the educational monopoly of the monasteries was subsiding. The striving for all-round knowledge had meanwhile passed into the consciousness of the towns and their citizens.

So the development of the art of gardening in the flourishing towns of Italy, Spain, France, Germany, the Netherlands and England lay in the hands of prosperous merchants or scholars who were also interested in matters

Plan and schematic representation of the botanical garden at Padua. The circular ground-plan is divided in beds, planted with various plant species in sections.

botanical. To this circumstance another must be added, the founding of numerous universities which greatly encouraged the construction of botanical gardens and supported the knowledge about plants and the passion for collecting them.

From the beginning of the 14th century the following botanical gardens came into existence: Salerno (1330), Venice (1333), Prague (1350), Erfurt (1525), Marburg (1530), Padua (1545), Pisa (1547), Leiden (1577), Leipzig (1580), Heidelberg, Montpellier, Strasbourg and Paris (1597) and Oxford in 1632.

The botanical garden in Padua served as a model for many other similar ones and, with its circular form, is the oldest of its kind. Italy not only stimulated the construction of botanical gardens, but also played a great role in introducing oriental and Indian plants and many from overseas, too. This passion for collecting foreign or unusual plants can be traced through all epochs in the history of gardening, right up to and including the present day.

Renaissance Gardening

When Europe, in the 14th century, was afflicted with starvation, plague and a flight from the land, a movement developed in central Italy in which Humanistic attitudes were the main cultural and spiritual guiding light. Life acquired a new meaning for the individual, whose thoughts no longer concentrated upon a transcendental world but on the realities of this world. This was accompanied by the awakening of a new attitude of people towards their environment. It was Petrarch (1304–1374) who first set forth the aims of Humanism, and Boccaccio (1313 to 1375) who encouraged an increasing interest in classical history and mythology. This movement unleashed a wave of creative activity; evidence of this is to be found in the writings of Erasmus of Rotterdam (1466–1536), Cervantes (1547–1616) and Thomas Moore (1477 to 1535), to name but a few. The new Humanistic current also stimulated scientific research and was a fertile breeding ground for discoveries. Copernicus (1473–1543), Kepler (1571–1630), and Galileo (1564–1642) recognized the position of the Earth in the universe.

Their ideas were brilliantly confirmed by the voyages of discovery of Columbus (1451–1506), Vasco da Gama (1468–1524) and Magellan (1480–1521). This period is also characterized by a new artistic tendency, orientated on Antiquity, which developed, above all, in Italy.

Florence became its artistic centre and attracted artists like Leonardo da Vinci (1452–1519), Raphael (1483 to 1520) and Michelangelo (1475–1564). The wealthy rising middle classes became patrons of the plastic and pictorial arts as well as of architecture and had themselves portrayed by famous artists. The new artistic tendency spread out from Florence to Rome, where artists like Albrecht Dürer (1471–1528) were inspirated and bore these new ideas across the Alps to Germany.

In Germany, too, it was the wealthy middle classes who became the supporters of this movement. Another cultural centre arose in Flanders. It was, in the main, Flemish painters like Jan van Eyck (1390–1441) who saw human beings as an integral part of Nature, portraying many details lovingly and integrating the landscape.

The Italian architect, art historian and writer Leone Battista Alberti (1404–1472) was greatly attracted to the new way of painting and building. His writings are evidence of an all-round education, an energy, a thirst for knowledge and an enthusiasm that are veritably astounding. In his work *Della Pittura* (On painting; 1435), he dealt with the new Florentine school of painting and attempted to lay bare its theoretical basis.

He concerned himself with questions of perspective, proportion and geometry, which were soon to acquire deep-reaching significance for gardening, too. His works also helped to create the beginnings of the Italian Renaissance garden. He laid down the basic tenets for the layout of these gardens in his work *De re aedificatoria* (On the art of building), completed in 1452 and published in 1485.

The early Renaissance villa is provided with open halls and betrays the influence of the Ancient Roman architect Vitruvius. According to Alberti, the guest should almost imperceptibly reach the heights where the house is erected by means of gently sloping paths, to be overcome with the beauty of the garden. Protection from the sun is provided by the portico and by pergolas along the side paths, as well as by grottoes of tufa that should resemble those of Antiquity.

He also praises the custom of the forbears to place plants in tubs and line paths with box. "Clear, bright brooklets should traverse the garden and bubble up everywhere unexpectedly. He wants the spring in a grotto framed by coloured mussel-shells. Circles and semi-circles, regarded as beautiful in the courtyards, he also demands in the garden" (Gothein) and statues as well.

All this is a clear reminder of the gardens described by writers of Antiquity. Undoubtedly he was influenced in his artistic outlooks by Pliny the Younger. However, the character of the garden had become quite different. For Alberti, the garden ushers us into the house and must have a bright and cheerful atmosphere, despite its formal, regular construction.

Terrace gardens
of the Italian Renaissance

Some time was to elapse until Alberti's ideas were realized. He forged ahead as a theoretician and laid the foundation stone for the garden designs of the Early Renaissance, until Donato Bramante (1444–1514) created the first real Renaissance garden. Prevailed upon by Pope Julius II (1443–1513), Bramante designed a plan in 1503 which foresaw the connecting of the Vatican Palace lying in the plain with the little palace Belvedere erected on a hill. Bramante combined the architectural aspects and garden planning in a masterly projection. A novelty was that he bridged the different levels of the terrain by steps which joined up the three flat areas on which the gardens were laid out. Upon climbing and descending these steps, changing perspectives opened to the eye, cleverly enhancing the effect of the buildings and gardens.

The rediscovery of the culture of Ancient Rome was a further influence on the development of the Renaissance garden. We would cite, for example, the excavation of sculptures, sometimes restored or copied and placed in gardens. New impulses for the art of gardening in the Early Renaissance came from Tuscany. Florence, situated in central Italy in a charming landscape — a cultural centre and, at the same time, a town of great political significance. Its economy prospered and trade received an even greater stimulus when Florence purchased the port of Livorno from Genoa in 1421. Banking houses increased in number and their transactions offered the opportunity for the realization of large-scale economic projects. The history of Italy was also closely tied up with the Medici family, the descendants of the rich banker Giovanni Bicci de Medici (1360–1429). This family gained a leading position in the field of politics and economy and furthered the careers of painters, sculptors and architects. Cosimo I de Medici (1389–1464) showed a great interest in the arts. He gave commissions to artists like Donatello (1386–1466) and Brunelleschi (1377–1446) and also had a great influence on gardening. Michelangelo was taken up by the Medicis as a young man and attended a school founded by Lorenzo de Medici (1449–1492) in the garden of San Marco.

The gardens of Tuscany displayed elements of a style which revealed the beginnings of a new epoch in garden design. Characteristic of this new approach was the sloping garden, whose origins are to be found in the natural relief of the terrain. In the first place, it offered favourable opportunities of an artistic revelation in the lay-out and design of the gardens and, at the same time, enriched the visitor's pleasure by the infinitely beautiful view of the fascinating landscape.

In order to deal with the difference in height, the architects constructed terraces, held up by supporting walls. The visitor went from one terrace to another by means of staircases which were usually to be found within the buildings. Outdoor stairs of the kind which later ornamented the gardens of the High Renaissance, were not in evidence at that time.

The areas on the terraces were divided into geometrical shapes, each enclosed by pruned boxtrees. Paths were arranged in stellar formation or ran parallel to each other; they made their best impression when seen from above. The terrace lying immediately in front of the building was mainly covered by lawns. There were seating accommodations, and visitors liked to linger there to enjoy the view.

Somewhat remote but still in the vicinity of the villa, small, enclosed spaces were to be found — so-called *giardini segreti,* secret or private gardens. The idea was to create an intimate domain into which persons could retreat for undisturbed discussion with their friends or where they could enjoy the pleasures of nature.

In some Tuscan gardens cavernous grottoes were already popular, like the one put up on the Medici castello. They became more numerous and significant in the gardens to follow in later times. Artists often decorated them with fantastic figures and groups of animals. So-called surprise fountains were also frequently to be found in these grottoes.

Ground-plans of Renaissance gardens make evident that the buildings were not yet part of the garden design — a feature so typical of the Baroque period, where villa and garden belonged to one architectural ensemble.

The Boboli gardens in Florence

The Boboli gardens next to the Palazzo Pitti in Florence represented a famous deed reminiscent of the Medici familiy. Work commenced in 1550, after drawings by the Florentine architect and sculptor Niccolò Broccini. Also involved in their construction was Bartolomeo Ammanati (1511–1592), who created the façades of the Palazzo Pitti and a great deal of garden architecture and waterworks. The palace and the gardens were not completed, however, until the middle of the 17th century.

The terrain is characterized by its division into two quite separate parts. The palace, with its courts and side wings, seems to lean against the rocky banks of the river Arno; its courtyards are enclosed by a wall cutting deep into the hillside. For the ground floor Ammanati created a grotto which caught up and carried away the watercourse that gushed forth from the cleft in the hillside — representing a special attraction.

The garden begins at about the height of the first storey, i.e., above the grotto. On this lowest level of the garden, a marvellous fountain rises up, creating an imposing foreground to the garden side of the palace. From the palace, one has a wonderful view of the imposing amphitheatre with its cascades.

The amphitheatre is surrounded by a wall with rows of seats and serves as an enclosed open space for festivities. Seemingly immeasurable labyrinthine paths in luxuriant woods stretch out from above and sidewards from the amphitheatre, although the main paths run in strictly geometrical order.

Two gently rising avenues lead to a particularly attractive water arrangement, the little Isola Bella, built in 1570 by the Italian painter, architect and writer Giorgio Vasari (1511–1574), which is surrounded by wild bushes. Here the eye is caught by an elliptical pool which is enhanced by balustrades, decorative vases of flowers and statues. In the middle of the pool, 94 metres long and 70 metres wide, lies a little island to be reached by two bridges and beautified by flower beds and a Neptune fountain.

The Boboli gardens of Florence provide an impressive picture of the High Renaissance, to be surpassed only by garden arrangements of Rome and its surroundings. It was here that Italian Renaissance gardening reached its climax, here that the art of gardening found its most beautiful expression, even by comparison with gardens in other European countries. Whether it is the Villa Medici in Rome, the Villa d'Este in Tivoli or the Villa Lante in Bagnaia, they all incorporate the finest unfolding of an artistic tendency which differs so much, both in size and decoration, from the little narrow gardens of the Middle Ages.

We can recognize changes in the ground-plans, too. The open spaces fuse together with the buildings to form a unity. By contrast with the Tuscan gardens, a new architectonic conception can be detected.

The sloping position of the gardens inspired the designers to ever new ideas. The steps that were necessary to overcome the problem of the different levels were no longer confined to the interior of the buildings. Magnificent open-air stairways appeared, and artists and craftsmen of the Renaissance can lay claim to having recognized the significance of outside terraced stairways for gardens.

Water arrangements and water tricks

The use of water also gained in favour and gave a completely new character to the gardens. This re-birth of an enlivening element already highly appreciated in Antiquity, evolved in a myriad of forms. Rippling, rustling, spluttering from now on it gushed over stairways and cascades into pools and basins, towered up into mighty pillars or made its appearance as delightful imaginative fountains, ranging from the elegantly dainty to the imposingly large. The arrangement of water developed as an art which changed the whole appearance of the gardens. At first, however, these gardens were only constructed around the outskirts of Rome, as this was the only area where water in sufficient quantity was available.

Famous villa gardens

The Villa d'Este in Tivoli is a significant example of what was new in the art of gardening. Here everything grew in great profusion. This garden was completed in the year 1580 according to the plans of the architect Pirro Ligorio (1510–1583), its splendour and exuberance being quite unique.

Using both natural and artificial elements, the artist has created a work whose basic conception rests on geometry and architecture. Here the unity of house and garden is in evidence. If one proceeds from the northwest to the building complex, the path leads along a nearly 200-metre main axis, crossed at right angles by many side paths. One passes four boskets around whose perimeters two labyrinths are arranged. At the point where the main axis is crossed by the main lateral axis, there is a circular stand of cypresses. Following the path further, we come to ponds stretching out on both sides. On the left, the famous water organ can be seen. The ground rises gradually and leads again through boskets to the Dragon Fountain. Behind it, the Terrace of the Hundred Fountains is visible and at the end of this, on the left-hand side, stands the water theatre. On the right, a model of the Ancient Rome has been built.

The ground continues to rise up to the building complex, so that, from the bottom of the garden to the villa, an elevation of nearly 50 metres has to be surmounted. It is, above all, the beauty and extravagance of its waterworks to which the garden owes its fame. One arm of the river Anio is drained along the western border and then straight across the garden. It was in this way that they were able to create the wonderful waterworks.

Of the many splendid fountains in this garden, the Ovato Fountain may be considered the growning glory. Its flow pours out into a broad, rounded cascade beneath the gigantic statue of the Albunean Sybil making us aware of a dull roar in the surroundings. Today, the Terrace of the Hundred Fountains is thickly covered with moss. Over the coat-of-arms with its eagles, ships and lilies flows a fine spray of tiny water courses. Once, a row of terracotta reliefs adorned the terrace that takes up the whole width of the garden. One of the innumerable water arrangements is the water organ, whose notes are brought forth by water pressure on its enclosed cylinders. Thus the air inside the organ pipes is squeezed out. The many tiny water courses and cascades along the ramps, the powerful stream of water in the Dragon Fountain and the ponds with their stock of fish are also evidence of the great variety of water arrangements.

Though the garden has not been destroyed, nonetheless, in the 18th century, it had already been robbed of its rich array of statues, and numerous waterworks are no longer working today. Many visitors who saw the garden in its prime wrote about their impressions. Michel de Montaigne (1533–1592), a French writer and essayist, described the water organ, observed the water-spouting dragon of the middle fountain and the singing birds in the western theatre with interest. In another place he de-

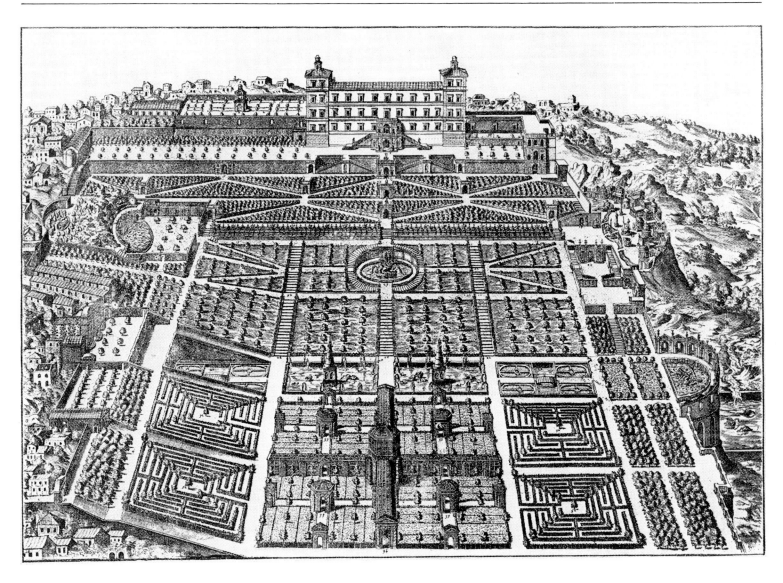

Total view of the Villa d'Este in Tivoli. Engraving by Etienne du Pérac.

scribes sounds like the thunder of cannon or rapid fire, all produced by the magic of water. He was aroused to greatest amazement by the water tricks which became increasingly important and numerous in the Italian Renaissance garden. The aim was to get the unsuspecting visitor wet through. Such water automatons existed in many Italian gardens.

The French philosopher Charles de Brosses (1709 to 1777) who, in 1739, many years after the construction of these gardens, visited several of them with friends, describes the working of such automatons very amusingly. "... in the Villa Mondragone, around a polypriapic pool; all round the rim of the basin there are leather hoses fitted with copper nozzles. These hoses lay there, inert and innocent, but when the water-cock was turned on, these strange creatures began to stand up in the most comical way and — as Rabelais puts it — to pee in an unbroken stream of water. Migieur took hold of one of them and directed it straight into Lacurne's face; the latter naturally retaliated in the same way and then we all began to take part in this pleasing sport until, after half an hour, we were wet through to the skin. One would think that winter was not the right season for such games but the day was so mild and warm that we couldn't resist the temptation.

We returned to our hostel to get changed. And guess what happened then! We were all sitting quite virtuously at the Belvedere in the Villa Aldobrandini and waiting for the Centaur (another water device) to begin to play on his trumpet. But we didn't notice the hundred treacherous water-hoses in the spaces between the stones until they burst forth and drenched us.

The Villa Medici in Rome. Earliest engraving from the 16th century.

Well, after our little romp at Mondragone, we had no more dry clothes, so we toddled along in good spirits to the dampest part of the palace where we spent the rest of the evening playing similar tricks. There's a particularly nice little curving staircase there; when you've climbed some steps the water begins to rain down on you from all sides, from above and below, left and right. At the top end of these steps, vengeance was meted out to Legouz who had been responsible for the watery adventure at the Belvedere. He had intended to turn on a water-cock to squirt water at us, but the water-cock was a trap that deceived the would-be deceiver; it shot out a stream of water as thick as your arm, and caught Legouz in the area of

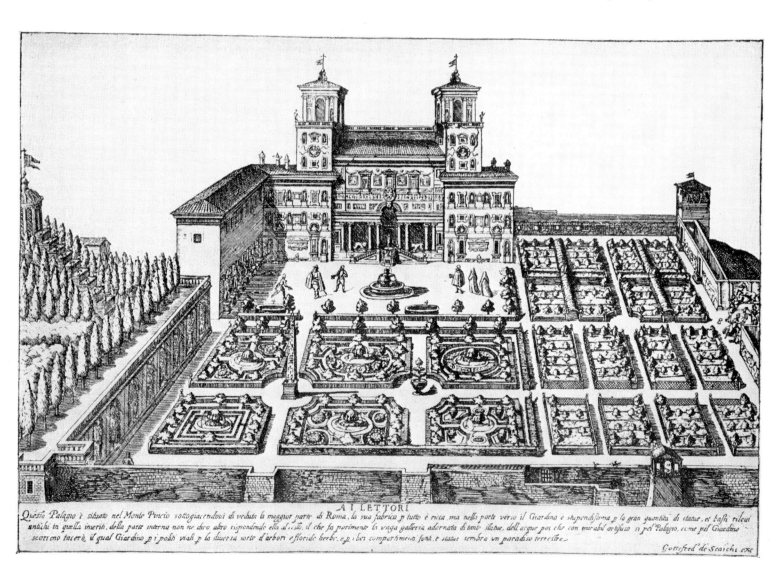

A I LETTORI

Questo Palagio è situato nel Monte Pincio sottogiacendoui di veduta la maggior parte di Roma, la sua fabrica p tutto è rica ma nella parte verso il Giardino è stupendissima p la gran quantità di statue, et bassi rilievi antichi in quella inseriti, della parte interna non ne dico altro rispondendo ella al resto, il che fa parimente la vaga galleria adornata di tante statue, dell'acque poi che con mirabil artifitio si pel Palagio, come pel Giardino scorreno tacerò, il qual Giardino p i polti vrali p la diuersa sorte d'arbori e floride herbe, e p i bei compartimenti fonti, e statue sembra vn paradiso terrestre.

Gottofred' de Scaichi ext.

the stomach with savage force. He was impelled backwards and the water streamed out of his water-logged trousers down into his shoes."

The best preserved garden of the Renaissance is that of Bagnaia near Viterbo which can still be admired today. The Villa Lante has been completely and meticulously restored; it is one of the few preserved masterworks of gardening. In 1564 the architect Giacomo Barozzi da Vignola (1507–1573) began to plan and to build the Villa Lante for Cardinal Giovanni Francesco Gambara. After his death, it was Cardinal Alessandro Montalto (1567 to 1623) who brought this important work to completion.

The garden has been kept narrow and rectangular and descends in terraces over a wooded slope. The villa stands in the first third of the grounds and is composed of two identical buildings, one on either side of the central axis. They fit in perfectly with the whole ensemble, an effect increased by the simplicity of their outside appearance. They seem to prefer to draw back in their effect and let the garden dominate. In this way they add to the effectiveness of the whole ensemble.

The lower parterre, cut off from the town by a high wall with a gate-house, is really splendid. The centre is dominated by a fountain; four quadratic pools, surrounded by balustrades, enclose a circular pond with their rounded corners. In the middle of this reservoir, four naked youths bear aloft the Montalto coat-of-arms. From this parterre, the garden rises gently in terraces and, from the balustrades, provides a wonderful view of the lower part. The uppermost terrace contains a grotto that was erected between two open buildings. From up here the water pursues its course along the main axis of the garden. It gushes out of the grotto down into a *bassin* and disappears, to emerge into daylight again in the Dolphin Fountain and then ripples quietly down into the *cordonata* or chain cascade, which lies between hedges and trees. By comparison with the Villa d'Este in Tivoli, this garden breathes a quiet elegance; the water's flow is barely audible as it seeks its course. The Fountain of the Giants and the Fountain of the Lambs dominate the picture on the middle terrace.

Apart from the water arrangement, the vegetation enhances the architectural impression in a perfect way. The higher one climbs from the flower beds of the lowest terrace, the more the dark vegetation dominates and the shadow comes to the fore. The geometrically formed gardens are bounded on one side by a park whose less formal shape somewhat softens their strict symmetry. There is still a labyrinth in this park and several fountains, such as the Pegasus Fountain. In other parts of the park loose groupings of bordering trees provide a contrast, and through this the architecture also gains in effectiveness.

As already mentioned, even in Rome the construction of such gardens was impossible for some time because the water supply was insufficient. Just such generous projects, with their water arrangements, were dependent upon the efficiently functioning waterpipes of the town. The aqueducts of Ancient Rome were dried up, and the only pipes which had been constructed in the time of Pope Sixtus IV (1414–1484) fell far short of these requirements. It was only when Sixtus V (1520–1590) had the Aqua Felice built, followed by the construction of Aqua Paola by Paul V (1552–1621) that water became available. Now great gardens with fountains and waterworks could be constructed on the hills upon which Rome was built.

Already in 1574, Pope Gregory XIII (1502–1585) decided to have the Quirinal Palace built on Monte Cavallo. For this purpose gardens of formal design were laid out with many fountains, stepped cascades and a water organ with four registers.

At almost the same time, the garden of the Villa Medici on Monte Pincio came into being. The lay-out of the garden presents a harmonic ensemble, nevertheless, the perfect unity of architecture and garden design is still missing. The façade of the villa, facing the garden, has an especially light, graceful character because of a retreating upper storey crowned by a tower. Arched niches between pillars are decorated with statues. The gardens are kept simple on a geometrical ground-plan. Special mention should be made of the many statues to be found here, too, a few of which stand among the attractive groves that form the main view.

The little park is strictly formal in construction and is characterized by quadratic parterres of flowers surrounded by box. In the middle of a square, a simple fountain sends forth its spray. By climbing a stairway which is guarded by hermae, one reaches a pavilion situated at the top of the hill.

From the Escorial to the gardens of Buen Retiro near Madrid

At this time, gardens pointing to a new conception of gardening also sprang up in Spain. Although they were strongly marked by Italian influence and were mainly constructed by Italian gardeners, they also strike a national note.

The Escorial was a magnificently proportioned building. This palace with its monastery and gardens was built between 1563 and 1584 under Philip II (1527 to 1598), King of Spain from 1556. The architects were Spanish, working under the guidance of Italian craftsmen like Giacomo Barozzi da Vignola. Strict lineation and the utmost architectural simplicity are its main characteristics; it is one of the most costly buildings of the Renaissance. The gardens are fastidious, but breathe the severity and cold reserve of the palace.

Theophile Gautier (1811–1872), the French poet, remarked about the palace: "To the east and south of this unsightly building the gardens stretch upon an uneven terrain supported by walls. There is more architecture to be met there than vegetation. There are great terraces; beds of pruned box form pictures similar to the crowns of branches to be found on old damasks. Some fountains and bits of greenish water decorate the dismal, boring garden. It is as stiff as a starched collar and fully worthy of the sombre building to which it is attached." Maybe this critical judgement is an unusual one; nevertheless, the gardens of the Escorial mirror the taste of Philip II.

Soon, however, in this century of festive celebration and glorification of power, Spain was called upon to abandon her restraint. For this, splendid palaces and gardens were necessary. Help in the planning came from Italy; the Medici sent architects and gardeners.

The main credit for the efflorescence of Spanish gardens at this time deserves the Florentine Cosimo Lotti (died *c.* 1650). Aranjuez, summer residence of the Spanish kings since the reign of Philip II, is an old garden that, although later partly re-modelled, nonetheless lost little of its original character.

The Tejo divides the garden into two halves and the available water was used in a really creative way. When it was re-modelled, the island garden was transformed into a bosket richly decorated with fountains. A large pool with a Hercules fountain was placed at the entrance. Circular or octagonal squares as well as crossing points were decorated in like manner by numerous fountains.

In front of the palace there is a richly formed parterre, while to the right attention is drawn to a cascade; another one tumbles down at the Tejo in the north. This island, full of the gurgling sound of water, is an Eldorado of water arrangements that need not fear comparison with the famous Italian water gardens. Later, Aranjuez was influenced by Le Nôtre, in that the woods bordering it were incorporated into its design.

Philip IV (1605–1665) lived in Madrid during the whole of his forty-year reign; whilst he took a great deal of trouble maintaining the interior decoration of his palace, improving the gardens was of little interest to him. Instead he was taken up with a different project, namely, Buen Retiro near Madrid. He obtained terrain near the Monastery San Jerónimo and here, in the course of two years, he had a stately home built with gardens which, from then on, served the Spanish Court. On the north side, the palace nestled up against the old monastery and was quite simple and without decoration. In accordance with building practices at that time, the rooms were grouped round courtyards. The parterre which appeared in this way was enhanced by two fountains. The main parterre — Jardín de la Reina (Queen's Garden) — was built to the north of this. As in Italian villas like those of the Medici and Borghese, a large square was provided, next to the parterre, for knightly sports. The park itself was constructed along generous lines, showing evidence of Italian models, but it lacked views into the distance which are typical in Italian parks. The central point in the eastern part of the park formed a great star. Eight covered ways led out from there towards various parts of the park.

Large pools and canals, boskets with fountains as well as flower parterres lent this garden a special charm. The flowers were brought in from all over the world: "... in 1633 thirteen wagon-loads arrived from Valencia, and Cardinal Pio di Savoya sent his gardener, Fabrizio, from Rome with flower bulbs worth 10,000 ducats."

The somewhat secluded parts of the park to the south had more of a rural character, with meadows and trees. Buen Retiro set the trend for the further development of gardening, largely because of the so-called hermit villas in its park. Small garden villas were erected, mainly on the periphery but also spread throughout the park. Each had a chapel, a little look-out tower and also small parterre gardens with a labyrinth and a grotto.

The summit of Spain's glory were the performances in the theatre of Buen Retiro built by Cosimo Lotti already in 1637. As the back wall of the stage could be removed, the park could serve as scenery and offered the theatre almost unlimited spaciousness.

Azulejos and cascades in Portugal

The Italian style of gardening was emulated in Portugal but enriched by and further developed with national elements. As in Spain, here, too, it was the Italians who sent the garden designers who introduced the Italian Renaissance garden in Portugal. The Moorish inheritance is more noticeable in Portugal than in Spain. *Azulejos* were of special importance for decorating buildings and gardens. Originally, these were blue tiles which were later produced in other colours, too. Brought by the Arabs from Asia Minor, they were used by the Portuguese on walls and floors much more frequently than in Spain.

They were enhanced with abstract geometrical patterns or with arabesques. It was not until the middle of the 16th century that pictorial art blossomed and that these tiles were decorated with pictures or used as sections of larger motifs.

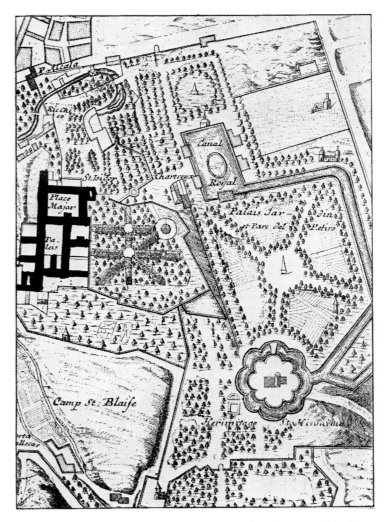

Buen Retiro near Madrid, plan of the park (after J. B. Homann).

In the villa of the Marquis de Fronteira in Bemfica the visitor is strangely moved by a pool that lies to one side. A high wall that supports a narrow terrace is divided by three gates. In between are twelve panels of faience tiles representing statues of riders. Into the wall supporting the upper terrace, five niches have been built, in which portraits of Portuguese kings stand out in red enamel; the spaces in between are decorated with terracotta ornaments.

A balustrade divides the pool from the rest of the garden, thus creating an independent domain. On the side, steps lead to the upper terrace. This landscaping is a typical Portuguese phenomenon. The large basins, mainly situated on high walls and enhanced with blue tiles, are the most eye-catching feature.

Another motif of Portuguese garden design are the cascades that were frequently made into a splendid arrangement of stepped waterfalls near monasteries situated at high altitudes. The earliest known example of such constructions was at the Bussaco Monastery. Amidst old cedars, stairways on both sides of a water course lead from one platform to another. Between the steps, the water drops down in little waterfalls and flows into a pool.

Somewhat more generously proportioned is the Monastery Bom Jesus do Monte in Braga. Here the platforms are decorated with niches, ornaments, statues and fountains. The steps to the highest terrace, which is crowned by a cathedral, are laid out in a semi-circle around a niche. This magnificent picture served as a model for other constructions.

We may regard these native elements of a Portuguese style as imposing, but no garden style was originated here that could materially influence developments outside the country's borders.

Gardens of the Loire Valley

Well before French gardens became famous, the dukes of Burgundy created great gardens in Hesdin. Under Philip the Good (1419–1467) they achieved a splendour which was unique for their time; there was nothing like them anywhere else in France. These gardens were destroyed by Charles V in 1533 but they have been preserved pictorially in miniatures by Burgundian artists.

The beginning of the French Renaissance coincided with the Italian campaign of Charles VIII (1407–1498) from 1495 to 1496. The king from the House of Anjou undertook the campaign to stress his right of inheritance of the Kingdom of Naples. The undertaking was not very successful from a military point of view but, to set against this, it had results of wide significance for cultural history. He became acquainted with many works of art that signalled the beginning of a new epoch — the Early Renaissance —, and this left him with impressions deeply affecting the king and arousing his enthusiasm.

It must have been in Italy that he made up his mind to transform his châteaux along the same lines, for he brought famous artists and architects with him from Italy to France. The transformation of the châteaux of Amboise and Blois was the beginning of the extension and re-modelling of several estates in the Loire Valley which became characteristic for French Renaissance style in architecture.

Because of political developments in France due to the Hundred Years' War with England, defended châteaux were necessary until the middle of the 15th century. So it was defence systems with towers, bastions and moats that determined the outward image of the towns and châteaux parklands. Even in new buildings at the beginning of the 16th century, moats and corner towers were predominant. So the gardens which existed at that time hardly differed from the castle gardens of the Middle Ages. In a narrow, level park, laid out like a chessboard, the square fields were surrounded by hedges. Pergolas softened the picture, fountains and pavilions were not lacking either. To obtain more space for gardens, Charles VIII had a high terrace extended in Amboise, later to be decorated with a gallery in the reign of Louis XII (1462–1515).

The dimensions of the gardens at Blois were much vaster; these were part of the royal château whose origins go right back to Roman times. What had formerly been a small mediaeval garden was laid out as the lowest parterre of a new garden. Massive quantities of earth were shifted to create three terraces, one above the other. However, as it was the custom in France at this time to have each separate part of the garden enclosed, steps were not necessary. So the three terraces were not connected and the result of this re-modelling left the three sections of the garden quite isolated from each other. Even the architecture of the château did not blend with the landscape.

Despite Charles VIII's enterprise and Louis XII's commitment to the transformation of the gardens, the breakthrough of the French Renaissance only came later. Francis I (1494–1547) began constructing larger gardens and buildings. The most magnificent château of the Loire Valley arose — Chambord. Two other châteaux of Francis I's reign were Fontainebleau and Chantilly.

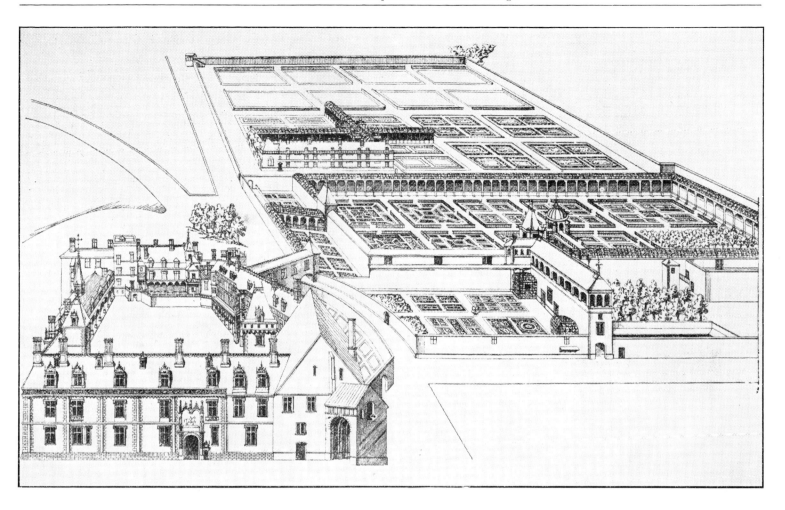

Total view of Blois. Engraving by Jacques Androuet du Cerceau.

Architects designate this Renaissance style with Gothic elements as Francis I style. But it was not until Henry IV (1553–1610), who came to the French throne in 1589, that there was a really new momentum in the approach to gardening. He could call upon a large number of architects of outstanding ability in Fontainebleau, Saint-Germain-en-Laye near Paris and around the royal palace at the Tuileries in the capital.

After the murder of Henry IV, when notable statesmen like Richelieu (1585–1642) influenced state politics and brought about social changes, this artistic tendency gained in strength and influence. But there was also another fact of significance for the development of the French garden in great style. The change of domicile to escape the summer heat, as, for instance, in Italy was not necessary in the cooler northern areas of France or in other countries north of the Alps. So the French Court stayed at the château for their vacation. The château and its grounds became their seat and later their official residence, with extended gardens that offered every opportunity for entertainment. These designs later on influenced the colossal spectacular gardens of Versailles.

Lakes and canals
as important elements in design

If the Italian influence was still evident, there were deviations from it — canals and lakelets, springs and fountains instead of the manifold cascades of the typical Italian villa garden. A native French perception of the garden began to shine through, a perception which very soon aspired to the unity of the buildings and the garden arrangement. At Fontainebleau a boggy area was transformed into a lake and the moat was consciously incorporated into the general design. This is how the French canal garden developed.

From now on lake and canal were an important element in French garden design. Such gardens quickly became popular. Where natural pre-conditions existed — subsoil water at high levels — these regions became the site where parks with large water areas could be created.

None of these gardens surrounding the châteaux are preserved in their original form. Only reconstructions — of which Villandry is the most painstaking — and the exceedingly numerous and accurate etchings of former artists can give us an idea of their design.

From the middle of the 16th century, exact regularity in the basic design was demanded in the planning of gardens, and within their borders all shapes had to be geometrical. Famous for their designs were the architects Philibert de l'Orme (1510/15–1570) and, even more, Jacques Androuet du Cerceau (1510–1589). The latter drew plans of châteaux grounds and gardens that were published in *Les plus excellents bâtiments de France* (The most excellent buildings of France) in 1576 and 1579.

Thanks to these drawings, we are able to trace the development of the most important forms of French gardens of the period. It is characteristic of French Renaissance gardens that the châteaux and the gardens were surrounded by a moat. The various elements like the parterre — composed of separate quadratic shapes — and the boskets did not blend with each other.

Verneuil is the perfect example of a French Renaissance garden based on Bramante's Belvedere. If it is not absolutely clear to what extent Du Cerceau, himself, contributed to this development, but one can assume that the plan of the moated garden at Verneuil was his brainchild. Amboise and Blois are largely the works of Pacello da Marcogliani. Between 1530 and 1533, Du Cerceau studied in Rome and knew the Belvedere from close inspection.

Grotto gardens, whose origins can be traced back to Roman times, became popular again in Italy from the 16th century onwards and spread to France. An early example is the grotto erected at Fontainebleau. As, in the middle of the 16th century, any garden worth its salt had to be furnished with a grotto, it became a question of constantly finding new ways of decorating them to make them real attractions. Adorned with mussel-shells, such grottoes became places for theatre performances well into the reign of Louis XIV. Later open-air theatres took over this function.

The famous French parterre

A new era in the development of gardening began during the reign of Henry IV. It is intimately connected with the names of notable men like Olivier de Serres (1539 to 1619), Claude Mollet (*c.* 1563–*c.* 1650), Du Pérac (1525–1610) and Jacques Boyceau (died *c.* 1630) who publicized their conceptions and plans.

In 1599, Olivier de Serres published a work entitled *Le Théâtre d'Agriculture,* whose 6th volume was largely devoted to gardening. He gives advice on the designing of parterres (Latin *partiri*), i.e., arranging the garden in sections. In the sequence of patterns and the planting of the beds, there must be the greatest diversity according to his opinion. He recommended low-lying shrubs like lavender, mint and many others as borders for the parterre; later on these were replaced by the durable box.

At the centre of the pattern, low-growing flowers like pansies, stocks, lilies-of-the-valley and others should be planted, though not a mixture of different flowers but only one species. He proposed that, around the pattern or bed, coloured gravel or sand should be strewn so that the whole should present a colourful picture at all seasons. The choice of variegated and attractive patterns was his criterion for an effective design of the parterre and a harmonious interplay of plants, colours and other elements.

Total view of Saint-Germain-en-Laye (after Braun and Hogenberg).

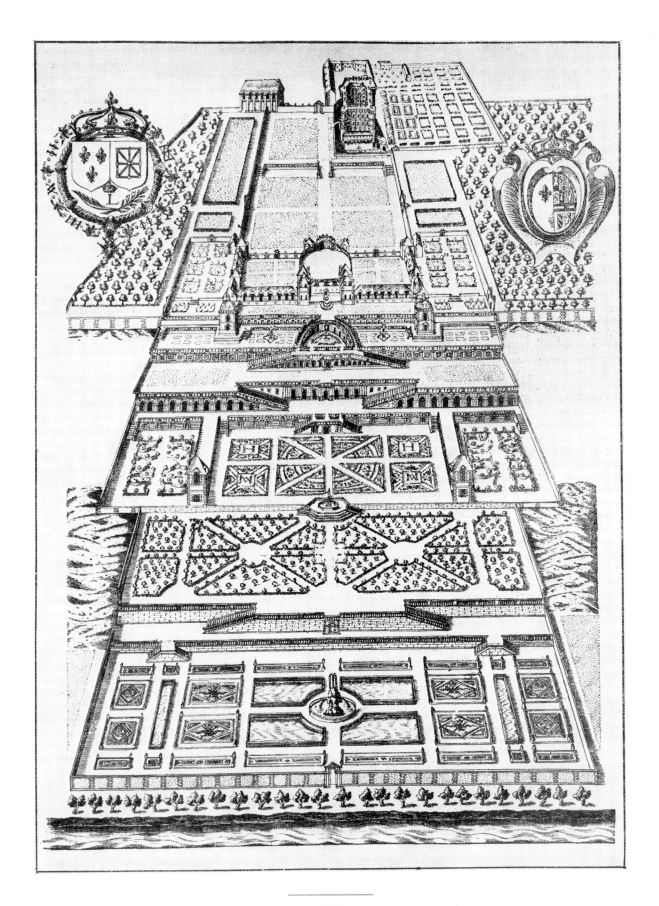

He believed that a cypress in the centre resembles the pin of a sun-dial; instead of a pyramid of trees he proposed to put up statues of all kinds, obelisks, pillars, marble pyramids, jasper or porphyry on those parterres — a grand sight when viewed from above.

Mollet's ideas corresponded with those of De Serres, though he already demanded various species of tall flowering bushes to border the sections of the parterre, so that the ribbon of blossoms flowered uninterruptedly throughout the seasons.

Mollet, mainly employed as a gardener at Fontainebleau under Henry IV and publisher of the book *Le Théâtre des Plants et Jardinages,* experienced the decisive development of the parterre garden during his actively creative period. At the end of the 16th century, the parterre began to be laid-out in a new way. When Du Pérac came back from Italy in 1582, after having eagerly studied ancient and Italian art, he brought with him valuable stimuli. He recommended that the individual parterres should be united into a single one. Boyceau, one of the most important parterre designers, in his sketches showed impressively the new type of parterre, using the

Jardin du Luxembourg as an example. Here, the parterre has closed around a central line in complete symmetry.

Instead of geometrical forms, lively lines of tendril-like ornaments dominate, giving the impression of delightful embroidery. The fashion of exquisite flowered, arabesque embroidery on clothes and furniture textiles of every kind, made of colourful silks, gold or silver, above all at the time of Henry IV and Louis XIII (1601–1643), all influenced the design of the parterre.

Although we should see Boyceau as a forerunner of the great French garden designers of Louis XIV's time, his greatest and most effective period was still during Henry IV's reign. For Henry he designed the new château at Saint Germain-en-Laye near Paris. Its position on the sloping bank of the Seine permitted the building of terraces; he constructed six in all and laid out attractive parterres on them with tendril ornaments. It was on the threshold of the age of Louis Quatorze who, with his Absolutist ambitions and his need for power and glory, created the conditions for the establishment of remarkable gardens, such as at Vaux-le-Vicomte and Versailles.

The English knotted flower beds
While the Italian art of gardening was reaching its zenith and France had already begun to realize its own horticultural ideas, England was still suffering from the effects

The *treillage* is one of the typical features in the château garden of Montargis. It is a rib-like, interwoven lattice framework with plastic adornments.

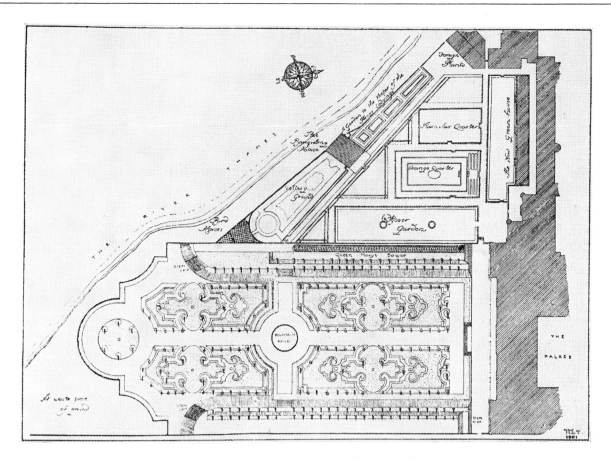

Hampton Court in the 17th century with the reconstructed flower garden. Contemporary engraving.

of her devastating civil war. The first evidence of any significant garden construction comes down to us from the twenties of the 16th century. Unfortunately, the few gardens that had been created up till then were completely altered in the course of time or have totally rotted away, so that today it is difficult to get a clear picture of them *in situ*. But written documentation does put us in a position to paint a graphic picture of the characteristics of the English Renaissance garden.

The first person to bring the new continental gardening trends across the Channel was Cardinal Wolsey (*c.* 1475 to 1530). This influential Lord Chancellor under Henry VIII (1491–1547) stood high in the king's favour until the latter, envious and jealous of his estate, brought about his fall from grace.

After consultation with famous physicians and scholars, the cardinal chose "the healthiest place within twenty miles of London" (Law) and had a summer house erected at Hampton Court, still using mediaeval architectonic elements like towers, battlements and moats, a style of building which only died out slowly. When Hampton Court fell to the throne, Henry VIII re-modelled this long desired country seat very quickly. So the building and the garden were given a magnificent appearance. The garden beds were laid-out in knotted patterns, called knotted beds; popular flowers of the time were planted there, like violets, carnations and primroses. The beds were bordered in various ways.

In the course of time, however, Hampton Court's image changed completely; the so-called pond garden was rearranged as an orangery; pot plants now stood on the paths at the side of the terraces. Its present form dates back to the time of William III (1650–1702) and Queen Mary II (1662–1694).

Labyrinths and mazes

Hampton Court had the most famous maze in England of that time. Such mazes were to be found at Hatfield House and Chatsworth as well. Labyrinths of this kind were constructed in practically every great garden of Europe in the 16th and 17th centuries; they were made of yew, privet and box. But the Renaissance was not the first period that mazes appeared on the scene. In the past they had a certain mythological significance. From China to Peru it was believed that evil spirits could not find their way so easily along tortuous paths as along straight ones. Troy, which lay behind a complicated system of walls, is another example of this attitude. Children in Rome played the Troy game, in which they drew labyrinths on the floor and had to find their way through them. In Rome, floors were often decorated with pictures of labyrinths. The labyrinth was a model for the European mazes of later date. Those that still exist today, however, are usually of a more recent date and are all composed of the same types of hedges, mostly head-high.

Isaac de Caus created one of the most important gardens of this time. He was called to Wilton House in Wiltshire in 1615, by the Earl of Pembroke. As De Caus published his own engravings and explanatory texts, so the erection of Wilton House was also depicted in a series of twenty-four copperplate engravings, published by him in 1615 under the title *Hortus Pembrochianus.*

These gardens measured a thousand feet long and four hundred feet wide and were laid out in three areas, one behind the other with paths crossing the terrain. Parterres formed the first section with beds artistically enclosed by low hedges; the parterres were held together in fours by a fountain and a marble statue in their midst. De Caus used the expression "embroidered parterres", as he was well acquainted with the *parterres de broderie* popular in France at that time which he introduced in England.

This was followed by two boskets with the river Nadder flowing through them which was fifty feet wide at this point. In the middle of the two boskets a broad path led across a bridge and to two great pools on either side of the path, with pillars between the pools. The third section was crowned at the centre by a statue, the Borghesian Swordsman, surrounded by concentric, oval paths.

De Caus thought it to be the most famous statue of Antiquity. At the end of this domain stretched a terrace with a balustrade along its full width. Marble statues and niches between the pillars divided the terrace into sections and made the front less stiff in appearance. In the middle, De Caus designed a grotto; on both sides of it steps with banisters, from which sea monsters spouted water, led upwards to the terrace. Here, above the grotto, lay a great pool with a fountain.

Unfortunately, nothing has remained of these gardens. Only the engravings by De Caus give us an idea of the rare beauty of this English Renaissance garden. A similar fate was suffered by the favourite garden of Queen Henrietta, wife of Charles I, in Wimbledon, that represents the highest perfection of the art of gardening in the middle of the 17th century. On the whole, no great inspirations for European gardening were transmitted by England and her gardeners, during this epoch. The English Renaissance garden differed little from the French, while the incidence of these gardens in England remained sparse.

Richly laid-out German citizens' gardens

While in Italy, France and England there were only very few centres of gardening, more or less exemplary for its development during the Renaissance, the situation was different in Germany. Here, at the end of the 15th century, the mighty wave which carried the new conception of art across the Alps from Italy, appealed to broad sections of the population. Representatives of the middle classes and the aristocracy had a common influence on the development of garden construction and inspired each other in a way unthinkable in the Middle Ages. On the one hand, the middle classes strove after a refined style of living and aristocratic forms of behaviour resembling

The garden of Christoph Peller in Nuremberg is one of those patrician gardens constructed, above all, in the great commercial cities by prosperous and influential personalities. Copperplate engraving by Michel Heer, 1655.

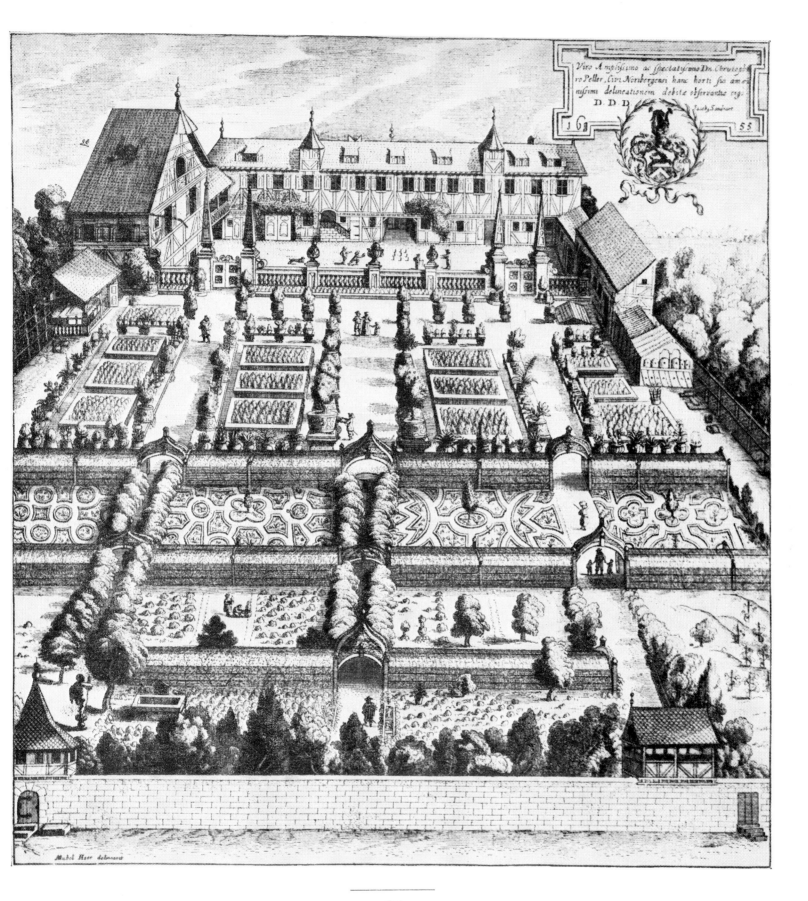

those of the nobility; on the other hand, the members of the aristocracy wanted to emulate the botanical propensities of the men of learning and the patricians. The basis for all this was created by the economic upswing and the far-reaching trading connections bound up with it, even though the various German principalities differed greatly in their development.

In South Germany, the expansion of the trade connections in the late Middle Ages had already led to the accumulation of large fortunes. So it was, in the main, the cities of Nuremberg, Augsburg and Frankfurt with their rich merchants who sponsored new conceptions in all fields of the arts. They were followed by Erfurt, Leipzig, Dresden, Breslau and Vienna.

Trade relations, themselves, created further practical preconditions for the great plans of the master builders and architects. The merchants travelling to the South were soon followed by physicians, naturalists and philosophers; artists set out on journeys to Italy to get inspirations from the great centres of art. They all were deeply impressed by the Italian way of life and told about the wonderful gardens and villas. Their narrations inflamed enthusiasm for the art of southern Europe, without, though, leading to imitations of the Roman or Tuscan garden. The models were used to stimulate the own creativity in designing gardens with a native touch.

True, certain elements, such as labyrinths, grottoes and artificial hills were incorporated, but they were modified and arranged in a new way. Further stimuli came from the Netherlands and France. In this way many foreign and native elements were combined, so that we cannot speak of a typically German style of gardening.

The growing interest in botany and the natural sciences encouraged the middle classes to collect plants; this was very soon to have a great influence on the garden lay-out in the 16th century. At first the new plants were regarded from the same viewpoint as in the Middle Ages and were valued largely for their medicinal properties; but soon interest arose not only in their beauty and their usefulness, but also in their location, their environmental condition, their cultivation and other aspects of their biotopes.

The new art of book printing furthered the spreading of botanical writings and introduced an important phase in the field of botany. At the head of this movement stand the German forefathers of botany, Otto Brunfels (1488 to 1534), who finished up as Medical Officer of Health in Berne and in 1532 wrote his book on herbs — *Contrafayt Kreuterbuch;* Hieronymus Bock (1498–1554), whose *New Kreuterbuch* appeared in 1539 and soon went into several editions; and Leonhard Fuchs (1501 to 1566), who was personal physician to the Count of Ansbach and, later, was professor at Tübingen (Hennebo/Hoffmann).

Most of the important botanists — who frequently were also physicians — owned beautiful gardens. In their case, this interest in gardening also arose from practical professional considerations. But for merchants and other middle-class citizens it came purely from the joy of collecting. Private collections were followed by the establishment of botanical gardens, for example in Königsberg (1551), Leipzig (1580) and Heidelberg (1597).

It was at this point that, in Germany, the town gardens increased in importance and, with the Fugger gardens in Augsburg, middle-class garden construction reached one of its high points. According to many contemporary documents they were quite comparable with the gardens of the Medici in Italy. In 1530 Charles V visited the Fugger gardens and admired their magnificence.

A year later Beatus Rhinatus wrote about them and thought them superior to the French royal gardens in Blois. Water tricks and a water garden, pergolas, fountains and statues were all components of these gardens. Botanical interest also provided an impetus here. In those days, everyone endeavoured almost jealously to collect new plants and make them bloom.

It was in pursuit of this aim that the famous botanist Karl Clusius (1526–1609), after whom the tulip *Tulipa clusii* is named, together with the heirs of the Fuggers went abroad in their search for new plants. Soon the Fugger gardens spread out so much that, in 1584, the citizens complained "that the residential areas were shrinking" (Gothein).

Page 93:
35 The enchanting gardens of the Vatican serve their inhabitants
as a place of rest and recuperation.

36 In 1954 the garden of the Villa Lante in Bagnaia
near Viterbo was completely restored.
The ballustrade of the fountain is enhanced by pine cones.

37 The Boboli gardens of Florence with the
horseshoe-shaped amphitheatre. View from the building.

38 View of the artificially constructed island,
the Isola Bella, in the Boboli gardens.
The fountain was created by Giovanni da Bologna.

39   The Terrace of the Hundred Fountains of the Villa d'Este in Tivoli.

40   The former water organ of the Villa d'Este in Tivoli.
Engraving by Venturini.

41   The Ovato Fountain in the Villa d'Este in Tivoli
is an example of the wealth of roaring waterfalls and
fountains of the Italian Renaissance garden.

42 The stepped cascade in the Portuguese monastery Bom Jesus
do Monte at Braga.

43 The garden of the villa of the Marquis de Fronteira
in Bemfica is laid-out in geometrical style with quadratic beds.

44 The Courtyard of the Evangelists is one of 16 courtyards of the
Escorial. It took 21 years to construct the huge building with its
12 cloisters, 86 stairways, 1,200 doors and more than 2,000 windows.

45 The gardens of Villandry were reconstructed by Carvallo
in the early 20th century after engravings
by Jacques Androuet du Cerceau. They are today among
the most famous restored Renaissance gardens.

46 The orangery of Fontainebleau. Engraving by Israel Silvestre.

47 The garden of Fontainebleau arose upon what was
formerly a swampy plain.

48 View of Hampton Court. Here Henry VIII had a
bowling alley and an indoor tennis court built.

49 Schloss Ambras with its spacious gardens was a favourite
retreat of Archduke Ferdinand and his wife, Philippine Welser.

50 Hellbrunn was famous for its waterworks.

Pages 104/105:
51 The impressively proportioned Jardin du Luxembourg
was designed by Jacques Boyceau.

52 The Waldstein garden at Prague was created
between 1625 and 1630. The statues, which are casts of works
created by Adrian de Vries, were made in 1626 and 1627.

53 In front of the Belvedere royal summer palace in Prague,
built in Renaissance style, stands the Singing Fountain;
the waterdrops falling on the bell metal
of the bowl produce various musical tones.

54 These gardens are situated on the grounds of the
former summer riding school at Prague castle.

Page 108:
55 The Waldstein palace with its five courtyards
and the extensive garden with many Baroque elements was erected
on a terrain originally destined for living quarters of the citizens.

The ideal garden of Erasmus of Rotterdam
and a Breslau scholar's garden

The gardens of the Humanists and scholars point to a connection with the philosophers' gardens of the ancient world. It was mainly in Florentine villas where scholars assembled, the small enclosed giardino segreto being the favourite place for their exchange of ideas. This model of the Italian Humanist garden combined with the mediaeval garden moulded Erasmus of Rotterdam's conceptions of the ideal garden.

This great Humanist pictured an ideal garden in his work *Convivium religiosum,* published in 1518. We find here a front garden leading into a flower garden with square ground-plan. In the midst of the beds is a fountain flowing out into a brook and dividing the garden into two halves. Surrounding the garden are three covered walks whose pillars are of simulated marble. According to Hennebo and Hoffmann the covered walks enclose a summer house resembling a pavilion, which rises up in the middle. This arrangement of garden architecture had existed in French gardens since the late Middle Ages and now extended to Germany. The walls of the summer house are painted with flowers and other garden motifs that rival the living plants growing outside and which, in winter, are intended to create the illusion of a blooming garden.

Parallels to the above are to be found, for example, in the Villa Livia at Primaporta and in the deceptive perspectives in Baroque gardens. The other gardens with fruit trees, vegetables and medicinal herbs are arranged around the flower garden. Near them are playgrounds, a meadow surrounded by hedges and a little summer house for taking meals. According to Erasmus' conceptions such a garden was also to contain a beehive and an aviary.

This garden planned as an ideal by a scholar, was actually created some fifty years after Erasmus' death — namely the garden of the Breslau physician and Humanist Laurentius Scholz (1556–1599). Its ground-plan is quadratic and it displays all the attributes recommended by Erasmus for an ingeniously designed garden. It is also interesting that Scholz commissioned a painter to make true-to-life illustrations of his plants, so giving us an idea of how richly stocked his garden was. The main delights of the flower garden were snowdrops, violets, crocuses, primroses, French cowslips and crown imperial, columbines, snapdragons, cornflowers, poppies and lilies. For the physician and botanist, the herbal garden was even more important. It contained many foreign plants from Spain, Italy and Austria, among others. Side by side with the medicinal plants that we know from the *Capitulare* and from the St. Gall Abbey plan, we find spices such as basil, sweet marjoram, melissa, hyssop, rosemary, rue and dittany. And then there are novelties, plants recently brought from India by Portuguese seafarers — like Indian cane and balsam and, worthy of special mention, the potato, unknown until then. In the orchard also ornamental trees are growing, like laburnum, guelder-rose and Turkish lilac.

The winding paths are bordered by trelliswork with climbing plants, there are imported oriental varieties in the rose garden. In a winter-house there are even pot-plants like oleander, myrtle and pomegranate.

From the Breslau scholar's garden — this typical German citizen's garden — we can trace the further development of middle-class garden design, as its distinctive features already mentioned remained until the end of the Renaissance.

While the princely gardens became, to some extent, more open, the citizens' gardens remained close, holding off, as it were, the outside world. Within its area, the many small details like hedges, covered walks and trelliswork covered with runners give rise to the impression of overloading. Where the rudiments of symmetrical axes emerge, these are broken up by hedges or lines of trees. So a basic concept is seldom in evidence (Hennebo/Hoffmann).

A letter of Benedict Factor, applying in 1579 for the position of Court gardener to the Elector of Saxony, is very instructive as he lists all preconditions necessary in the designing of a garden: "... to lay-out separate beautiful pleasure grounds, in a wonderful way, to provide much amusement and satisfaction, decorated with pretty little flowers to be used for medicaments, some for making oils, some for juices, some for perfumes, some for sweetmeats.

I may further be trusted to cultivate and trim trees in the shape of beautiful letters and coats-of-arms, to make sundials and do plantwork of all kinds in the most delicate shades; to create mysterious labyrinths and small enclosed places wonderful to behold, no matter what natural growths there be; to cultivate beautiful hawthorn plaited with hare's-twine, beautiful circular beds enhanced with trees so that one can see from their tops what sort of winds are prevailing and which winds they are. I may further be trusted to prepare water arrangements in the pleasure gardens, with leaping springs and fountains arranged with artistry, and to construct many other pieces in the pleasure gardens; further to make some simple little flowers double-flowered, and to create many other clever pieces in the garden that were never seen in this land" (Kaufmann).

The Thirty Years' War began with the defenestration of Prague in 1618, bringing the art of gardening gradually to languish or to stagnate in the countries concerned, while most of the existing gardens were destroyed. Very few new gardens came into being during this period, but among them were the Waldstein gardens in Prague, unfortunately, there are no contemporary representations. Today, the garden, still in its old position but lying hidden behind high walls in the heart of the city, is open to the public. Here, former Renaissance elements are still visible mingling with Baroque forms so that in this confined space a mixture of styles has developed.

Garden islands or island gardens

Germany, more torn up by the Thirty Years' War than before, only recovered slowly from its terrible effects. The post-war period was a time of re-building but also of transition. Foreign ideas and stimuli were again able slowly to penetrate into Germany; one source of these were the Netherlands. They were experiencing the heyday of their economic and cultural development. A garden city arose at Cleves under John Maurice of Nassau (1604–1679), reminiscent of the Dutch model. A once barren tract of land was turned into a blooming parkland with canals, avenues, country houses, terrace gardens, fountains and statues. It was the first attempt in Germany to blend several gardens into the landscape by means of avenues and canals. The Court garden of Celle, on the other hand, already features French influences.

Immediately upon taking over the government in Anhalt-Köthen, Prince Louis (1579–1650) re-erected a moated palace in his principality which had fallen victim to the flames fifty years earlier; the opportunity was taken to create wonderful gardens. In the main, the designs for the gardens were made by the prince himself, who spent part of his life in Italy.

So, in addition to the usual elements common to garden construction at that time, novelties were introduced which he had picked up on his travels (Salzmann). A great orchard and a vegetable garden resembled the one at the Villa d'Este in Tivoli, by reason of its cruciform covered walks, dividing the garden in four quarters. Various gardens lay next to each other, each provided with a specific motif without, however, giving the impression of a haphazard arrangement. No axial structure was perceptible, except two flower gardens where the main paths were stressed. Covered walks, acting as a partition, lessened the effect.

As a contrast to this colourful quartering, rich in motifs, the last garden had a pond in an open stretch of meadow; a round temple stood in the middle of the pond. The pond, with its temple, was surrounded by a round wall. This garden was depicted by Matthäus Merian the Elder (1593 to 1650) in his *Topographia* (Topography of Upper Saxony) in 1650.

According to Hennebo, such islands situated in gardens were typical for several European countries, as, for example, in Italy (e.g. Villa Lante and in the Boboli gardens), in France (Chenonceaux, Dampierre, Verneuil), in the Netherlands (Ghent) and in Germany (Munich, Hellbrunn) and in northern Europe (Hirschholm). Garden islands or, more properly, island gardens were to be found in the parks of Weimar in the 17th and 18th centuries as well as in the Berlin pleasure grounds. Such island gardens continued on from the Baroque to the landscape gardens and are regarded a popular element.

Members of the imperial House of Habsburg concerned themselves with the planning of gardens early on. Archduke Ferdinand (1529–1595) had Schloss Ambras in the Tyrol rebuilt for his wife, Philippine Welser (1527 to 1580), in 1564. A mediaeval castle near Innsbruck was transformed into a very beautiful princely residence. Even "hanging gardens" were included which could be situated on a substructure near the ladies' quarters, because of the elevation of the building. The actual gardens nestled at the foot of the hill with flower beds, labyrinths, grottoes with artificial springs drawing their water from natural brooks, all surrounded by pillared halls. Open pavilions were decorated with figures made of trimmed trees and bushes. These were called *opus topiarius,* a horticultural work of art known already in Antiquity and achieving a new efflorescence during the Renaissance. To this very day, Schloss Ambras is still admired for its wonderful gardens. That also applies to the grounds of the summer palace at Hellbrunn near Salzburg, with their water gardens, built between 1613 and 1619. Though the garden

was modified under French and English influence, it still retains the character given to it by the Salzburg Archbishop Markus Sittich (died 1619). Overall, the palace and the gardens are influenced by Italian garden art for, in addition to the architect Santini Solari (1576–1646), it was Italian craftsmen and artists who were employed at Hellbrunn. In the palace itself, on the front side and towards the garden side on the ground floor grottoes and automatic water contrivances were installed.

The royal way leads from the rear of the palace through a bosket to theatres, grottoes, fountains and statues. Here and there, treacherous water tricks pop up and accompany the visitor through the whole garden. This path leads to the ornamental pleasure garden which is no longer to be found in its original form. In the third part of the grounds, we find the stone theatre, which Markus Sittich had laid out as an open-air stage that probably represents the oldest open-air theatre situated in a garden.

The Belvedere in Prague
Emperor Ferdinand I (1503–1564), father of the builder of Schloss Ambras, married Anna, sister of Louis II, and thus secured his succession to the throne in Bohemia and Hungary after Louis' death in 1526. It was Ferdinand

The grounds at Schloss Ambras in the Tyrol epitomize the concept of a princely pleasure garden.

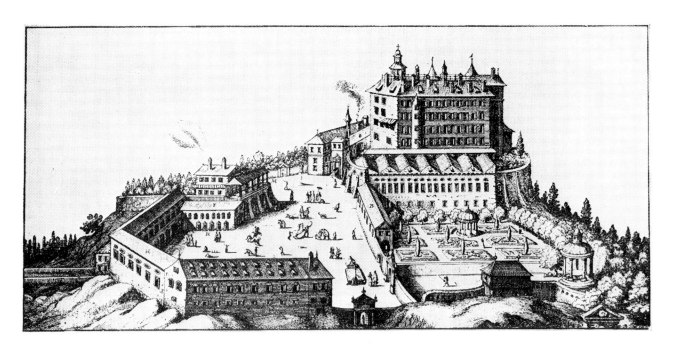

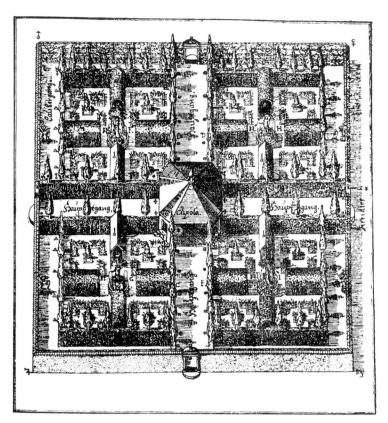

This copperplate engraving of a little "paradise" garden evidences the basic outlines of a school garden. Taken from Joseph Furttenbach, *Mannhafter Kunstspiegel ...*, Augsburg, 1633.

who constructed the gardens around Hradčany Castle. Famous at this time was the Belvedere, also called Anna Palais.

"This first summer palace stands at the beginning of a long line of similar buildings, from the summer palaces of the 16th and 17th centuries via the Baroque garden palaces and orangeries right up to the most gorgeous example, the Vienna Belvedere of Prince Eugene. Of the gardens around the Prague Belvedere, we only know they formed the background to fantastic festivals under Ferdinand" (Hennebo/Hoffmann).

When Prague became the official seat of Emperor Rudolf II (1576–1612), the fame of the Hradčany gardens waxed once more. The regent, a connoisseur, gave priority to the gardens surrounding the castle. One lay on a plateau situated parallel with the courtyard and separated from the castle by the Hirschgraben (stag-ditch); it could be reached by wooden bridges. There Ferdinand had the Anna Palais built. No documentation of the exact design of the gardens exists, but the Singing Fountain, decorated with figures created by Master Tomáš Jaroš between 1564 and 1568 and made of bell metal, has been preserved and still stands in the garden of the Anna Palais, surrounded by flower beds.

Plant collections as the beginning of orangeries

Those who held power made use of their far-reaching connections to lay the foundations for plant collections. Rudolf II had plants collected in Italy, Spain and Asia, and so did the Empress Anna. She was in touch with many ruling houses and plant experts with whom she exchanged plants and seeds. Brigitta von Trautson sent her Turkish flower bulbs from Vienna, others sent her rosemary, lavender, double-flowering peonies, laurel, myrtle and figs.

Botanical interests increased among feudal lords and prosperous citizens and the number of plant collections grew. Following the Italian example, botanists were employed by the aristocracy to look after these collections. We have the example of Karl Clusius, already mentioned, who served Emperor Maximilian II as well as Rudolf II. One result of this heightened interest was that, in addition to the collections in Prague and Vienna, others came into being in Stuttgart, Heidelberg and Dresden. They were the starting point for what later became the famous orangeries.

The Renaissance garden pictured in old engravings

At the Court of Rudolf II, both Adrian de Vries (*c.* 1550 to 1626), who created the fountains and statues for the emperor's gardens, and the architect and painter Hans Vredemann de Vries (1527–*c.* 1604) were employed.

Sketch of a citizen's garden by Joseph Furttenbach taken from *Architectura universalis ...*, Ulm, 1635. Copperplate engraving by Mathias Rumboldt after a drawing by Johann Jacob Campanus.

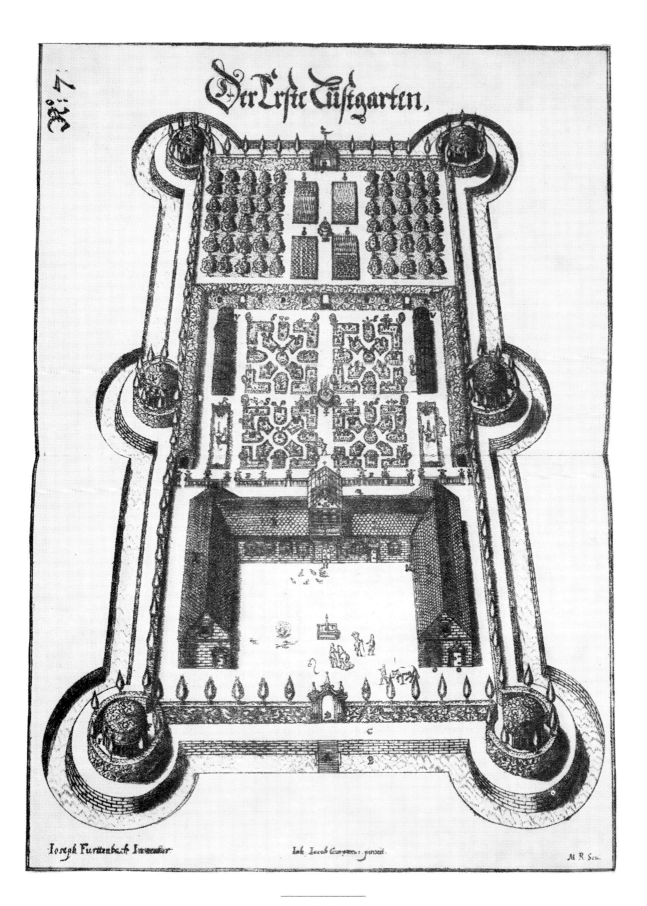

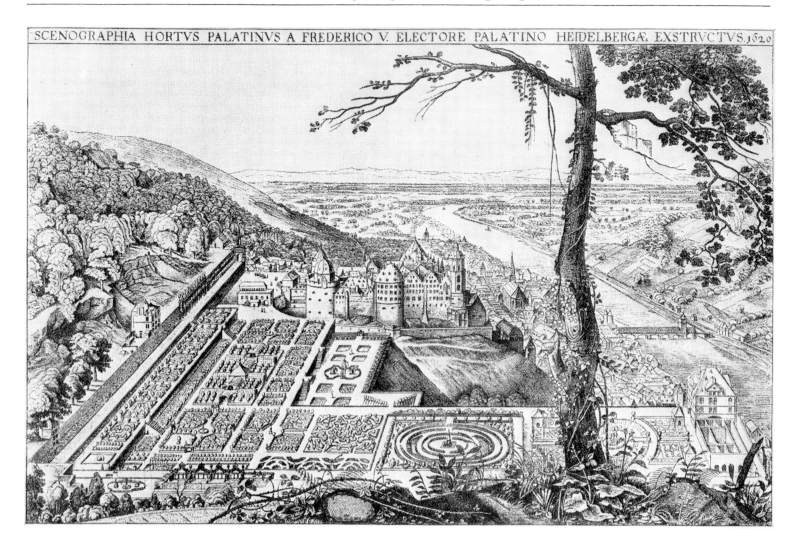

SCENOGRAPHIA HORTVS PALATINVS A FREDERICO V. ELECTORE PALATINO HEIDELBERGÆ EXSTRVCTVS 1620

View of the Heidelberg castle garden in 1620. In the eroded mountainside grottoes had been erected. From *Scenographia Hortus Palatinus …*

Through them, Dutch influence on German Renaissance gardening was again in evidence. The latter's famous edition of engravings *Hortorum viridariorumque elegantes et multiplices formae* contains numerous garden designs.

Copperplate engravers at that time found a new field of employment. Many lively impressions of the art of gardening in this period are derived from their oeuvre. One of the most significant copperplate engravers of the 17th century was the architect Joseph Furttenbach (1591 to 1667) of Ulm, who lived for ten years in Italy. It is, above all, in his designs for pleasure gardens that we may trace this Italian influence. It is true that after his return from Italy the garden at his own home was still constructed according to the ideas of the Dutch Humanist Erasmus of Rotterdam, but his later designs evince Italian influences.

There is a regular combination and strict sequence within the sections of the gardens. They all are surrounded by walls; the inner area sparkles with richness and variety. Complicated beds are bordered by flowers and box. Fountains, aviaries, fish-ponds, paths lined with statues, grottoes and areas of water are components of the garden, just as much as artistically designed trelliswork and fences.

Furttenbach was also concerned with the planning of public parks and gardens, so he designed a school-garden for children that he called "little paradise garden". But while Furttenbach's plans remained in the state of designs only, not to be put into practice, Matthäus Merian the Elder produced an abundance of engravings of palaces and gardens that were actually built.

Gardens of royal residences and the Hortus Palatinus

At the beginning of the 17th century, German residencies were provided with gardens, such as Bamberg, Güstrow, Kassel, Hechingen and, even more famous, Munich and Stuttgart. Mostly the gardens were laid out at a distance from the mansions or palaces and were enclosed by a wall. Even within one garden, the different parts — like flower parterres or orchards — were strictly separated from each other as, for example, at the Stuttgart residence. Some accounts of the Munich Court garden speak of a closer combination of individual parts.

A brilliant garden creation of the German Renaissance is the castle garden of Heidelberg, known as Hortus Palatinus. It was created by the Frenchman Salomon de Caus (*c.* 1576–1626). Because of his fame as engineer and physicist, after his return from England he was commissioned in 1616 to lay-out this garden. During his stay in England De Caus was in the service of Prince Henry of Wales and rearranged the parks of Greenwich and Richmond. He published the book *Les Raisons des Forces mouvantes* which contained an annex about grottoes and fountains for the decoration of summer-houses and gardens of the aristocracy. Additionally, a small illustrated volume was published by him in 1620 entitled *Hortus Palatinus,* with copperplate engravings by Theodor de Bry. Here he describes the garden grounds and their artistic arrangement — especially the waterworks and the grottoes in the castle garden of Heidelberg.

The little book is an imposing documentation of this wonderful Renaissance garden which, unfortunately, never was completed and soon fell in decay. So it is only the contemporary engravings and descriptions that survived to give us an idea of what the remarkable garden was like. It lay on the steep slope of a hill beside the mediaeval castle and had little relationship with its architecture. The relief of the terrain facilitated the construction of several terraces, one situated above the other. They were rich in variety, designed with arboured walks, many fountains, grotto motifs, labyrinths and a parterre with waterworks. The terraces were only connected with each other by narrow staircases.

Artistic Baroque
and Rococo Gardens

The building begins to occupy
the centre of the stage

Before the classical French garden experienced its birth pangs, in the middle of the 17th century, Italy had already hurried on in advance. At the end of the 16th century, a distinct change began to show itself in Italian art, a change which heralded the age of Baroque. It was an epoch of social contradictions — wealth and splendour of the rulers on the one side, poverty and misery for countless people of the lower strata of society on the other. The desire of the rulers to demonstrate their power, to impress and to put themselves in the limelight found its expression in their spacious gardens, too.

While the nature of the landscape was exploited in the Italian gardens of the Renaissance and, very frequently, of the Baroque period, and the structure of the terrain determined the lay-out, now the land was modified to suit the wishes and conception of the feudal owners of the estates. The level garden made its appearance, with depth as its special feature, earth tips, openings and supporting walls were enhanced with grottoes, niches for statues and stairways. The building began to occupy a central place in the whole conception and structure of the Baroque garden. In this way, even the entrance to the Baroque garden gained in significance; the main axis from this time forth ran in a straight line from the entrance to the palace. The waterworks were further extended and reached their heyday during this period. The famous water arrangements of the Villa d'Este in Tivoli were, among others, models for the fountains and cascades of the Italian Baroque gardens. Though traditional Renaissance elements were used in Italian Baroque — sometimes varied — an artistic advancement is clearly traceable which leaves behind a powerful impression on the visitor.

The great axis

It is the Villa Aldobrandini in Frascati that represents the new form in most remarkable way for the first time. Built by the architect Giacomo della Porta between 1598 and 1603, it is erected on a steep slope. High up on a wooded hill, water gushes forth from a grotto and, on its way down, displays surprising variations. It streams along the central axis over numerous falls and cascades and through canals and is forced upwards inside two columns which flank a stepped cascade. It soon emerges from the ends of the columns and pours down again. Finally, via another stepped cascade, it reaches a high-walled semi-circular pool which is enhanced by niches and statues.

This so-called water theatre is to be found opposite the villa, so that the spectacle may be admired from close range. The water arrangements at the Villa Aldobrandini were created by famous architects and engineers who had already shown their great ability at the Villa Lante and the Villa d'Este. What was already emerging at the Villa Lante in Bagnaia, finds its magnificent completion.

The boskets and labyrinths which had such a great significance in the Renaissance gardens were somewhat subdued, here. The main axis was a dominant element now, the flower gardens lying between the villa and the arboretum were shifted more to the sides. The house and the garden terrace had been fused into a unified whole.

An axial construction, proceeding from the main entrance, radiates in three directions, only one axis leading to the building; the others fan out from the entrance to the left and right, thus stressing the lateral extension of the gardens. The main axis leads upwards from the entrance of what was formerly a cultivated slope and is today covered by a lawn.

It runs through the terraces which, like a mighty plinth, support the villa with its palace-like character, and then seems to continue right through the building and out on the other side, to negotiate the eight steps of the cascade and climbs still further on. Today, the upper parts of the water axis are a sorry picture of destruction and, unfortunately, only a few statues remain of the once so rich sculptural decoration.

Le Nôtre and the golden age of the formal French garden

In France, the coming of the new style — the birth of the classical French garden — was inextricably linked with the age of Louis XIV.

The history of French landscape architecture is the history of its geniuses of the art of gardening. The most famous of them all is André le Nôtre (1613–1700). In the service of King Louis XIV (1638–1715), his great theoretical knowledge and creativity became evident. Le Nôtre was invited to design the château and the park of Vaux-le-Vicomte, on the recommendation of his friend Le Brun (1619–1690), a famous painter who had been responsible for the interior design of Nicolas Fouquet's château, minister of finance to the king.

With the execution of this work, Le Nôtre sprang into prominence. Not only Fouquet was entranced; many visitors to the French Court admired his creation. The envy of the king turned into hate when, in 1661, he was invited to take part in the ceremonial opening of Vaux-le-Vicomte, as he, himself, possessed no estate of equal magnificence. Hardly three weeks had elapsed when he had Fouquet arrested and charged with some vague financial misdemeanour; then he took over Fouquet's artists. It was in this way that the architect Le Vau (1612–1670), the painter Le Brun and the landscape architect Le Nôtre were commissioned to create Versailles.

Le Nôtre gained great fame; he was destined to enjoy another fifty years of high success as architect of the most famous French gardens of the Baroque period. His influence spread beyond the borders of France, "from England to Russia, from Scandinavia to Italy" (Fox). His

Ground-plan of the Villa Aldobrandini near Frascati.

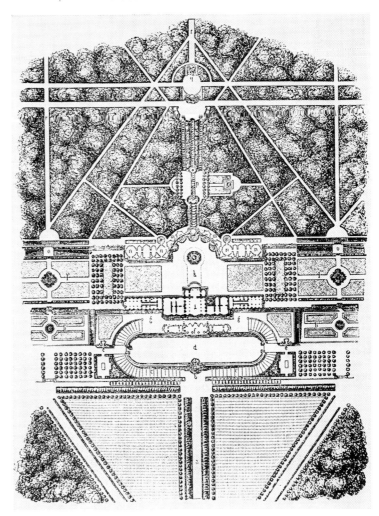

ideas also spread to Germany, a reflection of Le Nôtre's energy and unlimited creativity, manifested in more than ninety parks and gardens in many countries.

His most impressive work is, of course, the magnificent gardens of Versailles, though the basic ideas for the new French style of gardening already became evident in Vaux-le-Vicomte. His basic conception is founded on the formal French garden. It is here that we find all the elements which typify the Baroque garden and which constantly re-appear beyond the borders of his native France — even if partially transformed and later expanded.

In the formal French garden the main axis dominates, accentuating wide vistas and determining the garden's dimension. From this main axis "the whole network of allées is dynamically differentiated, firstly through diagonals which stretch out in all directions and which join the main axes and cross-ways to form stars or parts of stars, and then with the aid of free symmetrical path patterns" (Rommel).

Ornamental plant patterns and boskets

With the tendency to lay-out gardens on flat terrain covering wide areas in the first half of the 17th century, the construction of the parterre is of prime importance. Advice on their design is given in the model book of Jacques Boyceau, *Traité du Jardinage,* Paris, 1638; André Mollet, *Le Jardin de Plaisir,* Stockholm, 1651; and D'Argenville, *La Théorie et la Pratique du Jardinage,* Paris, 1709.

The parterre — a flat area very close to the building — has changed its appearance in the course of time. While it was mainly arranged as a sequence of independent but adjoining squares in the Renaissance garden, in the Baroque garden the squares and rectangles were joined together. The wavy pattern — especially suitable for a subtle design — gains precedence over the straight pattern..." (Rommel).

The borders were dispensed with and the various separate areas were brought together in a single unit. Several varieties of parterre appeared, made up of tendril and surface patterns, each with its own designation, like *par-*

Portrait of André le Nôtre.

terre en broderie, whose ornamentation imitated the embroidery patterns of those days, or the *parterre de compartiment,* of interest because of its mirror-image effect.

The parterre *à l'angloise* is a lawn whose sanded paths provided but blurred divisions of the surface. The decoration for these areas of the garden were remarkably manifold: there were simple patterns beside agraffes, arabesques, tendril and foliage designs as well as imitations of the leaves of bear's breech.

The spaces between the ornamental patterns were layed out with black powdered coal, red brick dust, rust-coloured iron filings and white or yellow gravel. The *plate bande,* the surrounding line, was planted with flowers, the artistic framework of the parterre was of box with a slightly raised inner surface. It could be "curved, cornered, drawn-in, split, sometimes pierced and spiralled outwards" (D'Argenville).

The recommended plants for this framework were mainly those grown from bulbs or tubers, like tulips, hyacinths and anemones but also primroses, violets and carnations, likewise lilies and peonies, wild thyme, marguerites and maiden pink. There was also frequently a mixture of pansies, common daisies and plumed pinks, giving the impression that the colours were running into each other. This was known as "enamel".

Narrow borders were set out with shrubs cut into globes, pyramids or other shapes, or with pot plants.

Vaux-le-Vicomte, view from the terrace of the château over the garden. Engraving by Israel Silvestre.

These were just as much a part of the parterre's adornment as waterworks, vases and statues.

The bosket is attached to the parterre and is delineated by a high screen of trees and truncated hedges. They called it a "little pleasure grove", even though with its trimmed truncated hedging and its niches it no longer retained any similarity to a grove. The bosket became very popular in France because of Le Nôtre that it is regarded as a typical feature of Baroque gardens. The social side of the bosket is also significant. Courtiers increasingly favoured the shady walks, the twisting ways and hidden resting places for conversation and contemplation, away from the turmoil of the Court. "So the boskets are the *buen retiro* of an extravagant society, tired of the courtly ceremonial, which

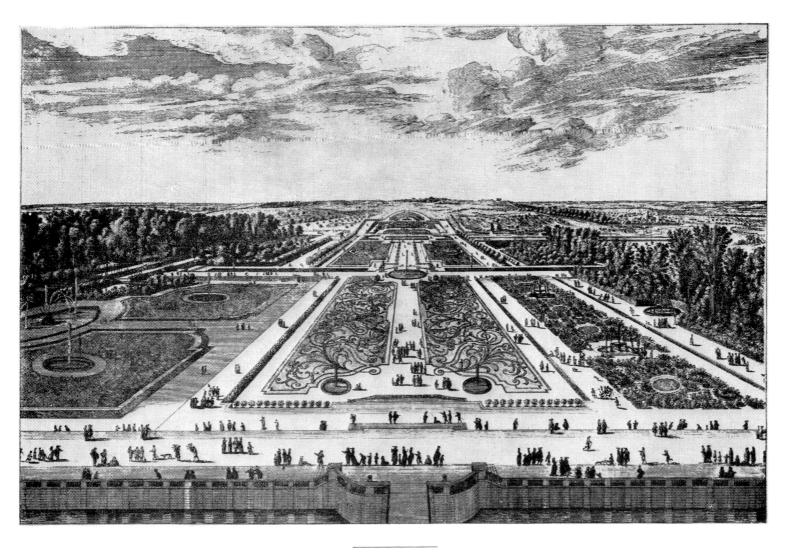

Sketch of a parterre, surrounded by grass and trees. Taken from the pattern book *Die Gaertnerey ...* by Alexandre le Blond, Augsburg, 1731.

Trees like the linden, chestnut, beech and elm were most frequently used for the outer screen, elm and box for the low hedges. Just as in the parterres, trees were trimmed into unusual shapes in the open spaces of the boskets. A great variety of forms created a play of light and shade that added another accent to the style of the Baroque gardens.

This play of light and shade was also effective in the pergolas. It was a delight to loiter here in the refreshing cool on hot sunny days. These wooden arcades, delicate and somewhat frail, were an important element in the Baroque pleasure garden.

Water as an enlivening element

Here we must again bring the reader's attention to the effect of water. It was a part of every Baroque garden not only in France, but also in the rest of Europe, yet there was a remarkable difference between Italian and French waterworks. As Rommel puts it: "While, in the Italian Baroque garden, varied combinations of jets are constantly appearing, the Italians manipulate the water *en masse,* in principle just like the tree plantations, and this is because of their historically determined inclination towards concentrated magnificence and roaring pathos. Here it is a question of bubbling over, of descending in a veil of mistiness, of a wild effervescence. These traits are brought to fruition by tectonic or rustic fountains, which may be in isolated locations or in niches but mainly by means of the crashing cascade which, as central axis, retains the main function of harmonizing the terrain (Villa Aldobrandini and Villa Ludovisi in Frascati). In France they were not able to adopt the monumental Italian style of handling the water *en masse.*" Except in the first half of the 17th century, Italian water tricks found no strong echo in French Baroque.

Fountains, springs and cascades

Other styles dominated the scene in all European Baroque gardens, varying a little from country to country, but the use of water as an enlivening element became extremely significant. We can hardly imagine Baroque gar-

amused itself within their safe embrace" (Neubauer). In the boskets the visitors expected a variety of effects and accommodations to entice them along the narrower ways — niches with benches or idyllic little places with statues. The enclosed nature of the bosket also offered favourable opportunities for romantic adventures or amorous interludes, such as the affair of the diamond necklace.

dens without the marvellous fountains, without water-spouts and quiet pools. There was no garden, however small it may have been, without at least a sparkling fountain or a pool.

The most impressive example is Versailles where, in Louis XIV's day, the water arrangements were the most spectacular in the world. Those fountains which still exist have long been less numerous than in those days and not nearly so eye-catching. The most interesting construction was the water theatre, built in 1671. Incidentally, this only existed for a hundred years. Similar to our present-day waterworks — if, indeed, a comparison is at all possible —, the water formed ten scenes, achieving a certain inner symmetry, by the play of hundred of jets with their high or low, straight or crooked, thick or thin streams of water. Within just six years after the construction of the water theatre, the Trois Fontaines appeared, which fell into ruins a hundred years later. The king is said to have designed these fountains himself.

The centre-piece of a raised flower bed, in a Baroque garden, was usually formed by a tub plant, artificially bedded in.

In 1687, when the Swedish architect Nicodemus Tessin the Younger was conducted through the gardens of Versailles by Le Nôtre, he subsequently wrote about the Trois Fontaines in a letter: "This bosket has been universally applauded and, because of its many fountains, is the most famous one. The middle fountain is the largest that ever has been built (it is composed of 140 jets) and the great mussel-shell *bassin* at the lower end of the bosket is simply wonderful with its fine threads of water, water curtains and cascades; in a word — the whole installation speaks of Le Nôtre's genius."

The fountains were activated in accordance with a plan specially worked out for the tour. Works were constructed at Marly-le-Roi to tap the Seine and to lead the water by channels to the gardens of Versailles. Since water was very scarce at Versailles, this installation was considered a great technical success. Yet, it proved impossible to set all the fountains of Versailles in motion at the same time. The king was constantly pressing Le Nôtre to build even more fountains.

From the early 17th century, a canal also became an element of the Baroque garden. Originally having more

a dividing function, it changed its position in the course of time. In Versailles, a great swamp had to be drained by means of a canal. Thus, a water area was created which served as axis. In this way, the canal moved, as it were, from its fringe position right into the centre of the picture and, with its length of 1560 metres, opened up a magnificent vista.

Boat and gondola rides were among the amusements of the Court, as well as parades and mock battles between ships of different kinds. The canal even served as transport means between the nearby gardens and the château

of Trianon. Venetian sailors were settled in one part of the garden; to this very day, that area is called "petite Venise".

At the same time as the canals were constructed for Baroque gardens, extensive *bassins* appeared; they dated back to earlier mediaeval pools. It is really a series of *bassins*, small and large ones, whose special effect was the reflection of the trees and the sky. To get nearly undisturbed areas of water, the ascending jet in the middle of the *bassin* had to be as fine as possible. As a contrast to the *bassins*, something quite different had to be achieved with the effect of the fountains. They displayed the gigantic strength and unbounded beauty of the richly flowing water and thus enlivened the whole environment at the same time.

The Trianon de Porcelaine was built in 1670 under the influence of Chinese stylistic elements. Engraving by Perelle.

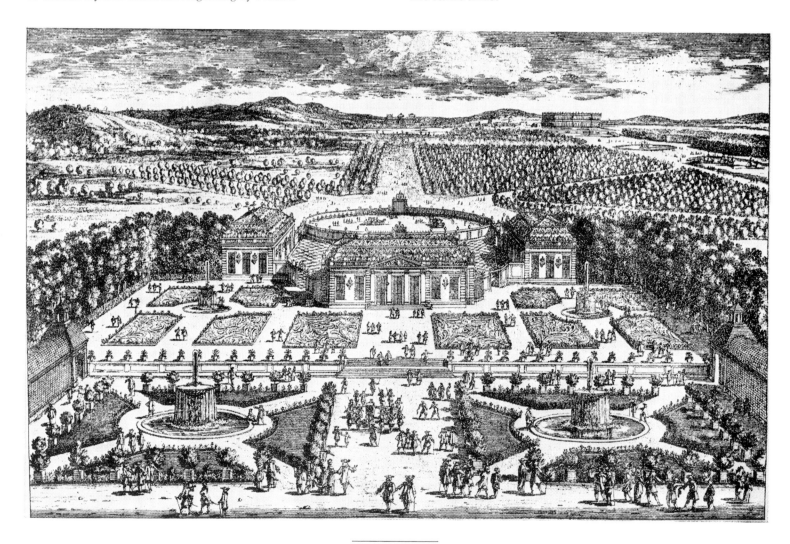

The grottoes are closely related to the water. Few Baroque gardens were without them; they played their part, too, in the design of fountains and cascades. The passion for grottoes continued, right through the age of symmetrical gardens on into the period of landscape gardening, when they again achieved significance. Like grottoes, plastics — either statues of the rulers, representations of the animal kingdom or allegorical figures — were a favourite and constantly recurring detail of the gardener's art of all times.

Exotic orangeries

The fondness for cultivating exotic plants in glass-houses and then planting them out in summer, already widespread during the Renaissance, reached its zenith in the Baroque era and is also very common in later periods. But it was not so much a question of a straightforward passion for collecting such rarities as it had been in the late Middle Ages and especially in the Renaissance; it was more a question of collecting southern plants.

It was mainly oranges, lemons, myrtle and laurel that were potted or planted in tubs, in order to winter. For this purpose, orangeries were built to protect the plants from frost during the cold season. In summer the surroundings of the orangeries were then enhanced by these ornamental or tub plants. They were valued for their beautifully shaped petals with their pleasant scent or because of their dark green decorative leaves. By overcoming climatic differences, the gardeners created a strange exotic world in these orangeries which also were the background to gay festivities.

The gardens of Louis XIV

Tired at last by the pomp and glitter of Versailles, Louis XIV longed for peace and quiet, so, in 1670, he had the charming little château Trianon de Porcelaine built, situated at the north end of the transverse canal of Versailles. It takes its name from its faiences and was one of the first indications of that fashion for chinoiseries which spread rapidly, especially during the Rococo period. It was built by D'Orbay after plans by Levau.

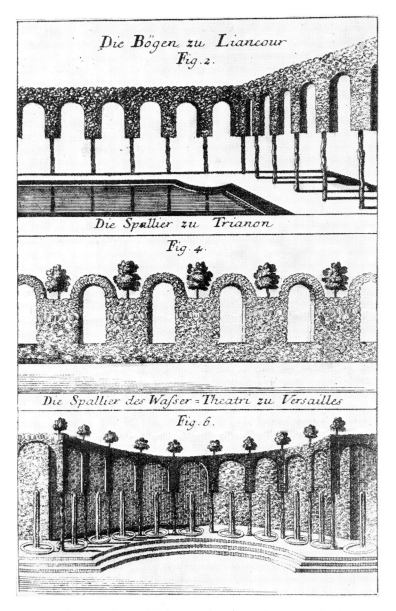

Frequently occurring trellis forms taken from the pattern book *Die Gaertnerey ...* by Alexandre le Blond, Augsburg, 1731.

The Trianon de Porcelaine — later re-named Grand Trianon after the Petit Trianon had been built in the second half of the 18th century — differed from Louis XIV's other gardens in the dazzling beauty of its flowers.

The parterres were decked out exclusively with potted flowers, which, where required, could be replaced by others several times a day. Le Nôtre commented in 1694 that there were two million potted flowers at the Grand

Trianon; they could be constantly re-arranged according to the seasons. He added that "at Trianon you never see a dead leaf nor any plant which is not in flower".

Not only the tall trees that shaded the avenues and the fountains in the parterre but also the gardens of springs — Bosquet des Sources — are especially worthy of mention. It is assumed that it was created by Le Nôtre as a contrast to the formal lay-out of the park and was made up of a triangular space overrun with meandering water courses, and composed of irregularly arranged sections. At the beginning of the 19th century, this garden was destroyed. Unfortunately not even an illustration exists.

Somewhat larger than the Trianon de Porcelaine was Marly-le-Roi, constructed about six kilometres from Versailles. Here was a spectacular palace garden with cascades and fountains which were also set in motion by the water machine. A mighty cascade foamed down through the valley to a comparatively small palace and into the Petit Parterre. This cascade, known as La Rivière, was the largest of its day, both with its dimensions and its beauty it surpassed all Italian cascades.

The sides of the Grand Parterre which, with its fountains and *bassins* lay on the other side of the palace, were adorned with pavilions; this formed an excellent contrast. Marly was a small, intimate summer palace in which rest and luxury could be enjoyed in equal measure. The Trianon and the Hermitage became popular models in other European countries, too.

Versailles

Versailles was and is the finest garden complex ever created in France. Having in mind contemporary landscape architecture, Hennebo explained the significance of Versailles in the following words: "The classical French garden has largely formed the image of an epoch of Court gardens. It was here that the royal society of the age of Absolutism found a garden lay-out that comprehensively satisfied its conceptions. In each of the countries concerned, of course, they modified it in accordance with their own approach or fused it with stimuli from other sources, but nowhere did they completely exclude its influence. In France, itself, Versailles represented the zenith and the culmination of this line of development in garden style."

After Versailles, Le Nôtre constructed further gardens, for the king did not lose sight of those gardens that already existed. In Chantilly, Le Nôtre came upon a Renaissance garden which he re-modelled. Here the abundant water flowed through numerous small canals, which Le Nôtre combined in one large canal. It was not possible to blend the mediaeval palace architecture with the design of the garden. A stairway formed the architectural background to the parterre which was penetrated by an arm of the canal.

The Versailles tradition was continued in other French gardens. Fontainebleau, which arose under Henry IV, was re-designed by Le Nôtre. Although the beginnings of the canal garden had already been in evidence here, it was only after its re-modelling that the canal gained its real significance. Saint-Cloud, just like Fontainebleau, also underwent a transformation and here, too, Le Nôtre created the marvellous effect of a Baroque garden. A very beautiful cascade — evidence of Italian influence — was re-fashioned by Le Nôtre into a tri-partite waterfall.

The broad spacious lawns
of the English Baroque garden

In England, the French style of gardening only spread in a very hesitant way and not to the extent that it did in several continental European countries. The puritanical outlook of the English and the frugality — compared with their French counterparts — of the English ruling class under parliamentary control, did not allow of the same degree of luxurious living. This was, to a large extent, an obstacle to the construction of generous Baroque gardens. That is why only few gardens were created in England in the 17th and 18th centuries that showed traces of an influence radiating from Versailles.

One of the most important examples that England has to show is Hampton Court. It was, above all, in the reign of William of Orange and his wife, Queen Mary II, who made it her seat, that these gardens achieved their modern

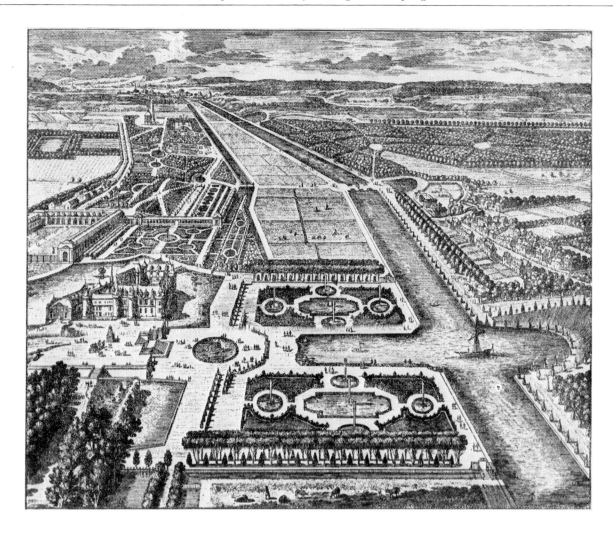

Total view of Chantilly. Engraving by N. Langlois.

form. It was at that time that the palace was added to the already existing Tudor building by the famous architect Christopher Wren (1632–1723); London and Wise, who were trained in London as pupils of Rose, designed the grounds.

Especially noticeable is the great semi-circular parterre enclosed in box, at the east wing of the palace with its fountains. The stellar paths leading to the palace and the canal forming the main axis are reminiscent of Versailles. Hampton Court did not remain for long as it had been constructed under William III. His successor, Queen Anne (1665–1714), had the borders planted and the box re-moved. The *allées* were later planted with oak trees to the right and left. However, Hampton Court is one of the few gardens of that time that remain basically the same today.

Some English nobility also had gardens constructed upon the great French model. One of these was at Blenheim, in whose fountain garden there was an imitation of the parterre with its water arrangements at Versailles; this was re-modelled in the 20th century by Achille Duchêne. Very beautiful gardens in imitation of the French style arose at Chatsworth. Today we only have the outlines of the gardens to hand and the great cascade. The latter was created by the Frenchman Grillet in the years 1694 and 1695 and is reminiscent of La Rivière at Marly. The two great parterres in the west and south of the gardens and the boskets on the upper terraces no longer exist.

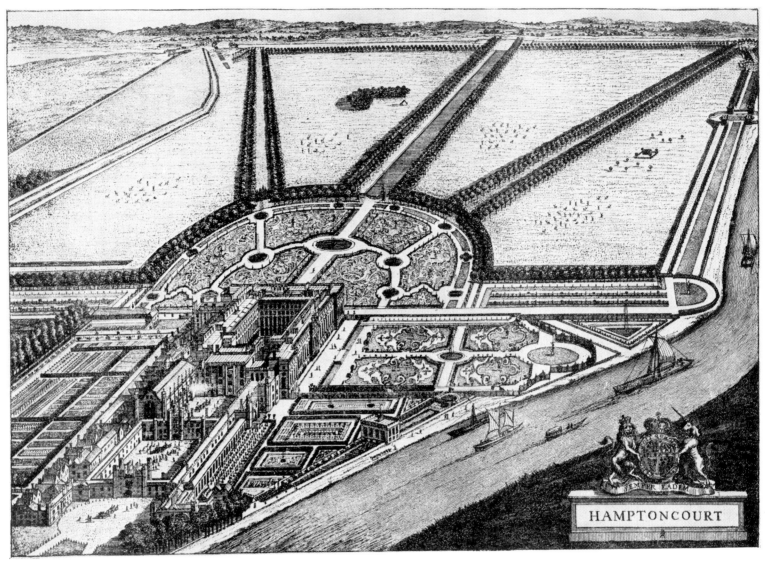

View of Hampton Court. Engraving by John Bowles.

Gardens divided by allées

Badminton, one of the most interesting Baroque creations in England, has been completely obliterated. The gardens with their parterres, boskets and fountains lay around the building in the middle of a great park, which was traversed by a central avenue, two-and-a-half miles long and starting from the entrance gate. The many *allées* which threaded through the gigantic parklands were noticeable. Just twenty of them ran outwards in stellar formation far out into the park terrain.

One of the few formal gardens that are still extant in England is St. Paul's Walden Bury in Hertfordshire. This garden — one of the largest in the world — came into existence between 1720 and 1760. Unfortunately, neither the exact date nor the designer are known to us.

"St. Paul's Walden Bury is in essence a garden of grassy, hedge-lined walks, which stretch straight and far into the distance, to terminate in temples, statuary, or glimpses of the wings of the house. One walk leads the eye to the village church, but otherwise it is largely a self-contained garden, interest and variety being maintained by the changing levels of the terrain and by the surprise effects at the multiple intersections of the walks.

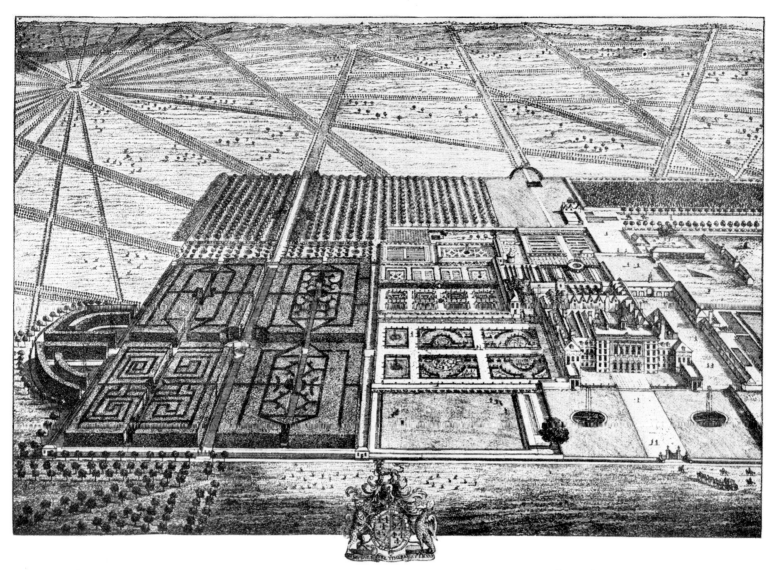

Total view of Badminton. Engraving by Johannes Kip.

The vertically clipped beech-hedges are eight-and-a-half to ten feet high and behind them rise the woods, so that the visitor never knows what awaits him around the corner. And where there are gravel rather than green paths, they are neither rigid, or stiff in effect but just as calming and gentle as those in Couranes in France.

Hidden behind the hedges in one large 'island' or woodland is the most successful *giardino segreto* in the British Isles, the oval enclosure of ... the Discobolos, whose statue stands down by the entrance. From there the land rises and, passing a formal pond, one reaches an open rotunda at the top.

The deep appeal of this part of the gardens comes from its private and tranquil nature — from outside, its existence is unsuspected and yet its generous grassy slopes inspire a feeling of spaciousness and repose — and from the contrast of its rounded outlines with the ruler-straight directness of the main walks" (Thacker).

Seen as a whole, we come to the conclusion that England lagged behind the great continental examples in the development of the formal garden lay-out until, in the 18th century, finally a completely new garden conception was born.

French influences on Swedish and Danish garden architecture

In Sweden in the middle of the 17th century, Queen Christina (1626–1689) showed herself very receptive to the French example. She invited André Mollet to Sweden and encouraged him to write his book *Le Jardin de Plaisir,* which was published in 1651 and exercised a great influence on gardening in northern Europe. The proximity of water is typical of Swedish palaces and their garden grounds.

Nicodemus Tessin's stay in France in the 80s of the 17th century and his acquaintance with Le Nôtre showed enduring results. Tessin created gardens in the French style, not only for the king but also for himself. This influence is particularly marked in Drottningholm on Lake Mälaren.

The parterre in this south-facing garden, made up of differing patterns, leaves behind a lively impression. By way of an open flight of stairs one reaches the Fountain of Hercules. This then leads on to the parterre enhanced by a waterway that ends in an oval pond; a cascade roars down on the opposite side. The boskets lie on the other side of the parterre.

Later, Queen Louise Ulrike (1720–1782), sister of Frederick II, had the gardens re-modelled according to the fashion of the times. She had a little colony built with miniature houses in Chinese style, a Chinese pagoda with a clock tower, Chinese porcelain vases and gilded statues.

The gardens at Carlsberg, the greatest Swedish palace, lack the uniformity of Drottningholm. Here the parterres only spread out beyond the dense boskets which are separated from the semi-circle of the palace by flower beds. The lateral parterres of the palace preserve a typical Renaissance character. The *allées* in the great park between the palace with its gardens and the sea are clearly visible in an engraving made after Dahlberg.

The canal, of such great significance in French gardens, is of somewhat less importance in Sweden. The reason for this is the frequently close proximity of the sea or the position of the gardens on islands. Similarly, in Denmark,

Engraving of the Carlsberg palace and gardens (after Erik Dahlberg).

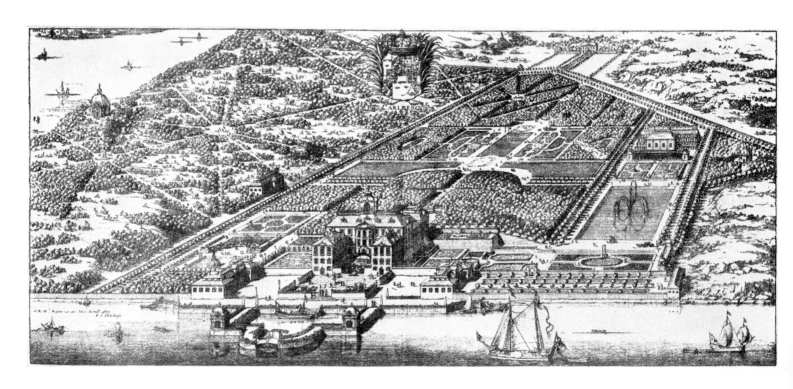

the gardens are mainly surrounded by water. The fore-courts and palace buildings of Frederiksborg in Copenhagen, for instance, are situated on three islands, linked by bridges. At the palace there is only space for a small parterre which also lies on an island.

The main garden is separated from the palace complex and the small parterre by the lake. An interesting phenomenon here is the main axis of the garden which runs in an imaginary line across the water and is continued across the parterre.

The little palace of Hirschholm with its parterres also spreads out over islands linked with each other by bridges. Only the boskets are on the mainland, grouped round the water. Unfortunately, Hirschholm is not very well preserved today.

Most typically French in style is Fredensborg, whose garden is still one of the most beautiful in Denmark. The palace is built around an octagonal courtyard and stands on an eminence at Lake Essommer, to which the gardens gravitate eastwards from the palace. Seven *allées* run right out into the park from the parterre and the boskets. The parterre is separated from the park by a semi-circular avenue of limes. The avenues run westwards right up to the lake.

Cascades and fountains
at Petrodvorets near Leningrad

In czarist Russia, too, the French art of gardening with a dash of Italian influence found favourable acceptance and Czar Peter I (1672–1725) devoted himself intensively to the construction of Petrodvorets. Outstanding architects and sculptors from Russia and abroad, like Johann Friedrich Braunstein, Mikhail Zemtsov (1688 to 1743), Bartolomeo Rastrelli (1700–1771), Niccolò Michetti (died 1759) and Mikhail Koslovski (1753–1802) were engaged for the work and created what is still today one of the jewels of the art of gardening of the Baroque period.

A masterly achievement of the Russian hydraulics engineer Vassili Tuvolkov was the waterworks which arose between 1721 and 1722. The whole irrigation system

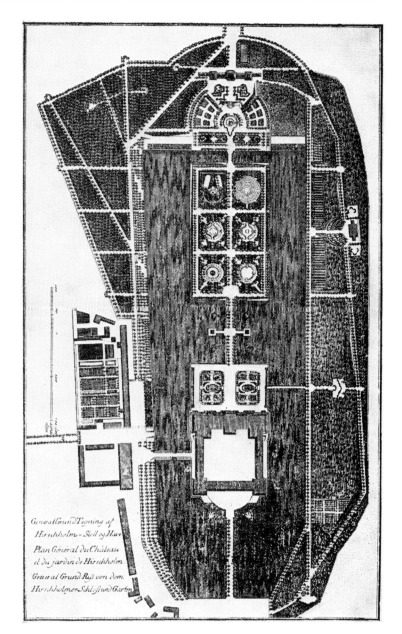

Ground-plan of the Hirschholm palace with its extensive gardens.

covers some 22 kilometres; the water is led through canals and pipes to gargoyles, cascades and fountains, without the aid of pumps. The greatest part of the park of Petrodvorets lies in the lower section of the grounds and for that reason is called the Lower Park. It is connected with the palace by three massive terraces, in whose central axis a cascade was erected. This cascade, consisting of seventeen high steps, is split up into sections linked with each other by the five niches of a grotto. It is adorned with 39 gilded bronze statues. 142 jets of water from 64 "water-throwers" of varied shapes bring forth a deafening roar.

The Grand Cascade was created in the first quarter of the 18th century but only acquired its present appearance in the middle of the 19th century. It is fed by two streams that spring forth from masks of Neptune, God of the Sea. Then, over steps adorned with gilded reliefs, the water reaches oval projections which are decorated with statues. From there it gushes forth from dolphins' jaws into a pool at whose centre rises a statue of Samson, the Old Testament figure, tearing open the jaws of a lion. The water shoots out of the lion's mouth in a 20-metre high jet up into the air. This fountain was erected in honour of the Battle of Poltava, which took place on 17th June, 1709 — Saint Samson's Day.

This Grand Cascade is the centre-piece of the park of Petrodvorets. It is a component of the Grand Palace, seen as a magnificent foundation of the whole, so to speak. The Grand Palace was erected between 1714 and 1724 by a team of architects like Johann Friedrich Braunstein, Jean-Baptiste Vallin de la Mothe, Niccolò Michetti and Le Blond (1679–1719) who was responsible for the total design of the park and had already worked under Le Nôtre for a long time.

The most important period of construction began under the direction of the world-famous architect Bartolomeo Rastrelli. He maintained the division of the palace into a central section, galeries and wings; however, he added further wings at the sides which stretched out southwards in the direction of the Upper Park. Rastrelli was outstandingly successful in combining old Russian architectural motifs with Baroque forms.

From the palace the visitor has a wonderful view of the Gulf of Finland. A large canal runs from the Pool of Samson right into the sea. Here, too, a magnificent vista opens up to the far distance.

To the west and to the east of the Pool of Samson and in front of the boskets which accompany the canal to the sea on both its sides we find two colonnades, created by the architect Andrei Voronitchin (1759–1814) at the beginning of the 19th century. They separate the lively squares from the quiet *allées*. The pillars of white and grey marble and of pink granite are adorned with lion sculptures and complete our impression of Petrodvorets.

Peter I's little garden palace

Numerous little garden palaces are to be found throughout the countryside here. Monplaisir is regarded as Peter's favourite creation. The German architect and sculptor Andreas Schlüter (1660–1714) contributed to its design. On the south side of Monplaisir is a little rectangular garden, its centre being graced with a fountain called the "sheaf of corn". The twenty-five water-jets are arranged like ears of corn in a sheaf. The other four fountains in the garden are called "bells", as their towering spurts of water form transparent bells from gaps under the plinths of gilded statues like Psyche, Apollo, a fawn with kids and Bacchus with Satyr. The garden of this little palace is terminated on its eastern side by a bath-house. Next to this, the little Chinese garden with a mussel-shell fountain is to be found. In that part of the park to the west of the great canal, via the Hermitage pavilion, the visitor reaches a part of the park where the Marly palace is situated. The garden of the palace impresses both by its breadth and by the great rectangular pond, in front of the main axis, in which Peter I kept exotic fishes. To the south of the pond lies the ensemble of fountains. It is here that the Golden Mountain cascade forms the centre-piece of this part of the park. It was based on a design by the czar and the architect Michetti and was built between 1721 and 1723. In 1732 it obtained its present form. The cascade is crowned by a marble wall decorated with statuary.

An examination of the axial system of the park reveals in several places that it is tri-radial. Taking a course from the Grand Palace, the canal forms one axis, another one runs on the right to the Palais Monplaisir, and the third leftwards to the Hermitage. From the Marly palace an *allée* leads to the Great Cascade with the Samson statue, and a central axis leads far into the parkland.

Spanish and Portuguese gardens

The inspiration of the French style of gardening was also traceable on the Iberian peninsula. Here, in Spain and Portugal, several gardens appeared in the Baroque period that bore traces of Le Nôtre's art.

In Portugal, a garden was created around the royal summer palace at Queluz, near Lisbon, that is reminiscent of an Italian Baroque garden. Although the Frenchman Robilion was engaged for the construction of the main parterre in 1762, this garden reminds us of the Villa Lante in Bagnaia. Thus it becomes evident that French designers not only constructed gardens in the French style but also adopted foreign traditions and bowed to the wishes of their patrons.

A river running along the side was incorporated in the garden and transformed into a canal. The side walls of the Ribeira de Jamar were clad with the blue tiles, *azulejos* — already used in the Renaissance gardens — and embellished with majolica urns. A bridge, similarly attired, spans the whole and has a decorative function.

La Granja — model for Caserta

With the end of the War of the Spanish Succession in 1714, the French influence on architecture and garden design in Spain made itself more overt. Philip V (1683 to 1746), grandson of Louis XIV, engaged the Frenchmen René Charlier (died 1722) and Boutelet to construct the palace and the park of La Granja at San Ildefonso. An ancient farm — La Granja, formerly in the possession of a monastic order — with its monastic courtyard, the Patio de la Fuente, formed its centre. The first thing to be built was a great church, attached to the monastery courtyard on its north-west side and consecrated already in the year 1724.

A vast number of people worked with great zeal for twenty years on the construction work, always with the picture of Versailles in their mind's eye. The location — at a height of 1,200 metres and surrounded by mountains — rendered their labours terribly difficult. They had to handle colossal quantities of earth in this valley to create the necessary flat areas and the terraces for the gardens. This is the reason why La Granja never completely equalled the generous lay-out of French gardens.

Vistas typical of the French garden could not be allowed for at La Granja; the proximity of the mountains prohibited such open views. Water was in plentiful supply and the architects made profitable use of this. The main parterre was comparatively simple in its design. A semi-circular pool, placed at the end of two parterre beds, lies at the base of a marble cascade together with the Fountain of Amphitrite. A beautiful twin-basin fountain of marble is the enchanting adornment of this cascade.

To the east of the palace sloping steps lead to a lower parterre, bordered on one side by the canal and ending in a very lovely water arrangement. This includes a gradually ascending pool with a Neptune fountain supported by little cupids riding on seahorses; something similar was later to be seen in Caserta. The Fountain of Andromeda is a most fascinating sight at the end of a broad parterre. The variety of water arrangements and waterworks is not yet finished. Many fountain structures, like, for instance, the Bath of Diana or the colossal fountain creation, the Fuente de la Fama in the great courtyard (Patio de la Herradura) at the south-west façade of the palace, are all murmuring or rippling treasures of this garden.

Charles III (1716–1788; King of Naples and Sicily from 1738 to 1759 and, from 1759, King of Spain) spent his early years in La Granja. In memory of his childhood home, he had a gigantic palace erected near Naples, which was to symbolize his power. So, in 1752, the architect Luigi Vanvitelli (1700–1773) constructed a palace near the little town of Caserta in the style of Italian Late Baroque which was to resemble Versailles.

With its parterres, boskets, fountains and cascades, with a canal, an orangery and wooded areas it is very impressive. It is very similar to La Granja in its basic conception, the latter serving as a model. At variance with the French style, we find here a kind of reversal of the perspective, just like at La Granja. The view, usually accentuated by the depth of the main axis and underlined by an almost endless canal, is limited here by the mountain range. At Caserta, no attempt was made to create a perceived axis leading into the far distance. While it would be unthinkable in a French garden of the period to allow a visible termination, it is not unusual in the Italian garden for the view to be cut off like this.

Canals, bulbs and little beds

When Dutch gardening experienced its heyday in the middle of the 17th century, the other arts had already passed their prime. When observing the development of garden construction in the Netherlands, a characteristic native style comes into view. While this does not imply any revolutionary changes on a European scale, it nevertheless found an echo outside the Netherlands. This native style has the mark of the country's geographical position as well as the mentality of its people. It must be added that the Netherlands cannot be thought of as a unified whole with a common foundation for the development of garden construction. While in the north of the country (Holland, Zeeland) the ideals of the Enlightenment were more in evidence among the citizens, the south (Flanders) in the middle of the 17th century retained its feudal order which can be traced back to its close ties with

View of Caserta. To supply the grand cascade with water, it had to be linked with the source in the mountains by a 40-kilometre aqueduct.

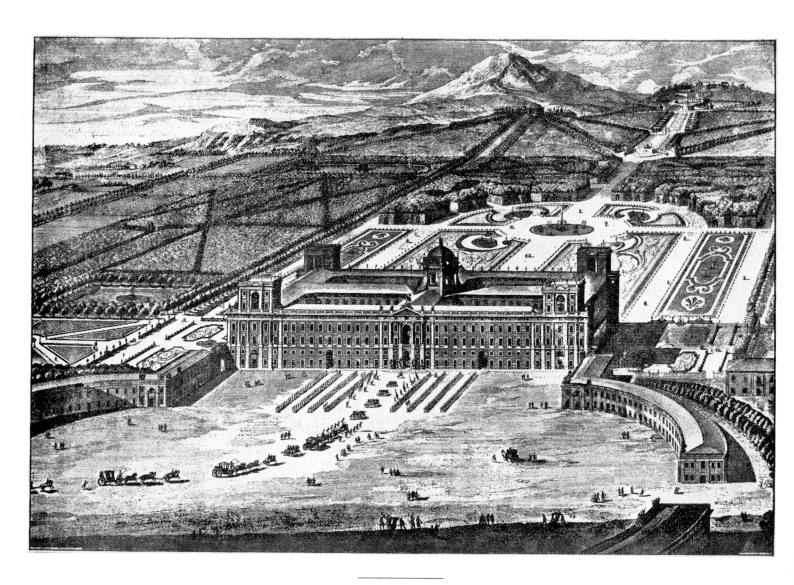

France. The dukes of Enghien, for example, in the mid-17th century had a garden constructed which, like other branches of Spanish-Netherlandish art, was clearly influenced by France.

In the north of the country, a whole number of country seats were set up by prosperous citizens. They were situated along the canals which drained the low-lying terrain. These canals, characteristic of the Netherlandish landscape, enclosed the gardens, were a means of transport and lined with paths. They were also a characteristic feature of the Dutch garden.

From time immemorial Holland was densely populated and the areas were painstakingly wrung from the sea and had to be utilized as effectively as possible. So, apart from a few exceptions, Dutch gardens are not very large.

The canal, which in the classical French garden was used as an axis accentuating the depth, had quite another function to perform in Holland. The want to surround the garden area and create an intimate atmosphere there was paramount. As well as the canals — which sometimes surrounded the garden on three sides — there were in addition hedges and trees, mainly fruit trees, which also served this delimiting purpose.

The little estates were characterized by a wealth of details that incidentally also pointed to the wealth of the owners. Statues, areas of sparkling flowers with tulips, hyacinths and narcissi as well as beds with myriads of summer flowers, plants set out in tubs and clipped trees lent the Dutch garden its individuality. The desired economic use of the garden found its expression in the fact that even the boskets were planted with fruit trees.

Such elements were also to be found in German gardens in the period of the Enlightenment. Frederick the Great had rows of fruit trees planted in the immediate vicinity of Schloss Rheinsberg and the terraces below the palace of Sanssouci were planted with vines and other types of fruit.

We also find features of Dutch burgher gardens in those of the ruling circles. They do not, it is true, come to the fore so much, but they are sufficiently influential to differentiate them from other European gardens based on the French or Italian style.

Already before Le Nôtre put his wonderful creations on display, there were French influences at work in the Netherlands. Stadholder Frederick Henry (1584–1647), for example, engaged André Mollet for the construction of his first estate in Honslaerdyk. In Huis Ter Nieuwburg, too, which arose around 1630, French influence is clearly discernible.

Although both gardens were later — after 1670 — remodelled, they retained the basic elements of their original conception. The delineation by canals was retained as was the arrangement of the boskets. The accentuation of the transverse axis was also maintained, making the grounds seem much wider than they are. Thus, seen in perspective, the stress on the main axis is reduced.

Richly stocked parterres were a characteristic element of the Dutch garden. It was in 1668 that Van der Groen, gardener to Prince William of Orange, published his famous work on gardening, *Den Nederlandschen Howenier* (The Dutch gardener). Its valuable gardening hints ensured its publication also in German and French translations. Among other things, it contained passages on the design of simple parterres.

French influence grew stronger especially under William of Orange and is traceable in the writings of Het Loo between 1684 and 1700. These describe a typical Dutch garden with French elements. The architect Daniel Marot (1663–1752), who co-operated with Het Loo in the planning of the palace and the gardens of Huis Ten Bosch and Heemstede, was responsible for the creation of a very special type of garden. One technique he used at Heemstede was to lengthen the main axis so that, in contrast to the typically Dutch terrain, it had a greater vision of depth, even where this is not to be measured by the criteria of the great French gardens of the mid-17th century. In Het Loo, larger boskets are traversed by numerous radial walks. But seen as a whole, in these later Dutch gardens the arrangement of equal axes was retained; also retained was the method of arranging the independent compartments in rows and the delineating function of the canal. One example is the summer palace of Honslaerdyk, where the canal not only flows round the garden that surrounds the great house on three sides, but also round the house itself which thus takes on the character of a moated palace.

We should also have in mind the evenness of the terrain. Terrace gardens as we know them from Italy and France could not be built on this flat land. Even the construction of cascades was difficult.

Neither was it in line with the middle-class ideology of the Dutch to raise the palace in order to make it an impressive symbol of Absolutist power. With the exception of Het Loo, where the main garden with its eight large parterres lies deeper, artificial alterations of the natural relief were avoided. The former glory of Het Loo was impressively depicted by engravers and painters. The tulip, then as now, made the Dutch gardens glow with a profusion of colour, together with other bulb plants, and called forth a wave of enthusiasm in Europe. In the years after 1554, Venetian merchants brought more and more tulips from Turkish gardens to western Europe.

It was somewhere around 1560 that the goblet-shaped flower was introduced into the Netherlands by the Leiden Professor of Botany, Karl Clusius, whom we have already mentioned. He began by growing them in his own garden and sent seeds and bulbs to his acquaintances; in this way he played a great part in their dispersal throughout Europe. The desire to possess them grew into a downright craving, especially in the years 1634 to 1637. For an especially beautiful specimen — variegated, feathered or striped blooms were the most eagerly sought after — incredibly high prices were demanded. Sums of up to 6,000 guilders were paid for one bulb and for a "Semper Augustus" as much as 13,000 guilders until, in the year 1638, the Amsterdam government introduced fixed prices.

In the independent German states

The Thirty Years' War (1618–1648) left its deep imprints on the Holy Roman Empire. Gardening also suffered and it was only the slow economic upswing following the end of the war that brought a new flowering in the development of this branch of the arts. The result of this impediment was that Baroque palaces and gardens in Germany appeared at a later date than in Italy, France, England or the Netherlands. So there was already a wealth of models that inspired the ruling circles in the principalities and the designers engaged by them. Because of the heterogenic nature of outstanding Baroque gardens — also brought about by historically constituted family ties and political connections — it is difficult to single out noteworthy examples.

The Gloriette at Schönbrunn

In the 17th century Vienna was the seat of the emperor and the cultural centre of the German states, also setting the tone for landscape architecture. Special mention must be made of the genius of Bernhard Fischer von Erlach (1656–1723), who produced the designs for the imperial residence at Schönbrunn near Vienna. Originally the hunting lodge was erected at the time of the Habsburg emperor, Maximilian II (1527–1576). But the real story of Schönbrunn began with the coronation of Joseph I (1678–1711) as German king, who became King of Hungary in 1687 and, from 1705, was Emperor of the Holy Roman Empire of the German Nation. This gave Schönbrunn its splendour and its favoured position in Europe. The newly awakened self-confidence of the Habsburgs — encouraged by the repulse of the Turkish attack on Vienna in 1683 — expressed itself in architecture just as it did in garden creation. Fischer von Erlach, returning from Italy around 1686, probably designed the first project — as early as 1690 — largely orientated on Italy.

The original site for the palace was that which is now graced by the Gloriette, certainly for its beautiful view which would have given the garden an Italian air. However, the resources of the court did not allow this plan to be realized.

In 1694 Fischer von Erlach designed a second project, one that displayed unmistakable French features, but underwent alterations during the period of construction. We cannot be quite sure whether the garden architect Jean

Trehet, born in Paris in 1654 and engaged from 1690 to 1692 at the imperial summer residence Favorita auf der Wieden, worked at Schönbrunn after plans by Fischer von Erlach, or whether he had already submitted designs of his own. What is certain, however, is that Trehet continued his activities at Schönbrunn after interrupting his work to journey to Paris on behalf of the king.

The result was a typically French, stretched-out main parterre in the axis of the palace. Inspired by the impressions he had gained on his journey, he also created boskets which framed the garden. After the death of the Emperor Leopold I (1640–1705), the work was not continued. In the reign of Maria Theresa (1717–1780) the gardens achieved their present form by transformations and additions. The Gloriette only came into existence after 1770, at the same time as the Fountain of Neptune.

The palace and garden at Het Loo were constructed in 1686, but extended already in 1692. Engraving by L. Seberin.

The Viennese Belvederes

Johann Lucas von Hildebrandt (1668–1745) created one of the most magnificent palaces in the world – the Belvedere which he constructed for Prince Eugene of Savoy (1663–1736) before the gates of Vienna. Here again we meet both garden styles, the French and the Italian, yet in a clearly differentiated composition.

The Lower Belvedere displayed a conception that was obviously widely popular in Vienna at that time. It was also expressed in the neighbouring Schwarzenberg Garden, in the Staremberg Garden as well as in the second design of Fischer von Erlach at Schönbrunn. The main building stood in the valley at the beginning of the garden, which was terminated, on rising ground, by a Belvedere; the sequence of the partitions thus began from below.

The upper part of the estate — also called the Upper Belvedere — was constructed upon quite different principles, largely connected with the participation of Le Nôtre's pupil, Dominique Girard (died 1738), who had

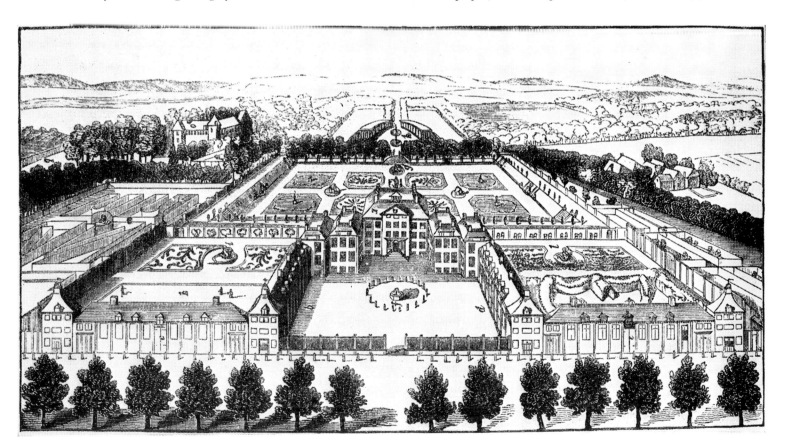

been invited to Vienna in 1717. Aurenhammer compares this conception with that of Vaux-le-Vicomte, as follows: "The pupil of Le Nôtre, Girard, in constructing the garden seems to have incorporated elements of a previous work of his teacher, the Vaux-le-Vicomte; common to both are the relief of the terrain, the strict axiality, the borders planted with box next to the palace and the cascades in the central axis. The difference lies in the fact that, instead of the typically French pool, a second palace borders the garden from below; and this may be seen, looking upwards from below, as an example of the manneristic Italian terraced garden."

The Vienna Belvedere is a jewel of garden architecture, in which the blending of many different elements is brought to fruition in a work of rare perfection.

Fertöd

So that he might remain close to Vienna, the spiritual metropolis, Prince Nicolaus Eszterházy (1714–1790) initiated the building of the greatest palace ensemble in Hungary in 1762. It was of this creation that Louis Prince of Rohan-Guémémé, French ambassador in Vienna, wrote: "In Eszterháza I have found a Versailles." The death of Prince Eszterházy also heralded the demise of the glory of the palace and gardens. The estate declined, and only the description of visitors and engravings give us some inkling of its former beauty.

The palace itself was, of course, also a remarkable creation of Hungarian Baroque architecture, but the special effectiveness of Fertöd lay in the complexity of the whole ensemble. The estate, with its buildings, the park, the deer park and the surrounding villages, formed a uniquely harmonious composition that, right from the start, was consciously planned.

The palace was the centre and, from its semi-circular parterre, the *allées* feathered out into the distance. A wide parkland spread out behind the palace and, in the axis leading to the main building, was delimited by cascades. Behind it lay another park, vast in size, richly decorated with statues, vases and fountains. Next to this an ensemble of buildings followed: a Chinese garden house,

the Hermitage and four pavilions — temples of Diana, Fortuna, the Sun and Venus. The ceiling and the façade of the Sun Temple were decorated with representations of the sun; in each of the others there was a statue of the goddess.

The Chinese garden house was the largest of all the pavilions. Narrow pilasters divided the main façade of this one-storey building; seated on the highest point of the roof was a Chinese with an umbrella, and tiny bells at the corners of the little house tinkled in the wind. The interior decoration and the furniture likewise were in Chinese style.

An especially beautiful monument to Hungarian wrought-ironwork has been preserved in the gate to the great house. This trisected gate was made from a drawing by Melchior Hefele. The work is attributed to the smith Johann Carl Franke; in the course of time a number of alterations were undertaken. Even at the time it was constructed it was greatly admired for its excellent plant ornamentation.

Canals and gondoliers in Bavaria

In Bavaria, the Baroque art of gardening had its heyday during the reign of Elector Maximilian II Emanuel of Bavaria. One reason for this seems to have been the elector's long sojourn in the Netherlands and France, forced on him by the political exigencies of the time. So French influence is of special significance here and, in garden construction, finds its main echo in the creation of Schleissheim and Nymphenburg. In the gardens of both these palaces the main object of attention is the situation of the canal which forms the main axis from the palace.

An extensive canal system was constructed which connects the parks. It was built under the direction of Enrico Zuccali (1642–1724) who was architect to the Court of Bavaria from 1669. The canals run from Nymphenburg to the river Würm, via the Würm canal to Schleissheim and then continues to Dachau and Dirnismannig. Another canal, starting at Nymphenburg, was planned and was to join up with Schleissheim in a circular course eastwards, but it was never completed.

Alongside their obvious agricultural purpose, i.e., as land drainage, these water arteries of Dutch origin also served as a means of transport and kept the waterworks going. As in Versailles or at the Dresden Court, there were also gondoliers in Bavaria to look after the fleet of pleasure gondolas.

In Schleissheim, the canal runs to a small casino — known as Lustheim — that was already in existence in the nineties of the 17th century. Completed sooner than the palace, it was to become the "Trianon" of the Bavarian elector. This is indicated by two flanking pavilions which were later to be connected by a semi-circular gallery with the small mansion in the middle. Lustheim bounded the garden at one end and so became a special attraction for the garden area.

The basic outlines of the Schleissheim palace seem to have been laid down shortly after the turn of the century, jointly, by Zuccali and Charles Charbonet (died 1720) — a Belgian pupil of Le Nôtre. But it was Joseph Effner (1687–1745) who set his seal on the final version of the palace which by the addition of laterally extending galleries and corner pavilions eventually stretched right across the whole width of the garden. He also continued work on the garden. In this he was supported by Dominique Girard, "master of the wells, inspector of the pleasure gardens and waterworks". Thus Schleissheim can compete with outstanding Baroque gardens — especially with regard to its water installations (Berckenhagen).

Nymphenburg — an imitation of the great French model

The fruitful cooperation of the two artists is also in evidence at Nymphenburg, which even surpasses Schleissheim in its dimensions and its variety of water installations. Just like Schleissheim, Nymphenburg was already in existence as summer palace of the electors of Bavaria when Maximilian II made his appearance as patron of the works, thanks to the activities of his mother, the Electress Maria Henrietta Adelaide. When she died in 1676, the little pleasure palace in Italian style was nearly finished. But as it did not satisfy the elector's demands, it was ex-

tended bit by bit over several periods of construction so that finally a great summer residence had been created. It is probable that the decision to lay-out gardens after the great French model was already made in 1701. French influence is indeed extraordinarily strong in Nymphenburg. The construction of radial axes — so well known from Versailles — was strictly adhered to at Nymphenburg. The optical illusion of a sloping terrain was achieved and has become a Nymphenburg phenomenon. The electors wanted the palace to stand somewhat above the level ground, as in the French gardens. In reality, however, it stands on what is only a very slight, almost unnoticeable rise in the land. As the natural relief could not be suited to the lay-out of the gardens, another way had to be found. The front section of the canal up to the cascade was constructed without the usual step for damming up the water; the row of trees which bordered the canal were shortened in height as they receded into the distance.

The actual extension of the gardens into grounds which blended with the architecture and the dimensions and adornment of the palace was only carried out after the War of the Spanish Succession. The original state of this Baroque garden ground is documented in plans of 1720, 1736 and 1755 and in miniatures by Maximilian von Geer (1680–1768) and from views by Mathias Diesel.

Seldom has the basic scheme of the French garden been so strictly adhered to. Three separate sections merge together in a totality. The first section comprised the forecourt and great courtyard with the junction of the avenues and of the canal, as well as the palace with two miniature cabinet gardens at the side — the so-called *giardini segreti*. The second section is made up of the Petit Parc with its main parterre and the boskets at the sides, as well as the wooded belt. The Petit Parc is surrounded by canals which, on the one hand, demonstrate their close relationship but, on the other, accentuate a certain unusual separation from the other sections. It is remarkable that just at Nymphenburg, which in other respects follows the French example, the canal does not disappear as an outer moat running off into a central canal, but appears here as a surrounding girdle of water.

Nymphenburg is primarily famous for its water arrangement. More than six hundred "leaping and running" watercourses are referred to in an inventory (Hager). Of its one-time splendour a traveller, the nobleman von Rothenstein, who visited Nymphenburg in 1781, reported: "The garden has nineteen fountains with 285 water jets; to behold so many waterworks, gilded vases and statues and myriad flowers is nearly beyond description. The great flower parterre has a span of 138 *Klafter* (*c.* 250 metres); it has a large fountain, four smaller ones and one that is sexagonal … The parterre has 28 gilded statues, vases and urns; the beech trellises are adorned with 17 statues of white marble. After the Fountains of the Dragons there follow two fountains with sculptures of

The great canal of Nymphenburg (after Mathias Diesel).

children, each child riding on a gilded whale … at last, right at the centre, the Fountain of Flora — octagonal and set in white marble, it has a circumference of over 100 feet … Then there are eight little gilded hillocks in the pool, four of them crowned with cupids, the other four with Tritons, holding corals, pearls and the like in their hands.

Around the rim of this pool eight gilded frogs spout forth parabolic streams of water. This gorgeous fountain costs 60,000 guilders and required 250 hundredweight of lead. After that, you again come to a large pool from which twelve-foot high streams of water gush forth — six in a row; this pool is connected with the canal which leads on to the great cascade" (Bernoulli).

In the incomparable effects of its fusion of tamed nature and fashioned stone, Nymphenburg stands at the crest of central European Baroque gardens.

The palace terrace of Sanssouci, where plants and choice fruit trees grew behind glass panes.

The Augustusburg at Brühl

With the elevation of Prince Ernest of Bavaria (1554 to 1612) to Archbishop of Cologne, the Electorate of Cologne remained tied to the House of Wittelsbach for nearly two hundred years (until 1761). It was largely through the policy of Maximilian II Emanuel of Bavaria who decided upon the clerical career for his brother, Joseph Clemens (1671–1723) and some of his sons, that he secured the Bavarian succession in the northwestern bishoprics.

Among some other princely seats in the district of Bonn and Cologne, the summer residence of Augustusburg at Brühl arose. Joseph Clemens determined as early as 1715 to reconstruct the hunting grounds and its moated castle that had existed there since the high Middle Ages, and to lay-out gardens here. This plan was not carried out and it was only under his successor, Clemens Augustus (1700–1761), that the Baroque Augustusburg and its gardens came into being.

It was under the guidance of the Westphalian Johann Conrad Schlaun (1695–1773) that an estate was built with a fortified moated palace in the middle of three gardens; Dutch influence seems in evidence here. The Frenchman François Cuvilliés the Elder (1695–1768) was the one who had the moat filled in and turned the castle into a summer palace.

The main axis of the garden proceeds from the south wing of the palace; it was here that the above-mentioned Dominique Girard erected the great terrace whose steps connect the interior of the palace with the main area of the garden. For the re-modelling of the gardens which had now become necessary, the prince-bishop again appointed Girard who designed the main garden strictly in accordance with the "classical" order of individual sections. The sequence of terrace, parterre, bosket and park was based on the Le Nôtre pattern.

Orangeries and menageries
for exotic plants and animals

Inspired by the brilliant courts maintained by the high European nobility, the young Duke of Wurttemberg, Eberhard Louis, who came to power in 1693, determined to imitate them. Because of the wars carried out on the borders with France, Wurttemberg was under economic duress all the time, and was only able to recuperate very slowly after the peace treaties of Rijswik (1697) and Rastatt (1714). So it was only in this peaceful period, at the beginning of the 18th century, that the real flowering of Baroque garden design could begin with the construction of Ludwigsburg.

Several building phases preceded the large-scale project put forward by the Italian Giuseppe Frisoni (1683 to 1735) in the year 1721, who gave the palace and the garden their final form. From 1703 to 1707, Matthias Weiss (1636–1707) put forward plans for the gardens on the north side of the Erlachhof hunting lodge; they included an orangery and a menagerie. The actual extension into

View from the orangery over the garden grounds of the Gaibach palace (after Salomon Kleiner).

a Baroque palace began under the architect Johann Friedrich Nette (1672–1714), and, after his death, was continued by Frisoni. It was then that the Ludwigsburg Baroque ensemble attained its present beauty. The accentuation of the transverse axis is a noteworthy feature. This stressing of the widening effect was achieved by the demolition of the orangery building in the second section of the garden. Now, two one-storey orangeries appeared athwart the main axis. The accentuation of the width is also visible in the third section; here it is brought about by the labyrinths and the *broderies*. This tendency became evident in France particularly after Louis XIV.

The new residence of the Margrave of Baden-Durlach deviates from the rest of the schema, both in the construction of the palace and in the positioning of the individual parts of the garden. The construction of the palace and gardens was influenced, above all, by a division of the terrain at Hardtwald in 1715.

There, Margrave Charles William III (1679–1738) had a large circular area cleared, from which thirty-two rides and avenues led in all directions. In the middle, as focal point, arose a tower, visible from afar. The avenue leading southwards served as a kind of base line, towards which the palace — built later — opened out. The extensive side wings follow the radial walks and flank a great courtyard in the shape of a trapezium. The erection of pavilions with quadratic, sexagonal or circular bases, at the beginning of the avenues, may be seen as a special feature. They served as small menageries for poultry, songbirds, dogs, cats, monkeys; they were also used as rest areas for sentries, as bath- and wash-houses and were painted and stuccoed in a most original manner.

The pleasure gardens lay in the area bordered by stables, orangeries and pavilions between the town and the great courtyard. The beds in the pleasure garden formed rectangles of various dimensions. The triangular spandrels — created by the system of radial walks — were filled in artistically. The middle section was made up of a *broderie* parterre on both of whose sides were ponds for waterfowl, glass-houses for foreign plants and aviaries. A sunken menagerie had a fourteen-cornered pavilion in the middle, used as a bird-house underneath and as a dining-room on top.

The park, split up by rides radiating from the centre, began just behind the palace. Certainly the idea was to create a great princely residence — like Marly, for example. There is evidence for this in an inscription attached to the palace entrance. "A lover of tranquility wished to pass the time here in peace and quiet, in contemplation of God's creatures, scorning vanity, greatly honouring the Creator. The people, alone, came hither, built what thou seest here …" (Hennebo).

In this southwestern German area, the most outstanding garden designers were the two closely related families, the Petris and the Sckells; they were decisively involved in the fashioning of a whole number of smaller garden establishments. The Sckell line achieved fame, especially in the later landscape garden, through Friedrich Ludwig Sckell.

In the central Franconian area and the central Rhineland, Baroque garden design is primarily marked with the stamp of the House of Schönborn. As Bishop of Bamberg (1693), Archbishop-Elector of Mainz (1695), First Prince and Arch-Chancellor of the Empire, Lothar Franz von Schönborn (1655–1729) combined the highest honours in his person. He has also gone down in history as one of the greatest patrons of building in the Baroque period.

Artists like Johann Dientzenhofer (1665–1726), Johann Lucas von Hildebrandt (1668–1745), Maximilian von Welsch (1671–1745) and Johann Balthasar Neumann (1687–1753) were all employed by him and his successors. Old engravings of the wonderful gardens and the palace ensemble with its four wings, at Seehof near Bamberg, or the Schönborn family seat in Gaibach near Würzburg are examples of their ingenious deeds.

The Favorite at Mainz

The most interesting and, at the same time, most beautiful and significant architectural and horticultural creation of Lothar Franz von Schönborn was his summer palace — the Favorite at Mainz. The opportunity to obtain a residence worthy of his office as Archbishop of Mainz offered itself in 1700, when he was able to get a suitable plot of land with a pleasure garden, on the banks of the Rhine opposite the junction with the Main. The construction took many years and was probably largely completed in 1722. As an expression of respect for the imperial house in Vienna, it was named after the Favorite in Vienna; Marly-le-Roi at Versailles was the model for its design.

In 1717, Lothar Franz von Schönborn wrote in one of his letters: "I am at the moment imitating therein the petit Marly, that is six pavilions, namely, three on each side seen in perspective, and yet each separated from the other by a special terrace and above, to close it off in the middle, an orangery of 120 feet ..." (Hennebo).

The basic outlines of this —on German soil completely new — type of garden design were laid down by Maximilian von Welsch. This ingenious work points the way to the continuation of what was begun at Marly. It consists of a "system of relatively independent gardens, arranged parallel to each other ... pointing the way to the next epoch of garden design. The gradual dissolving of the 'great Baroque forms into fascinating detail, of strict uniformity into loose juxtaposition ...' begins here" (Landau).

The course of this development may be seen if one compares the Favorite with Rococo gardens like Veitshöchheim or Sanssouci. The axial structure rigidly adhered to in the Baroque garden is dissolved and the concept of the Favorite further developed; as Hennebo formulates it with regard to Sanssouci, "... by the positioning of its buildings (Gallery of Painting – Palace – New Chambers), by placing them next to the adjoining gardens, by their opening out to the landscape and by the axis which draws them together at the foot af the hilly country". Besides a clear accentuation of the transverse axes, peculiar to Dutch gardens, is recognizable.

At Mainz, the palace stands sideways at the end of the main axis — so that it is not the only dominant feature —, what also points to a deviation from the French ideal. Unfortunately, this interesting work of art no longer exists; only surviving engravings give us an idea of its former beauty.

Gripped by a lust for building

In Weissenstein near Pommersfelden a summer residence came into existence between 1711 and 1718, under the aegis of Lothar Franz von Schönborn; Johann Dientzenhofer, assisted by Lucas von Hildebrandt, drew up the plans. It was Maximilian von Welsch who was responsible for the whole construction. With the death of the patron, the building work was brought to a close. At the turn of the century, the Baroque garden was turned into a landscape park, which still surrounds the palace.

On each side of the palace accompanying buildings were used as orangeries, "... for, in 1720, the first tubplants arrived from Austria and Bamberg; among them were 70 laurel trees and 166 orange trees". Orangeries were generally popular among the Schönborns. A report from Rudolf Franz Erwein (1677–1754), a nephew of the archbishop, tells of the acquisition of whole orangeries, and the reigning prince-bishop in Fulda — who maintained close friendly relations with the Schönborns — engaged F. J. Stengel (1694–1787) and Andreas Gallarini to build an orangery resembling the one at the Mainz Favorite between 1721 and 1730.

The Prince-Bishop of Bamberg and Würzburg, Friedrich Karl von Schönborn (1674–1746), was also gripped by the building fever. In 1733, he had a garden constructed at Werneck — which lies between Würzburg and Kissingen —by Balthasar Neumann and Lucas von Hildebrandt; however, it lacked parterres, fountains and cascades. It was designed in a rustic manner with meadows and tree plantations and already showed indications of that new outlook which, a few years later, was to give a thoroughly new image to the garden.

The magnificent Baroque garden at Kassel-Wilhelmshöhe

The trends in the art of gardening that find expression in the Italian villa gardens, reveal themselves in the grandest manner in the creation of Wilhelmshöhe near Kassel. Landgrave Charles of Hesse-Kassel (1677–1730) has left behind a gigantic work to posterity, a work that, in view of the limited size of his domain, must seem even

The Favorite at Mainz with the waterworks and boskets. In the foreground the Fountain of Neptune.

more prodigious. He had toured Italy in the winter of 1699 to 1700 and was so impressed with the beauty of the great villas situated on hills that he travelled home with the idea of creating "something really wonderful" before the gates of his own residence at Habichtswald.

The relief of his estate, on the slopes of hilly country at the rivers Werra and Fulda, seemed peculiarly suitable for his purpose. Now the problem was to find an artist capable of executing his design after the Italian fashion. He found one in the person of Giovanni Francesco Guernieri (*c.* 1665–1745), whom he invited to Kassel in 1701. Guernieri's design was the basis for the construction. In all essentials it has the hallmark of the typical Italian highland villa. There is great similarity, for instance, with the Villa Aldobrandini in Frascati in respect of its position and the arrangement of its individual parts, though it should be added that Wilhelmshöhe was enhanced by many of the landgrave's own ideas, which Guernieri incorporated into the design.

"Out of this harmonization of the German and the Italian perceptions in artistic matters, there arose what is perhaps the most magnificent creation that Baroque style, in a coalescence of landscape and architecture, has dared to bring about anywhere" (Dehio).

The difference from the Italian highland villa is to be seen, above all, in the extra-dimensional expansion of the "borrowed" features. The plans — published as copperplate engravings in Rome in 1705 and in Kassel a year later — point to the similarities. The crossing axes, for example, consist of a main axis directed towards the upward slope, and several transverse axes running parallel to the slope. The palace stands at the foot of the actual garden axis but can be clearly seen from the valley and, from it, one has a magnificent vista of the valley. (The park axis is continued by an avenue leading to the town.) A particularly obvious similarity with the Villa Aldobrandini is to be found in the fountains, grottoes and cascades with their gurgling and roaring waters.

No thought has been given here to what is usual in most Baroque gardens — the position of the elevated palace as a symbol of power. Here it is an octagonal olympus on the hill; we have a parallel for this in the Belvedere of Prince Eugene in Vienna. The work did not proceed very rapidly; by 1713, for example, only a third of the planned cascades were finished.

The mighty figure of Hercules still dominates the skyline of Kassel and its surrounding district, as a symbol to this very day. Created by the Augsburg coppersmith Johann Jakob Anthoni, it was completed in 1717. The statue is nine-and-a-half metres high and can be entered. Its erection marked the climax of the construction at Wilhelmshöhe.

Guernieri had already left for Rome in 1715. After his departure the work was carried on but proceeded very slowly until, with the death of the landgrave, it finally came to a complete halt. Nothing stirred in Kassel for the next thirty years until a fresh stream of garden culture began to flow through; this new impetus carried with it the re-fashioning of the garden into one of the most beautiful landscape gardens in Germany.

Dutch influences
in North German garden design

From the north of Lower Saxony to the Oder, we can trace a development under quite different influences. Here, despite the evidence of French inspiration, Dutch influence was clearly discernable.

It was the Electress Sophia (1630–1714), wife of Ernest Augustus (1629–1698), whose initiative gave rise to one of the most famous gardens of this area. It was she,

too, who assembled at her residence important personages, notably Handel and Leibniz. In 1713 she wrote to Leibniz: "It is only with the Herrenhausen garden that we can make a show; it really is lovely and neatly kept" (Hennebo).

Until the great days of the Herrenhausen gardens came to pass, in the reign of Ernest Augustus, numerous transformations took place. After Duke John Frederick (1625 to 1679) decided to make the place his summer residence, the gardener Michael Grosse installed a little garden on the south side of the summer house which had been built in 1666. Already in 1670, the duke had several plans for the transformation of the garden produced by unknown artists; these, however, were largely neglected.

The construction of waterworks was problematic right up to the 19th century because of the insufficient water supply. As early as 1676 the Frenchman Cadart (died 1687), working with the specialist Michael Riggus of Augsburg, busied himself at Herrenhausen, building a grotto beside the palace. To complement this, a great cascade resembling a water theatre was erected, on the other side of the palace. It is still in existence. But on the whole, Cadart had little success with his water arrangements. The project for a water pumping station, put forward by Leibniz in 1696, was not carried out. Only English mechanics were partly successful. They dammed up the river Leine to the south of the garden and branched off a canal above the dam steps; its waters worked blade-wheels that set forty pumps in motion and thus set the waterworks in motion, too.

From 1680 until her death, the electress' technicians were busy extending and re-fashioning the Herrenhausen gardens. Now the Dutch influence emerged clearly. The reason for this was that, for the whole of her life, she maintained a close relationship with the House of Orange. So the Great Garden was to be transformed along the lines of the Orange residences at Het Loo, Honslaerdyk and Nieuwburg. The work began in 1696, after she had invited an expert from the Court of William III of Orange and sent the French gardener Martin Charbonnier (died 1720), engaged at Herrenhausen since 1682, to Holland again to pursue his studies there. In addition to this, a gardener of Italian descent was invited from the Netherlands to take part in the work.

An encircling canal, the *gracht,* flanked by an avenue of limes, epitomized the Dutch model. Charbonnier even refrained from using the continuation of the central axis right up to the banks of the river Leine. What had formerly been a square garden was doubled in length and now falls into two square halves, one of which, lying to the north of the palace, is richly endowed with parterres. The boskets lie in the southern one.

In the vicinity of Herrenhausen, Duke Anton Ulrich (1633–1714) had transformed Salzdahlum into his residence. His artistic ambition far outran his political strivings. His journeys took him through the whole of Europe — to Venice and the Netherlands, among other places. These experiences left the deepest impression, which found their reflection in the construction of the palace and the garden.

Unfortunately, nothing has remained of the estate, begun in 1688, a "masterwork of secular Baroque architecture in the Guelph domains" (Hennebo), in the whole of the north German area. We have to rely on descriptions and engravings. As at Herrenhausen, the palace was arranged around numerous courtyards and special gardens. The ends of its wings enclosed the garden, as in the Dutch style, and formed arcades.

These arcades looked out on the parterre with its water arrangements. (Berckenhagen sees a resemblance to the Boboli gardens in Florence; no doubt the amphitheatre's embracing of the parterre plays a role in this. Hennebo goes back to the gardens of Het Loo as a possible source of inspiration, where the parterre is bordered by a raised walk.)

The garden of Salzdahlum consists of two halves, as does that of Herrenhausen. The two parts were linked by a main axis, but through the separating transverse axis each appeared as an independent ensemble, equipped with fountains in the middle. A Belvedere and a pagoda, thought to stem from Dutch inspiration, are regarded as an early example of chinoiserie in central Europe.

View of the palace and gardens of Charlottenburg. Engraving by Johann August Corvinus.

As a result of the marriage of Elector Frederick (from 1701 Frederick I of Prussia) to Princess Sophia Charlotte of Hanover, by such places as Herrenhausen and Salzdahlum an influence was exercised over the March of Brandenburg with regard to the construction of mansions and gardens, as various establishments there, in the French and Dutch styles, reveal.

The gardens of the palace of Oranienburg display the same Dutch influences as Rosenfelde near Berlin, which was only renamed Friedrichsfelde in 1661.

The loveliest construction in the Brandenburg area is the ensemble of the palace and the garden at Charlottenburg — formerly Lützenburg. It has to thank the young Electress (later Queen) Sophia Charlotte (1668–1705) for its existence and was, for a long time, the main residence. In contrast to most of the other North German creations, Dutch elements are hardly in evidence, allowing French taste to come to the fore. It can no longer be established who designed the plans for the project. Simeon Godeau was engaged in 1696 as "designateur et conducteur de ... jardins de Lützenburg" and thus it was he who presented the first plan. As evidence that the design was based on principles laid down by Le Nôtre, Kühn writes: "... the enclosed nature of the estate is breached at its most important point — with a mighty impulse the main axis surges powerfully forward into the surrounding countryside".

The function of the Grand Canal at Versailles is taken over by an extended, semi-circular enclosed pond, hard by the Spree; that river, itself, accompanies the garden for the whole of its length. Charlottenburg is, in general, characterized by an impressive abundance of water. Several watercourses flow through the back section of the garden, just as the Dutch canals do. The palace was begun in 1695 by Johann Arnold Nehring (1659–1695) and, after the turn of the century, was enlarged mainly by Johann Friedrich Eosander von Göthe, who also built the orangery.

The principality of Anhalt-Dessau had both family and political connections with Prussia, as the Princess Henrietta Catherine (1637–1708) was a princess of the House of Nassau-Oranien. Oranienbaum, between Dessau and Wörlitz, can be traced back to her line. This was the time when Dutch architects, engineers and craftsmen came to Anhalt-Dessau. One of these was Cornelius Ryckwaert (died 1693), who had drawn up the plans for the palace and also — it is assumed — for the park. The transverse axis is stressed here, following the Dutch style. The continuation of the deep axis links the palace with the market place. The palace was built in horse-shoe shape in the homely style of the Dutch country seat, and is sur-rounded by a moat. One reaches the courtyard across a bridge and then proceeds to the garden over another bridge which leads to the parterre; this formerly was planted with box and pyramids of yew, the whole being enlivened in the middle by a *bassin* with a fountain. In summer, tub-plants were set in this parterre. According to a plan of 1719, this garden was composed of eight sections, but not all of these have been preserved. On the one-time island garden, a Chinese garden arose between 1793 and 1797. It still exists and is — with its buildings — a special delight. The centre of attraction is the Chinese tea-house. This brick building is decorated with numerous East Asian motifs and Chinese pillars. On the border of the garden on a small hill, a five-storey pagoda rises up; it is modelled on the famous Kew Gardens pagoda of William Chambers.

As there was originally only a small stock of tub-plants available at Oranienbaum, a small building was all that was necessary for the orangery. By 1754, however, the stock had increased to 417 orange and lemon trees, as well as other tub-plants, so that in 1812 a new orangery was built, measuring 175 metres, which still exists today.

Baroque gardens
of Elector Augustus the Strong

When many artists engaged in Prussia were dismissed or had restrictions imposed upon them in the reign of Frederick William I (1688–1740), they emigrated to the Electorate of Saxony. There, under Elector Augustus the Strong (1670–1733) — from 1697 also King of Poland —, the courtly splendour and the cultural life approached its zenith. He made Dresden into one of the loveliest Baroque residences; gardening, too, experienced a remarkable development.

Matthias Daniel Pöppelmann (1662–1736), Johann Christoph Knöffel (1686–1752) and J. F. Karcher (1650 to 1726) were engaged to construct gardens as well as summer palaces and hunting lodges together with Z. Longuelune (1669–1748), Jean de Bodt (1670–1745) and others. An extravagant efflorescence of magnificent estates began, orientated on the Court of Louis XIV, the

Sun King. French and Italian influences replaced the Dutch model in garden construction.

Pöppelmann's designs for the erection of a new palace, after the old one had burned down in 1701, could not be put into effect within a short time because of the political and economic conditions prevailing at the beginning of the 18th century.

He was not only an architectural genius but also an outstanding garden designer. The numerous journeys he undertook, on behalf of the elector, to Italy, Prague, Vienna and Salzburg, provided him with stimuli of many kinds.

But prior to these journeys, his building plans for the palace had been completed and already contained the location for the Zwinger. The main work on the palace began in 1711.

Parts of the fortifications were incorporated in the structure. The moat, for instance, remained filled with water in front of the Crown Gate. The Zwinger served as a place for tournaments and festive displays, as an amphitheatre and grandstand; it was both orangery and gallery, a garden with waterworks and grottoes. In all, it proved a grandiose setting for the elector's festivities. The boskets, tree screens, hedges and trellises to be found in other aristocratic gardens were replaced by stone pavilions and galleries which enclosed the open spaces. Orange trees in tubs served as decoration.

View of the Grosse Garten in Dresden with the palace seen from the west. Engraving from about 1840.

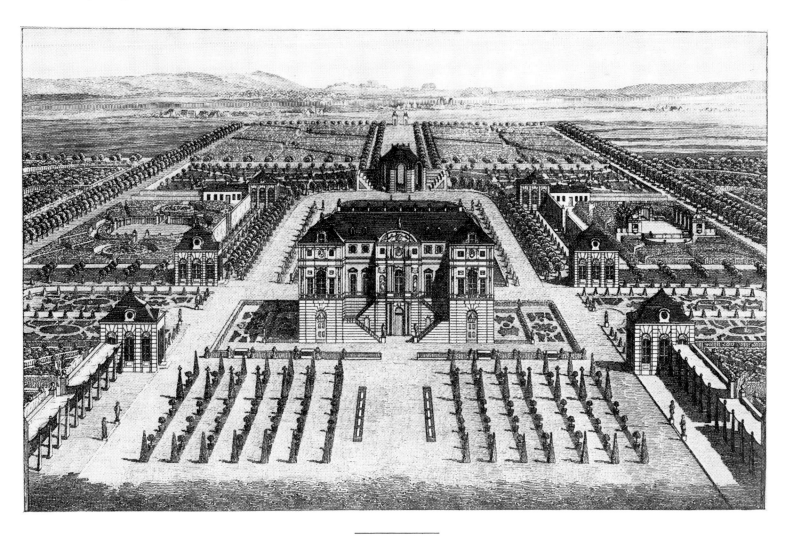

Plastic garden decorations

The Zwinger with all its ensembles is strongly influenced by Italian taste. The nymphaeum in the Villa d'Este in Tivoli, the water theatre and cascades of the Baroque villa at Frascati and the amphitheatre of the Boboli gardens could all have been the instigators of what we see here. The *broderies* and water areas, as planned by Pöppelmann for the Zwinger courtyard, were not constructed at that time. It was Balthasar Permoser (1651–1732) who created the plastic decorations and many garden sculptures in the Zwinger.

Longuelune, working together with Jean de Bodt, Knöffel and Karcher, achieved a significant transformation of the gardens. The conspicuous opening of the central prospect towards the Elbe is described by Sulze as follows: "Here the garden becomes the prelude to the landscape. The steps leading to the Elbe were transformed into a gondola harbour and decorated with the colossal figures of Eurytus, Hippodamia, Nessus and Dejaniera, sculpted by Antonio Corradini; these were later exhibited in the Grosse Garten."

The Grosse Garten outside the town was the third of Augustus' pleasure gardens. Already at the end of the 17th century, John George II (1630–1680) had a hunting lodge built on this site. It was in 1715 that the extension and transformation of the Grosse Garten was begun, after a design by Karcher. The palace stood at the crossing point of symmetrical longitudinal and transverse axes.

Parterre gardens and boskets formed the central Petit Parc around the palace. Beyond this were extensive wooded regions in cruciform shape, sheltering a variety of game. In its basic plan the palace corresponds to the French style of château, though its builder, J. G. Starcke, modified this with Baroque elements. Later, alterations were undertaken in the park, until well into the 19th century. Friedrich Bouché, who belonged to the Lenné school, carried out a transformation in landscape style.

While wood-like boskets are suggestive of a park in the Grosse Garten, at Moritzburg an extensive wooded area was used as a grand park. In 1720 Pöppelmann designed plans for the reconstruction of the old Renaissance palace.

These plans were put into effect under Longuelune, and completed in 1736. The beautiful Baroque palace stands on a mighty terrace, surrounded by stretches of lawn with conifers and deciduous trees. The garden of the palace carries on northwards, behind stretches of water. Today it is bordered by *allées* and is not laid-out as a Baroque garden, as originally planned. At Moritzburg, the architecture blends with the garden, the woods and the water courses in an imposing way.

Grossedlitz offered other developmental possibilities than Moritzburg. However, the estate in its present form corresponds only in parts to the plans of Longuelune. When it came into the hands of Augustus the Strong in 1723, the eastern part of the grounds — with the orangery and the palace — were already completed.

The Baroque garden of the estate stands in stark contrast to other parks created at that time. Here Italian influence is more in evidence. Most Baroque gardens are situated on plain terrain. At Grossedlitz, on the contrary, the terrain of the park falls southwards sharply from a plateau in the north, to rise again from the depth of a valley. This relief was skilfully used for the creation of terraces and broad outdoor stairways. The level surfaces were covered with flower parterres and waterworks. Two narrow canals underline the centre of the lawn parterre beneath the orangery. (Vaux-le-Vicomte has such canals with gargoyles along the main avenue.)

Plastic decoration is used far more extensively than was usual at that time. The abundance of sandstone figures is especially noteworthy, being crowned by a stairway construction — a Pöppelmann creation. The balustrades of its curved landings form a platform for music-playing Tritons. These latter give their name to the whole construction: "Silent Music".

One of the palace estates of Augustus the Strong is Pillnitz near Dresden. The graceful structures there, built with fine flourishes, and the foreign plants exert their exotic charm over the visitor to this very day. The Far East conjured up a picture of lively yet playful elegance; so they liked to decorate the buildings — not primarily used for official purposes — with oriental features.

Page 149:

56 Aerial photograph of the gardens at Blenheim, Oxfordshire.

57 The flat *broderie* parterre in front of the château
Vaux-le-Vicomte, with its characteristic arabesque patterns.

58 Versailles with the Latona Fountain. To hasten the work of
construction, 35,000 workers were employed in the year 1685;
in this marshy area they were struck down
in droves by fever, from which many died.

59 Louis XIV had 18 million tulip bulbs imported from
Holland in the course of a single year to decorate the
flower parterres and other parts of the gardens. Nowadays
the plants are changed according to fashion and taste.

150

151

60   The water-raising machine at Marly was constructed
between 1681 and 1685. Coloured copperplate engraving,
about 1700. Deutsches Museum, Munich.

61   View of the palace and garden of Jakobsdal, Sweden.
Engraving by Perelle.

62   Using the royal estate at Drottningholm as their model,
the nobility had gardens of the same kind laid-out,
though on a smaller scale. Engraving by Jean Benoit Winkler.

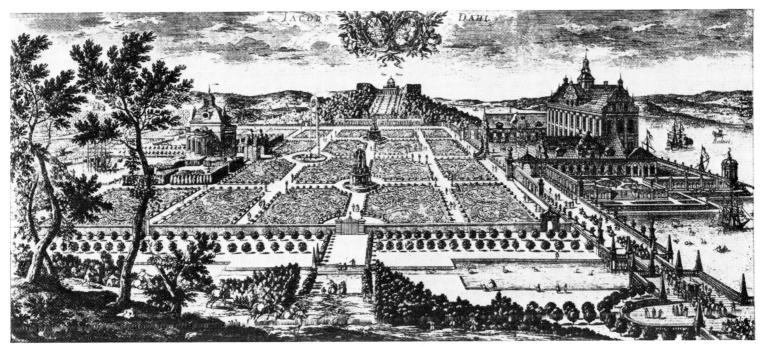

63 The palace and gardens of Frederiksborg are situated on islands
in a lake. The parterre and the boskets are laid-out on the
other shore of the lake through the axis of the great house.

64   Het Loo is regarded as a typical Dutch garden
under French influence.

65   The royal summer residence at Fredensborg was built
on the pattern of a French château. The long *allée* leads
to the forecourt of the great house.

66　The Grand Cascade of Petrodvorets is situated
below the palace. The water tricks are a constant
source of amusement to the visitors.

67　The distant parkland area is visible from the cascade
of the Marly garden in Petrodvorets.

68　The Grand Canal at Petrodvorets is artistically lined
by boskets. View from the palace.

69   The extensive water gardens with the fountains
at La Granja were created in 1720.

70   The parterre in front of the royal palace of Queluz
is laid-out in formal style.

71   The fame of the Aeolus Fountain is only surpassed
by that of the stepped cascade in Caserta, which stretches out
into the countryside for nearly a mile.

72   The palace and gardens of Schönbrunn
impress by their dimensions.

73   View of the garden frontage from behind the Fountain
of the Naiads at Schönbrunn.

74 The Belvedere palace near Vienna, seen from the north.

75 The open hall of the Belvedere palace is situated
between the inner rooms of the palace and the grounds.
Engraving by Johann Jacob Gräsmann and Salomon Kleiner.

76 View of the menagerie of Belvedere. Copperplate engraving
by Johann August Corvinus after Salomon Kleiner.

Pages 164/165:
77 View of the rose garden of the palace of Konopiště.

78 The former hunting lodge at Süttor was reconstructed
after 1764 and became the Eszterházy palace.

79 Topiary at Sanssouci. It was mainly linden, hornbeam
and yew that was clipped in this way.

80 The former Wilanow royal summer residence is situated
on the outskirts of Warsaw and is one of the
most beautiful creations of Baroque landscape architecture.

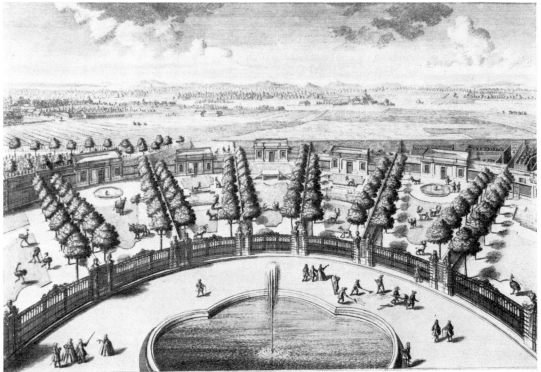

165

81 The Baroque palace of Ludwigsburg as seen from the garden.
The new Corps de Logis was probably completed in 1728.

82 View of the main *allée* in the formal garden
of Nymphenburg near Munich.

83 View from the Nymphenburg palace
to the *allées* lined by statues.

Pages 168/169:
84 Aerial photograph of the Karls-Aue in Kassel.

85   This aerial photograph of Pillnitz represents
the formal style of the garden design.

86   A bird's eye view of the ensemble of the Dresden Zwinger.

87 Part of the outdoor stairway with the curved landing
in the park of Grossedlitz.

88 Detail of the extensive garden grounds of Herrenhausen.

89 In the Baroque garden at Grossedlitz it was originally
intended that two side-axes should be attached
to the central east-west axis.

90   The Rococo garden at Schwetzingen,
designed by J. L. Petri and N. Pigage.

91   Stuttgart has been famous for its municipal gardens
since Renaissance times. The building of the Neues Schloss
commenced in 1746, the square in front
of it shows Baroque elements.

92   The tea-house in the park of Sanssouci stands
in most picturesque surroundings.
It is one of the best-known examples of the craze
for chinoiserie in the 18th century.

93   The orangery at Sanssouci was erected between 1851 and 1857
and leans towards the Italian Renaissance style.

94   A characteristic feature of the Rococo garden
of Veitshöchheim is its rich adornment with statuary.
This statue was created by Adam Ferdinand Dietz.

95   The hedge garden of Veitshöchheim measures 450 by 250 metres
and was laid-out by Adam von Seinsheim.

96   The somewhat raised palace of Veitshöchheim
with the ornamental parterre.

Page 180:
97   The Moritzburg palace and grounds blend harmoniously
with the landscape.

As far back as 1403, a document mentions two palaces, one of which stood on the banks of the Elbe. It was here that a moated palace was built after 1720, with a gondola harbour watched over by sphinxes, where Venetian gondolas of the Dresden royal household tied up at the landing stage, with its beautifully designed steps. From 1722 to 1723, the other building on the landward side was turned into a hillside palace. Both palaces enclose a courtyard, enhanced in the middle by a fountain and designed as a decorative garden. The visitor is especially delighted with the many beautiful tub-plants here, as well as by roses and summer flowers. A special delight is the camellia. It is one of four plants introduced into Europe in the 18th century: at Herrenhausen, at Kew Gardens and at Schönbrunn near Vienna. The other three plants faded away, but the Pillnitz camellia lives on. It is interesting to note that it was already planted in the open in 1801 and today has developed into a strong tree. To preserve this arboreal rarity it is protected by glass in winter. The influence of the English style of garden, coming into fashion at the end of the 18th century, was also in evidence at Pillnitz.

Gardens in Saxe-Weimar

To round off the picture of German Baroque gardens, we must take a look at the efforts of Duke Charles Augustus of Saxe-Weimar (1757–1828). Here we are especially interested in the Fasanenhaus (Pheasant House) lying to the south of Weimar on a slope called the Eichene Leite, named after a mountain. The palace was later known as Belvedere, but in the early days — it was erected in 1724 — it was still referred to as the Fasanenhaus. After 1806, the park was completely re-fashioned into a landscape park; the Russian Grand-Duchess Maria Pavlovna (1786 to 1859) had a considerable hand in this. Remains of this Baroque estate are to be found today in the courtyard structure and the horseshoe-shaped orangery. This once contained a rich assortment of plants with over 500 orange trees, 68 coffee trees, 50 laurel pyramids, olives, figs, myrtle, oleander and agaves among many others. The southern semi-circle was occupied by a menagerie divided into segments by radial walks. It housed rare exotic wildfowl and is a faithful replica of the one at Versailles.

The cascades planned by Charles Augustus and his attempts to utilize water from the river Ilm to feed them by means of a water machine à la Marly, never got beyond the planning stage.

Tea-houses, pavilions and pagodas

In the second third of the 18th century, new lines of development in garden design became apparent which revealed a style that somewhat departed from those of Baroque. If Baroque incorporates the larger, the mighty, even the monumental, then we now find an elegance with a touch of sentimentality expressing the age of Rococo with its floating lightness. It is precisely the works of plastic arts that entered into a remarkable association with those of the gardeners' art of the new epoch; they drew mutual sustenance from each other. What would a Rococo garden be without statues of the gods like Amor and Apollo, without the playful nimbleness of amoretti, without the muses, nymphs and graces from the world of sweet illusion.

The Baroque garden assumed different forms. The strictly formal lines occasionally even dissolved to be replaced by flourishing lines. Fountains, springs and grottoes were retained but were fashioned in the elegant, graceful Rococo forms. Water as a bubbling, murmuring or dripping fluid experienced varied forms of expression.

Some elements, like orangeries and hermitages, were frequently used — indeed, a kind of renascence in the Rococo period. Recourse to chinoiseries was fashionable, though this was also significant already at the Court of Louis XIV at Versailles, in the Trianon de Porcelaine; now it reached its peak. Tea-houses and pavilions and, later, pagodas gave a new tone to the landscape.

Buildings of the Rococo period also include temples based on those of Antiquity and artificial ruins. Climbers were planted to act as symbols of movement, almost playfully scaling the heights. Altogether, special attention was paid to plants as a means of delineation but also to enliven the scene by the play of light and shade.

The "surprise" effect

Screens of trees and hedges divide, shut in and therefore create the intimate hideaways which find their fullest development in the Rococo period. The visitor finds it hard to orientate himself, for with the changing impressions he loses the overview, the symmetry so pronounced in the Baroque is missing. Now it is difficult, if not impossible to gain a total conception of the garden in traversing it. The stroller is led with playful lightheartedness from one idyllic spot to another and is each time delighted anew by the surprising variety of impressions. The varying scenes make a lively impression on the guest and keep him on tenterhooks in joyous anticipation of the next "surprise". One of the outstanding patrons of this style of construction was King Frederick II of Prussia (1712 to 1786) who, as crown prince, already had the margrave's fief at Rheinsberg re-fashioned. After the Court architect Von Kemmeter (died 1748) had altered the mansion, adding another wing *(corps de logis)* at right angles to the Renaissance wing with a round tower (also known as Klingenberg wing), the further re-building and extension of the mansion was undertaken by Georg Wenzeslaus von Knobelsdorff (1699–1753) in 1737. As a result of his journey to Italy, he was still completely under the spell of the buildings he had seen there and, naturally, this found an echo in his designs for the house and the grounds. He sought symmetry in the total conception of the house and added a new wing so that the ground-plan of the estate now included round towers bordering the side wing, thus creating a great courtyard delineated by a colonnade.

Knobelsdorff was the most important representative of the so-called Frederician Rococo. He made use of a formal garden design — which was in any case usual at the time —, but in doing so always tried to incorporate the natural surroundings into his composition; he made the park fit in well with the whole landscape. An *allée,* straight as a die, begins at the Klingenberg wing, leads on across a bridge over the river Rhin and ends at a portal with flanking groups of pillars and a semi-circular balustrade. Incidentally, Knobelsdorff repeated this same idea later for a gate at Sanssouci.

The obelisk, too, made an appearance again at Sanssouci as a focal point outside the garden, at the end of the *allée* — no longer there today. In the orangery parterre, the difference in levels in the main *allée* were overcome by a stairway at which Glume (1714–1752) posted two sphinxes, which later were also copied at Sanssouci. Above the orangery parterre a cross-walk led eastwards to the "Heckentheater" (open-air theatre) constructed in 1758 by Reisewitz.

Somewhere near the middle of the main *allée,* a cross-axis was laid out at right angles; it ran parallel to the narrow side of Lake Grienerick and ended at the Egeria grotto. This grotto was decorated with corals, mussel-shells and coloured pieces of glass. On this cross-axis lay a great roundel that boasted a pavilion as its centre-piece, originally planned to house an orangery. This building was never completed and, in 1753, parts of both side wings were dismantled.

Various boskets surrounded the orangery. A special feature of the Rheinsberg garden were the hedged-in fruit tree sections which also again appeared at Sanssouci and are regarded as hallmarks of Frederick II's gardens. If one proceeds on the transverse axis behind the place with the orangery, one passes the former vineyard on the left-hand side with the Temple of Fortuna. The dome was supported by eight Ionic pillars. The temple was the centre-piece of a tripartite system of paths. One of these paths runs right across the transverse axis to a roundel planted with larchs.

Gradually the character of the landscape style became more marked. The garden was enriched with a Chinese tea-house and a Chinese tent and an open-air theatre. The former vineyard became the site of the temple and of boskets. Ancient, Gothic and Chinese elements are to be seen; also the "recourse to the natural may be clearly observed, especially in those sections done in the English taste, distinguished by the rich variety of species of woody plants … The French style especially extolled by Heinrich, the shepherd idyl and the dream of an Arcadian rural life, Rococo and Romantic are the features of this style of garden design" (Badstübner/Karg).

According to Siedler, some of the elements of the Rheinsberg conception are already a clear pointer to Sanssouci. Thus, for example, ideas which could not be carried out at Rheinsberg were again taken up at Sanssouci. Especially to be noted is the fact that the palace — built by Knobelsdorff between 1745 and 1747 — stands to one side in contrast to the French style. It lies at a height on a range of hills and almost has the character of a hermitage. The six terraced vineyards that spread out at the foot of the palace were neither to be enhanced by balustrades nor by other plastic decoration but, apart from pyramids of yew, were to serve purely utilitarian purposes.

The niches which, because of their glass windows, have the appearance of a glass-house, were intended for finer fruit sorts. Additional buildings, like the orangery to the west of the palace — later the Neue Kammern (New Chambers) — and the glass-house to the east — later the picture gallery — stressed the breadth of the palace, making it more prominent. Parallel to this tripartite complex and at the foot of the hills runs the main *allée*. It begins at the entrance portal with the obelisk and ends at the Neue Palais (New Palace). When the visitor strolls along this *allée*, the character of the Rococo garden with its ever changing impressions becomes clear. The first bosket lies at the same height as the Neptune Grotto. Following the hedges, we soon reach the Dutch garden that stretches out on both sides of the main *allée*.

A pool in the middle is lined with busts that document the family ties with the House of Orange. The avenue leads on through rows of trees and walls until the whole scene opens to a wonderful panorama. In the centre is a *bassin* with marble figures; to the right, the terraces can be seen, at the top of them the palace.

The *allée* continues straight ahead, walled in by rows of trees in boskets, walks leading off radially in all directions. It then leads on further to two circular places with sculptures of the Muses at the centre of radial *allées* with another sculpture, until it arrives at the Neue Palais, in whose vicinity a rocky grotto was only partly erected and then broken up again.

But the grotto motif remained and is reflected in the grotto hall. The interior of the Neue Palais, with a length of 213 metres, was decorated in Rococo style. Here we meet the "peculiarity of Potsdam Rococo — the effective contrast between smooth white walls and rich ornamentation" (Wagner).

A passion for chinoiseries and grottoes and a predilection for ruins

The delight in chinoiseries finds expression at Sanssouci in the tea-house, among other things, created in 1755 by Johann Gottfried Büring (1723–1782). It highlights the extravagance of this fashion, with imaginative sparkling golden figures and palm trunks. The tea-house area seems detached and is only connected to the rest of the park by a winding path — later a common feature of the English garden style.

Similarly isolated were the Temple of Antiquity and the Temple of Friendship erected in 1768 by Karl Philipp Christian von Gontard (1731–1791). The Belvedere was also modelled on an antique building; it was created in 1770 and served as a lookout. One can get an excellent overall view of the whole Sanssouci park from there. The little Dragon House, not far from there, was built for the vintner of the vineyard and was modelled on the Great Pagoda at Kew. In the 19th century, the Prussian crown prince, later King Frederick William IV (1795–1861), had Sanssouci extended and engaged Joseph Peter Lenné (1789–1866) to re-fashion it in the style of an open landscape garden.

The Bayreuth Hermitage is also worth a mention. An abundance of grottoes, buildings of natural tufa and ruins reveal the obvious sentimentality of the Margravine Wilhelmina (1709–1758). Of artificial ruins alone — including both hermitages — seven remain and the theatre ruin, erected in 1743 by J. Saint-Pierre, is the earliest building of this kind in Germany. A sunken lawn is surrounded by a raised auditorium; behind this there are five raised pairs of pillars joined together by flat arches.

The sentimental nature of the patroness is also expressed in her designation of a ruin as a gravestone for her favourite hound. The whole charm of its abandoned look was enhanced by the fact that these structures were everywhere overgrown by climbing plants like ivy, and so looked wild and deserted — like a wilderness. The ruins, whilst portraying evanescence and sorrow, were also pervaded with her historicizing inclinations.

The margravine was equally enamoured of the fashion for things Chinese as an outlet for her exotic tastes. The garden had a Japanese house with a dragon's cave on the ground floor, constructed in the form of a grotto. The interior of the New Palace also showed signs of this trend, an outstanding example of which was the Chinese cabinet especially created for the purpose.

With the sunken parterre, a charming pool was created. As centre of attraction there was a large pond decorated with mythological creatures. Fountains and jets created a gushing and glittering display whose attractiveness was increased by the enchanting, colourful decoration, even more enhanced by the inlay work on the outer walls of the palace.

The whole was enclosed by semi-circular arcades with the Sun Temple in the middle — a domed building. The garden was laid-out symmetrically but, despite this, constantly provided the visitor with surprises such as its boskets and hedged quarterings. There was a wooded area immediately adjoining the rest of the garden; one can already see here the tendency towards a natural style of garden which, at that time, was just beginning to take shape in England.

The spirit of the age also showed itself in the garden at Sanspareil. Bizarre-shaped rocks dominated the garden and the buildings. One can almost place Sanspareil in the ranks of the landscape garden, but it still shows features of a more formal lay-out.

The Würzburg palace gardens

The prince-bishops of Würzburg erected their residence on a site east of the Old Town, right in front of a bastion of the town fortifications. So it was impossible to create extensive gardens on the grounds in front of the palace complex with depth effect.

Famous architects like Balthasar Neumann, Maximilian von Welsch and Johann Dientzenhofer drew up the plans for the palace and gardens. In their considerations, they included the areas to the side of the palace for the garden; this gave rise to a quite peculiar ground-plan for the ensemble. The fundamental relationship between the gardens and the palace did not change from the very beginning of the planning, in 1744, to the completion of the construction in 1770.

Earlier plans, in addition to an accentuation of depth, also attempted to achieve a broadening effect in the orchard — situated symmetrically on the garden side of the palace —, but Johann Prokop Mayer (1737–1804), from 1770 head gardener at Würzburg, concentrated his main efforts on achieving depth. He went in for an abundance of divisions and a rich assortment of plants, so to counter the limitation on space. In addition, he let the garden run out to a point at the top. As a crowning glory, he erected a pavilion standing on top of the bastion. In order to get there from the palace, one has to traverse a whole number of terraces. The path leads across a circular area composed largely of tub-plants, through an opening in the arboured walk to the terraces, which are supported by a curved buttress. Before one reaches the garden pavilion, the path goes past two cascades, lying behind each other in the Italian manner.

The lay-out of the south garden gives no effect of height; it is separated from the south wing of the palace by a path. There are tub-plants here, too. Beautiful to behold, with its richly imaginative curves, is the triangular parterre, whose apex penetrates a rectangular parterre, up to more than half its length. The remainder of this area is occupied by fruit trees.

Behind the fountain *bassin* there is a further garden area with an oval section whose surface is likewise largely covered with fruit trees. In order to produce a visual coalescence of all the parts of the south garden, they are bordered by arboured walks. The Flora Temple rises at the south end; this is surrounded by further garden areas. Hedged gardens, similar to the labyrinths of the Rococo period, lie in the western part of the south garden.

Veitshöchheim —
a typical Rococo garden

The planning and construction of the gardens at Veitshöchheim, in the neighbourhood of Würzburg, were so protracted that it took more than fifty years to complete them.

But do not look for an especially large size or outstanding position, a link with the palace or axes with wide views — Veitshöchheim has none of these to offer. And yet, it is *the* German Rococo garden. Gracefulness and elegance in a confined space are as typical of this place as its rich adornment of statues, which present an excellent picture of Rococo garden statuary.

A circular place known as the Circus acts as a garden centre-piece. Thirty-two sculptures by Ferdinand Tietz (died 1780) are harmoniously blended with stone

View of the labyrinth in the castle park at Würzburg (after J. P. Mayer).

benches. "And so that these plastic riches should not confront us all at once, the ensemble is divided by thirty-two short hedge walls, converging on the centre and forming niches which are roofed over with arches. Dancers and musicians, characters from four continents, animal vases and fancy pieces with musical instruments, give the Circus its cheerful, graceful, capricious touch" (Hoffmann) and delineate the garden's appearance for us — a highly picturesque sight.

From the Circus one axis leads in a straight line eastwards to the great cascade, created from 1772 to 1773 by Materno Bossi (1735–1802) with figures by Johann Peter Alexander Wagner (1730–1809). A stroll through this garden leads, as it were, from one green cabinet to another; figures loom up constantly which sometimes appear phantom-like in the moving shadows. According to Kreisel, "the figures were created in colours, mainly white, to give the sandstone the appearance of shining marble; some were highly coloured and others — like Pegasus at Parnassus — were gilt".

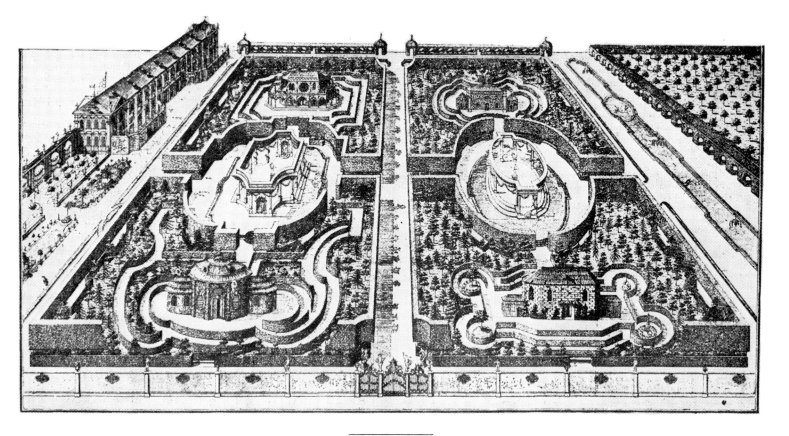

Apollo Temple and bath-house
at Schwetzingen

It was the head gardener of Pfalz-Zweibrücken, Johann Ludwig Petri (1714–1794), who designed the plan for Schwetzingen, a plan based upon the French textbook of gardening, *La théorie et la pratique du jardinage*. Although the garden is modelled on very strict lines, Petri was able to score "an outstanding success in the interplay of the formal and the ornamental" (Lohmeyer). A large circular area is broken up by a rectangular parterre that follows the axis to the palace. A further section of parterre, with a row of trees, cuts it up in such a way that a cross is formed.

The sections thus remaining are laid-out with boskets and green cabinets as well as fountains. "The parterre, itself, has two bowling-greens at each end, all exactly the same and enhanced by surrounding flower borders and with foliage at the narrower sides; each bowling-green also has a round fountain *bassin*. The centre-piece, where the axes cross, displays four corner sections adorned with box around a large circular fountain *bassin*.

The whole parterre is shut off by a semi-circular pool containing two high fountains and flanked by water-spouting stags" (Hoffmann). A long middle perspective was, apparently, originally not planned, as the view along the depth axis is obstructed by a facing row of trees behind the last *bassin*. In 1761, Nikolaus von Pigage (1723 to 1796) extended the garden, especially westwards, so that the new terrain in its extension equalled two diameters of a circle. In doing so he directed his attention principally towards an opening in the depth axis, which even ends up crossing a transverse canal, continues through a meadow and becomes a forest ride.

The extension largely benefited two boskets of differing character. Although the northern one seems more austere than the southern one, it contains interesting winding paths reminiscent of a labyrinth.

The sections adjoining the boskets are richly decorated with figures. An Apollo temple stands royally behind the open-air theatre; a grottoed slope is decorated with cascades, naiads and sphinxes. The attractive bath-house stands near the open-air theatre, with a small free area enclosed by fences and walls.

The water-bell, the wild-boar fountain, the antique busts and the Bacchic putti enliven these lovely surroundings. Some buildings in the park of Schwetzingen, like, for example, the mosque, ruins of a moated Roman castle or the Temple of Mercury, arose after 1776 and already belong to the landscape garden period, whose development did not pass Schwetzingen by.

A Glance to China, Japan and India

In Chinese gardens nature is copied *en miniature;* mountains, rivers, trees and plants serve as formative material for fascinating garden landscapes, or unspoiled countryside — untouched by human hand — is completely absorbed into the whole design. We know of similar features in the English landscape garden and its imitators throughout the whole of Europe.

Mountains and waters

As well as in its completely different topography and its own distinctive forms of expression, the Chinese art of gardening differs from European landscape gardens above all in the interpretation and significance of the individual elements, from which emerges a combination and arrangement which depict a symbolization of nature. This desire goes back to Taoism, a philosophy which believes in an immanent order and harmony in nature which remain hidden from man and will only materialize in the moment of "enlightenment".

Mountains and waters most frequently reveal the very being of the Chinese garden and both expressions recur in the Chinese word for landscape painting — *shan-shui.* One may see the art of gardening as closely associated with landscape painting. Chinese picture scrolls with portrayals of landscapes are famous; they demonstrate the affinity between garden and landscape. While vertically painted scrolls allow the representations to be perceived at a glance, the idea of the horizontally painted scroll is to open the picture up bit by bit just as nature reveals itself to our eyes. With a few exceptions, the Chinese garden is not to be perceived in its entirety, all at once, either.

Chinoiseries — pavilions, bridges, ceramics — spread throughout Europe in the second half of the 17th century and convey a tiny impression of the manifold designs in the Rococo gardens or — until the beginning of the 19th century — in numerous landscape gardens.

Sacred groves

As in Greece of Antiquity, there were no ornamental gardens in our sense of the word in ancient China, but only arboured groves. One of the oldest groves we know of lies around the tomb of the Chinese philosopher Confucius (551–478 B.C.). This grove stands near the town of Ku Fou in the Province of Shantung, where the philosopher spent many years of his life. As a sign of the respect in which he was held, memorials and temples were erected in other places, too, and people planted trees nearby. In Ku Fou, notice-boards tell us that the cedars there were planted during the Ch'in and Yüan Dynasties between the 12th and 14th centuries (Thacker).

In the neighbourhood of this same town stands Mount Tai Shan with its many temples and trees. To reach the summit of this sacred mountain one climbs seven thousand steps, the path leading through defiles and gorges and past monuments, caves and waterfalls. On top we find a shrine that is also surrounded by a grove. At an-

The Emperor Wu Ti also sought the legendary islands — dwelling place of the Immortals — which was supposedly to be found in the mists of the Yellow Sea. As he did not discover them, he decided to create them from his fantasy and thus a garden with lakes and islands came into being that was constantly imitated both in China and Japan.

The secret of the stones

Wu portrayed the animals of the island garden symbolically by stones. Stones were also used to indicate the islands; they were, in fact, a symbol of the infinite. This depiction of the infinite, of immortality is, from now on, frequently demonstrated and is a key to the conception of the Chinese garden. There were also many artists, writers and scholars who identified themselves with Wu's ideas and who were attracted to the garden design of the time.

After the fall of the Han Dynasty — a time of economic and cultural flowering for China —, many painters and poets withdrew to the loneliness of the mountains. The impressions they got there, of the rough unpolished stones, were so strong that — spread far and wide — they led to new impulses. The lake- and island-gardens became popular again but the soft contours disappeared and bizarre shapes met the visitor's wondering gaze. Strange forms were just as much in demand as stones with holes in them.

In 618 China achieved a new cultural flowering which stemmed from the first emperor of the T'ang Dynasty; this was when artists again began to paint on silk, the origins of which go back to the 5th century B.C. Many beautiful flower and landscape paintings have been preserved from this period.

Landscape painting and the art of gardening evolved hand in hand and reached their zenith in the 13th century under the aegis of the Sung emperor Hui Tsung. He ruled in Hangchow until 1279. Other emperors of this dynasty also had their seat there, surrounded by a "paradise" with lakes, bamboo, lotos, magnolia, chrysanthemums, plums, peaches, almonds, apricots and other lovely flowering plants could be found there (Cowell).

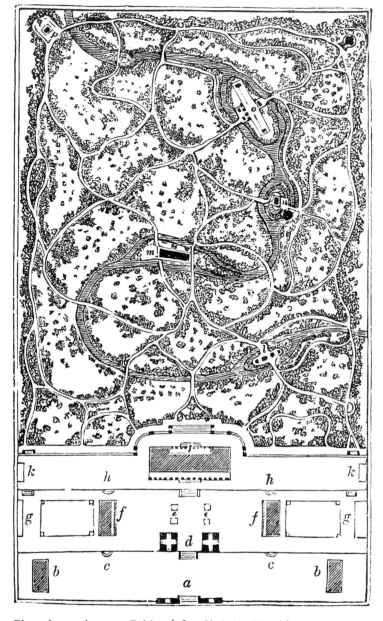

Plan of a garden near Peking (after Christian Krafft).

other place in the Tai Temple, there are six cedars that Emperor Wu Ti (*c.* 140–86 B.C.) of the Han Dynasty is supposed to have planted. He had a passion for collecting plants and is said to have enclosed an area with a wall of 250 kilometres length for this purpose. All the provinces of the land had to contribute towards this collection by specially selecting plants and large stones, typical of their area, and sending them to him (Jäger).

Page 189:

98　The Chinese lacquered wall screen represents
garden scenes from various centuries. It is a work
of Master Dshou Dshou of Ru-nan, Honan province, 1756.
The lacquered, black surface is decorated with paintings
and inlay-work of jadeite, malachite, steatite and ivory.
Museum für Völkerkunde, Leipzig.

99　"The Garden Ch'in-ku Yüan". Painting by Ch'ou Ying,
ink and water-colours on paper, about 1500.

100　A rock called *tai-hu;* these bizarre stones
are an essential component of Chinese gardens.
Östasiatiska Museet, Stockholm.

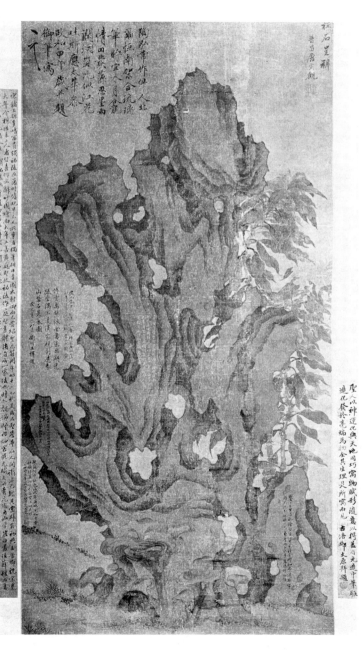

101 The tomb of Confucius in Ku Fou, Shantung province.

102 Wall carpet with Chinese motifs. Lewin Collection.

Pages 192/193:
103 The Silver Pavilion – Ginkakuji – in Kyoto was begun
in 1482 and is a copy of the Golden Pavilion.
Both of them were based on the Great Hall in Seiho-ji,
the most famous of the great Japanese temple gardens.

104 The tea ceremony in the tea gardens had its heyday
in the 17th century.

105 The Ritsuren garden of Takamatsu is one of the
most famous and most beautiful of Japan.

106   The Katsura garden in Kyoto.

107   The Zen garden in Kyoto belongs to the
so-called level-ground gardens.

108   Following Buddhist models, the capital Haij-ko,
present-day Nara, arose in 710 and,
with the help of Chinese and Korean craftsmen, many gardens
were constructed. Byodoin Temple in Nara.

109 The garden palace of Dig in Rajasthan, India, stretches out along the waterside; the gardens extend behind the façade.

110 The waters of the mountain rivers are directed through the garden of Shalimar in Kashmir to supply the fountains and gargoyles.

111 The Jain Temple in Sonagir, Madhya Pradesh.

112 The Taj Mahal gives an excellent example
of the integration of a memorial and a garden.

113 Mogul palace garden portrayed in perspective.
Miniature of the late Mogul school, 18th century.
Staatliche Museen zu Berlin, Islamisches Museum.

114 This Mogul miniature shows a garden from Baber's time
with an artificial pond. British Museum. London.

Page 200:
115 The Shalimar garden of Kashmir is one of the
famous Indian gardens.

Famous imperial gardens

The great Mongolian Emperor Kublai Khan (died 1294), who founded the Yüan Dynasty, became ruler of China in 1280 and took over the wonderful gardens of Hangchow. Marco Polo (1254–1324), a Venetian merchant, whose account is our most important mediaeval source of information on East Asia, also wrote of this imperial palace with its groves, lakes, gardens and animal preserves.

A peasant uprising which lasted ten years, from 1351 to 1361, finally brought about the end of Mongol rule. In 1368 the leader of the peasants, Chu Yang-chang, took over power. This was the beginning of the Ming Dynasty which lasted until 1644. The gardens of this period tended towards romance and sentimentality and had plenty of stones. The Lion Grove — Shih Tzu Lin — in Soochou can still be seen today as an example of that kind of garden. It was laid-out in 1530 on Mount Tien Mu, surrounding a temple. Buildings and trees enclose a lake with islands which are reached by bridges. "The Hall of the Artificial Cloud" stands enthroned on top of a man-made mountain. It is reached by paths that lead past bizarre, fantastically shaped rocks, "which seem, with the play of light and shade, and the reflections in the water of the lake, to portray not merely lions but stranger and more alarming monsters" (Thacker).

At the end of the 16th century, a new emperor had a further lake- and island-garden laid-out, a work which was accomplished by a million men; it covered an area of 1,110 square kilometres. Between the lotos-covered lakes and the bizarre-shaped stones stood red palaces and pavilions whose roofs were made of glittering, colourfully glazed tiles and had raised gutters at the corners (Johnson).

Just as European landscape gardens are closely connected with painting and poetry, these art forms are also intertwined with Chinese garden design. This is demonstrated by the painter-poet, Wen Cheng-ming (1470 to 1559), whose paintings and poems of Cho Cheng Yüan (garden of the unsuccessful politician) in Soochow give us a vivid impression of this garden.

The garden art of China has probably changed very little since the above description. Many gardens appeared in the course of time, large and small ones, but the common pattern was repeated again and again, of mountains, stones, buildings, flowers and trees. From this plethora of gardens, a few stood out, especially the Yüan Ming Yüan (garden of perfect light), Ch'ang Ch'un Yüan (garden of everlasting spring) and Wan Shou Yüan (garden of untold years) which lay to the north-west of Peking. This ensemble was begun in 1709 by Emperor K'ang-hsi (1654–1723) and later extended and embellished by his son and — even more so — by his grandson, Quian-long (1736–1796).

Nothing remains of these gardens today, but forty paintings shed light on their most beautiful aspects. Quian-long produced a literary work, entitled *Yüan Ming Yüan,* which illustrates these views with woodcuts. According to a description by the Jesuit missionary J. D. Attiret from the first half of the 18th century, an exotic impression was created. He writes of artificial hills and infinitely numerous little valleys with canals of clear water. Earth and stones which were dug to create the artificial lake and the river beds, were piled up into artificial hills.

"The real jewel is an island or rock, rough and desolate, rising six feet above the water in the midst of the lake. A little palace is erected on this rock, which has more than a hundred rooms. A magnificent panorama opens up from there — one sees all the palaces, one after another situated along the shore and the mountains beyond, the canals and bridges, the pavilions and the triumphal arches decorating the bridges, and the clumps of trees which screen the palaces," these are the words of a contemporary report.

Flowers and shrubs

Among the favourite subjects of poets and painters, flowers have a prominent place and, as in the Middle Ages in Europe, they seem to have attained a symbolical significance. Chinese poetry reveals great admiration for the beauty of flowers, but reference is also made to those that are utilized for medicine or perfume. However, for Chinese garden design flowers were of less significance than, for example, for European Baroque gardens. Here, greater interest was shown in flowering shrubs and trees. An exception to this is the lotos which could not be omitted from any Chinese garden. Those with the greatest symbol-

ical significance were orchids, bamboos, chrysanthemums and the Japanese apricot. They represent the four seasons. In addition, the orchid symbolizes feminine charm and tenderness, the chrysanthemum stood for a long life while bamboo — a garden without it was unthinkable — was a sign of suppleness and strength. As early as the Sung Dynasty (960–1279), more than a hundred species of bamboo had been recorded. The "queen of flowers" is the tree peony, which was already highly appreciated in the Sung period. Many cultivars were grown and espe-

The Yüan Ming Yüan garden. The most attractive views of this garden were depicted in twenty paintings by T'ang Tai and Shen Yüan in 1744.

cially beautiful specimens fetched enormous sums, just as was the case with the tulip craze in Europe. In China there were several species of hibiscus which were held in high esteem and assiduously nurtured. Rose-mallow was called *fu-sang* by the Chinese and was connected in their minds with the Tree of Immortality. The Chinese hibiscus was called "flower of wonderland". Also esteemed were roses, peach blossoms, guelder roses, magnolia, azaleas, wisteria, lilies, jasmine and pines.

Poets and painters dedicated their works to their favourite flowers. The artist T'ao Yüang Ming, for example, had a special passion for chrysanthemums. A painting by Kao Feng Han (1683–1747) portrays the poet in his garden, which is covered with chrysanthemums that he cultivates. In the book *The Garden Flowers of China* it is recorded that by 1708, already three hundred species (he means cultivars, of course) had been described. The Japanese apricot is also one of the most frequently painted flowering trees of China.

Japanese temple gardens

In Japan, too, the oldest "gardens" were to be found in temple grounds and constructed as sacred groves or paradises. In and around Kyoto, the development of Japanese garden design with its various types can be studied. It is here that the renowned Shinto Shrine in Ise is dedicated to the Sun Goddess Amaterasu. The shrine originated in the 5th century and is surrounded by an open area of gravel arranged in accordance with strict rules. Shintoism worships natural deities and elevates mountains, rocks, rivers, waterfalls and trees to symbols, which embellish the gardens in miniature form.

Later, too, when Buddhism spread to Japan in the 6th century and rapidly established its teachings, the sacred grove had religious significance. The stones laid-out there in the gravel represented the relationship of Buddha with his pupils.

The temple gardens of the Zen monasteries were influenced by Zen Buddhism. It was in these monasteries that the symbolical type of garden gradually developed; these were also called "dried-up gardens". By arranging stones, sand, bushes and trees in a special way, mountains, waterfalls, rivers and lakes were symbolized. There are no flowers in these abstract gardens.

The rules of Japanese garden design were already laid down in the 11th century in the *Sakuteiki*, a treatise on garden planning which, later further developed, formed the basis for a work by Kitamura Enkin, entitled *The layout of landscape gardens* (1735). In this work, the two main garden types were described. It differentiated between the landscape garden with hills *(tsuki-yama)* and the level ground *(hira-niwa)*. In addition, various stages of design were delineated. *Shin* is the elaborate construction (e.g., Katsura), *gyo* indicates an intermediate stage (e.g., Daisen-in) and *so* is the abbreviated form (e. g., Ryoanji).

Although the same rules governed the lay-out of all mediaeval gardens, there is an impressive abundance of idiosyncratic details. Their appearance and its effect on the visitor differs from garden to garden.

The famous Daisen-in garden of the Daitokuji Monastery in Kyoto is one of the most outstanding creations. It originated in 1513 and is enclosed by walls and by the buildings. It can be viewed from a veranda. In a corner a line of jagged stones are visible, that jut out and are supposed to represent a mountain chain. Fern, mosses and little bushes give the impression of a wood. A waterfall with a cascade is imitated simply by stones and sand. It continues under a bridge, the latter being represented by a stone.

The garden of the Ryoanji Temple, with its downright simplicity, represents the zenith of the Japanese garden of contemplation. Purity and austerity is the first impression one gets of this garden. A relatively small area of only twenty-three metres by nine metres is bordered on three sides by a plastered wall which frames the structures of sand and stone. Viewing the artwork from the wooden veranda, one can make out the flat, gravel-strewn white area from which fifteen stones, arranged in groups, stand out. The only colourful element in the "ascetic monochrome of the garden" (Vinogradova) is the moss that grows around the stones and partly covers them. The gravel is smoothed out in parallel lines by a rake, and these lines symbolize the waves of the sea. In ellipses and rings they encircle the stones and stimulate the illusion of surging and retreating waters. The foremost aim of the artist was to arouse the observer's imagination. The whole garden is framed by tall trees which stand outside the grounds.

In addition to these "dried-up gardens" there are a number of temple gardens which also arose on the basis of the *Sakuteiki,* though significantly extended by the temple atmosphere. One of the most famous of these gardens is the Saiho-ji in Kyoto. Probably begun in the 8th century, it received its present form in 1339 by the Buddhist priest Muso Soseki (1276–1351). It is also known as the moss garden because it is the most richly covered in moss of all Japanese gardens.

As well as the moss, it is also composed of stones and a dry waterfall. Along a winding path, over bridges and "mossy seas" interrupted by heaps of jagged stones, one can get a good view of this garden. It is intended for meditation and at the same time to display its beauties to the visitor, like the Tortoise Island or the ship sailing to the Elysian Isles — indicated by a double line of stones.

Also to be found in this garden were the predecessors of the two famous buildings in the garden grounds at Kyoto, the Golden Pavilion (Kinkakuji) and the Silver Pavilion (Ginkakuji). The Golden Pavilion was begun in 1397 and the surrounding grounds and the lake were constructed exactly along the lines of Saiho-ji. The present-day building is a copy, as the old one burned down in 1950.

The pavilion is used for religious and secular purposes and stands on the shore of the lake; right next to it, four ships are represented by stones. The Tortoise and Crane Islands lie on the other side and are covered with pine, signifying a long life.

The Silver Pavilion is a copy of its golden neighbour; it is smaller and was begun in 1482. The Japanese have even picked out specific times of day recommended for observation. The silhouette of the Silver Pavilion and the romantic atmosphere of the silversand lake should be enjoyed by moonlight in the stillness of the night.

As against this, on the other side of the pavilion the visitor is confronted with a richly varied picture — a lake, small islands with a wooded slope as an attractive background.

The traditional tea ceremony

An examination of the Japanese garden would be incomplete if the influence of the traditional tea ceremony were to be ignored. It is the subject of innumerable works of painting, calligraphy, ceramics and architecture, and has necessitated a special form of garden — the tea garden.

It was the Zen Buddhists who, from the very beginning, invested tea-drinking with a ritual significance. The priest Murato Yuko (1423–1502) is credited with having created the tea ceremony; he first developed this Japanese art in the garden of the Silver Pavilion and raised it to a ritual. It was named *cha-no-yu* — tea ceremony — and was to be carried out in a little hut made of wood, straw and bamboo.

This corresponded to the whole conception of the ritual, in which modesty was the highest commandment. It was the famous "Master of Tea", poet and garden lover, Sen-no Rikyu (1522–1591), who first laid down the procedural rules. He also created the architectural conception of the building, the garden grounds and the necessary utensils for the tea ceremony. He simplified the tea-house even further. A tiny window sufficed to let in enough light, without revealing a diverting view and, for the same reason, there was only a narrow door.

In the tea garden — *chaniwa* — the visitor comes to stepping stones. These indicate the direction he should take but also, by the way they are arranged, diminish the speed at which he should proceed. On small, closely spaced stones, the visitor must walk slowly; large stones are a clear hint that he should pause and admire the surroundings. The regulations for laying down the stones are very complicated; it is not just a question of choosing the right size but it is also the structure and colour of the stones that are highly significant. The passage through the tea garden serves as a mental preparation for the tea ceremony.

In the Katsura garden

The 17th-century Katsura garden is regarded as the crowning glory of the Japanese tea garden. It stretches along the western banks of the river of the same name and covers an area of 66,000 square metres; it was designed by Prince Toshihito. His son, Prince Noritata, carried the plans further and achieved renown by the Shugakuin Garden.

The construction of the imperial palace and its gardens lasted from 1620 to 1659 and produced a work that stands out for its variety of form, splendour and richness. Special attention should be paid to the work of the "Master of Tea", Kobori Enshu. By his arrangement of the stones in the ring path he presents the visitor with a panoramic view of the garden.

The many different tea-houses and the details connected with them make a substantial contribution to the

The stepping stones in the Seshu garden in Kyoto, arranged to strict rules, give the impression of symmetry.

peaceful atmosphere of the garden. It is possible to enter the garden and approach the Katsura palace through many entrance gates: one for daily use, the ceremonial gate (Onorigomon), the imperial gate and the central gate. The rooms of the palace are in angled juxtaposition like a folding screen and so a few brief movements suffice to let them fuse with the garden in all its amplitude. The palace is largely composed of three *shoin* buildings; the old *shoin,* the middle *shoin* and the new palace. The Sickle-moon Pavilion (Gepparo) stands on the shore of the pond; its name refers to a verse by the Chinese poet Po Chu-i, "The sickle-moon, a pearl, dear to the heart of man" (Hrdlička, Hrdličková and Thoma).

A particularly graceful pavilion lies on the opposite bank. One reaches it across a bridge of stone monoliths and along a narrow path beside the lake. This pavilion — Shokintei — is harmoniously enclosed by a number of fir trees. The highest point of the main island is crowned by the "Pavilion of the Enjoyment of Flowers", known as Shokatei. On a slope in front of it, pieces of moss-bor-

dered rock are strewn. The Shoiken tea house completes the complex; it stands somewhat to one side, in the south-west corner of the garden.

"The Katsura complex is an unusual masterpiece. At first sight it may seem inconspicuous. Only those who have grasped the essence of Japanese taste will be able to achieve a full understanding of this work, its aesthetic worth conveyed in the Japanese expression *shibui*; it means quiet charm and dignity but with a lingering taste of bitterness, arousing the senses to seek and understand the beauty in everything that is part of nature and human life. In this, Katsura has permanently influenced the design of Japanese buildings and gardens" (Hrdlička, Hrdličková and Thoma).

The Garden of Learning

Shugakuin, the Garden of Learning, lies in the Northeast, at the foot of Mount Hiei. This famous Japanese garden is constructed on three levels and this strikes a special note. The bushes, planted in long, ribbon-like strips, are famous; they are clipped round or oval and border gently-winding paths. The beginnings of the garden go back to 1655, when the Emperor Gomizunoo revived the old tradition of Japanese garden art. While the upper level is intended for people to stroll around, the two lower-lying areas are primarily tea gardens. At the highest point stands the cloud-scraping pavilion called Riuntei. From there one has a wonderful view of the lake and the garden as well as the surrounding mountains. This pavilion is very simple in form and clad in grained wood.

Shugakuin is a ring garden — called *kaiyu-teien* — from the Edo period. Such gardens were very demanding elements in the composition of a garden complex; their aim was to touch the human soul and to arouse emotions by the rich variety of the scenery and to influence aesthetic sensibility. Bridges were an important component of such gardens.

The symbolism of flowers

Flowers are not very widely represented in Japanese gardens. Yet they form an important element in daily life and flower and twig arrangement in the house can be traced back to an ancient tradition. *Rikkwa* is a special way of displaying flowers in which twelve different sorts are used; this contrasts with the more refined method known as *ikebana,* where only a few flowers are used. This cultural expression of the Japanese also includes the erection of a landscape of stones in a black-lacquered bowl known as *bon-seki,* and the Japanese dwarf-tree culture, known far and wide as *bon-sai.*

A constantly recurring blossom motif of the various branches of art is the cherry blossom, which has now almost become a cliché through the opera *Madame Butterfly.* The cherry has a special place in the Japanese garden. Incidentally, characteristically Chinese flowers are also favoured by Japanese garden designers and always have a symbolical significance.

Gardens in the heroic epics of India

The first references to a garden culture in India are contained in two heroic epics — the *Mahabharata* (4th century B.C.) and the *Ramayana* (4th or 3rd century B.C.). The first epic refers to the palace area of the Pandu ruler Arjuna with the palace, several other buildings and a number of gardens surrounding the buildings. It speaks of a pond with artificial lilies and other water plants, with leaves of precious metal and precious stones. One could see gilded fish and tortoises on its bed and blooming lotos on the surface.

The descriptions of gardens are even more detailed in the *Ramayana.* In this epic, the Monkey-god Hanuman tells of beautiful gardens which he saw on his way to the royal palace of Ravana. First he walked through a blooming land of gardens, with different fruit trees and lotos ponds. Arriving in the royal city through a gate in the wall, he saw magnificent houses with columns adorned with foliage and blossoms. Behind a further wall, more palaces of high dignitaries were to be found, with gardens around them. Beyond the next wall he glimpsed the magic palace of the prince amid lotos ponds and tall trees. But the Asoka Grove surpassed all these gardens. There, lianas were slung from branch to branch along the *allées,* whose trees were all abloom; golden steps led to crystal clear ponds. The hub of the whole garden was formed by the asoka tree with its red and gold umbels.

Artificial ponds

Around 300 B.C., the Greek ambassador to India, Megastenes, reported on his impressions. He described great parks with pavilions and artificial ponds which adjoined the houses of prosperous citizens. People sought to keep cool in open-air baths; there was frequent use of the opportunity to construct underground rooms to rest in, near the water. The water was stored in bath-tanks and a kind of revolving water-spray in the garden helped to keep people fresh.

Already before the Mogul period, there were public gardens and groves which were situated on the outskirts of towns. Wealthy merchants and princes had parks constructed as gifts for Buddhist monasteries. The most famous garden was Jetavana, the summer park of the Jeta. The Chinese pilgrim Fa Hian visited this park in the 5th century and enthused over the beauty of the clear water of the pools, the trees burgeoning in many colours and the luxurious greenery.

The showpiece of Indian gardens is always the artificial pond. It was used just as much for bathing as for irrigation. In the construction and equipping of these ponds the Indians achieved a high degree of artistic mastery; the technical mastery that lay behind it was equally impressive. Ancient inscriptions, in addition to lauding the man-made irrigation equipment, also especially extol the planting of trees.

Followers of the Jains also honoured the previously mentioned asoka tree. According to the story handed down to us, the founder of this sect, Mahavira, experienced theopneusty — like Buddha — under a tree. Jain temples are mainly erected on top of mountains amid groves. From various descriptions we can deduce that the Indian garden was primarily an arboretum. In such a cli-

mate where everything grew abundantly without the help of human hand, flower beds were seldom cultivated. Only lotos was cultivated. It is very closely associated with East Asian culture and is frequently depicted by artists. In Buddhism it is regarded as a holy symbol and is therefore never missing from any temple garden.

It was only some centuries later that a new chapter in the history of Indian garden design began. A successor to the Mongolian world conqueror Timur (1336–1405) was Baber (1483–1530). After entering Delhi in 1526 and founding the Great Mogul Empire in India, he established himself in Agra. This area, deserted and devastated by war, offered no shade-providing gardens essential for man's welfare — so he began to construct them. He had water-wheels provided for irrigating the gardens, planted roses and narcissi in flower beds.

Baber's gardens, like those of his successors, leaned towards the Persian style, for the Mongolians — a nomadic people — had no tradition in this field. They copied the Persian quartering of the garden, equipped it with a large pond and closed it off from the surrounding country. The Mogul gardens also had so-called sunken flower beds, which lay at a lower level than the paths, crowded with roses, tulips and narcissi but mostly only with one of these.

With the consolidation of Mogul rule under Akhbar (1556–1605), Jahangir (1569–1627) and Shah-Jahan (1627–1658), art, architecture and literature reached their summit, despite continuing wars. Akhbar's name is closely associated with Fatehpur, Agra, Delhi and Lahore. And it is in those cities that we must seek the many beautiful gardens which, today, only display a mere shadow of their former glory. Their dazzling colourfulness is today only to behold in Mogul miniatures. Emperor Jahangir created a particularly splendid estate in the picturesque valley of Kashmir — the Shalimar and Nisat gardens.

The Taj Mahal
and the Dig garden

It is not only the gardens of rulers that reflect the high cultural level that existed in India. There are also examples of gardens of a special kind connected with memorials. One of these is the Taj Mahal. This structure was erected in Agra for the Mogul Emperor Shah-Jahan between 1630 and 1648. The dome is of white marble with artistic stone mosaics; surrounded by four minarets, it dominates the landscape.

In contrast with the arrangement in other memorials, the mausoleum and the neighbouring buildings are not in the middle of the garden but at the end of it. A long, central canal leads from the entrance gate to the memorial, accompanied by several avenues. Previously, beds covered with flowers were laid-out. Today, only the stone setting of the flower beds, along the main avenue, remains. There are very few flowers there today, and the many shade-providing trees of former times are gone. Now they are only to be found in narrow rows along the *allées*. The domes of the Taj Mahal are reflected in the water of the raised pond. So today the garden does not distract the viewer but rather leads his gaze directly towards the building with its richly adorned walls and towers.

After the collapse of the Mogul Empire in India, many gardens in Islamic style arose under the patronage of wealthy Hindus and maharajahs. Especially well-known is the Dig garden, which originated in 1725. It had the Persian motif of the cross axis as basic design.

Descriptions of Indian gardens by eye-witnesses began to reach Europe, especially England, where certain influences of Mogul garden design and architecture were to be observed. The English trading companies of the 17th century and British colonial policy lasting for several centuries form the background to this horticultural and agricultural imitation.

From Landscape Gardens to Public Parks

Large areas of Europe saw the creation of great Baroque gardens like Nymphenburg, Brühl, Schönbrunn, Würzburg and Schwetzingen, to name but a few. This was accompanied by some sharp criticism, not to say downright opposition — in accordance with the development in each individual country — for different reasons. For example, the economic reason for this development can be seen as the change from arable to pastoral farming in southern England. It was here that the closely-cropped meadows with their isolated trees and hedges increasingly determined the landscape. So the basis was given for the kind of garden that seems to harmonize with the landscape because of its apparently natural design.

The new feeling towards nature
in England

The spiritual source is the energetic pursuit of free development, the determined rejection of constraint and oppression, an opposition to the formal lay-out of the Baroque garden, to the interference with natural growth. Philosophers, poets, artists took up this movement and carried these new ideas into wider circles. Powerful impulses came from England.

The two English poets and essayists, Joseph Addison (1672–1719) and Alexander Pope (1688–1744), were part of this movement that was marked by a new feeling for nature. Addison did not deny the artistic merit of the formal garden, neither did he plead only for the wild

beauty of nature. He sought a compromise, differentiated between the "artistically beautiful" and the "naturally beautiful" (Hoffmann), and believed that both would gain by inclining towards each other. *The Spectator* published an article of his, describing the ideal garden. This was to contain what we today would regard as many odd things. The kitchen garden, flower garden and orchard were so intermixed that one might take the area for a wilderness. A wild abandon was deliberately created out of kitchen plants and natural elements like a little watercourse, wild-growing flowers or naturally growing trees.

Pope, a major figure of classical English literature, expressed himself in similar vein to Addison in *The Guardian,* in 1716. He inveighed against excessive formality and symmetry in design and championed the study of nature that it might be copied in the garden. He also recommended the study of landscape paintings and the practical application of what had been learned therefrom. And he put his own conceptions into practice on his estate at Twickenham.

We cannot yet regard this garden as a real landscape garden but rather as a Rococo garden in the process of dissolving, but, nonetheless, symmetry and tree-lopping are, here, already completely dispensed with. The contrasting effects of light and shade are suitably brought forth, too, and are a necessary part of the whole. In addition to this, Pope is looking for surprise effects for the observer and no visible circumscription for the terrain.

Every one of these points is to be found in all subsequent works on landscape parks, though sometimes in modified form.

A plan of 1744 shows Pope's garden at Twickenham, quite small and therefore allowing of very little possibility to imitate nature run wild. One interesting feature is the joy he seems to have in a grotto he has fitted out with an entrance that looks like a ruin. This preference for grottoes is not new; what is new is the design of the entrance, as artificial ruins in landscape gardens later acquired quite a significance (Jäger).

The landscape gardener William Kent

Decisive influence on the composition of new gardens was exercised by the architect and painter William Kent (1685–1748). He went on to become a landscape gardener, a profession in which he used the rules of composition to be found in landscape painting. He selected his motifs from nature and recognized that the curved line is an essential element in the natural garden. He took as his model the landscape of Claude Lorrain (1600–1682), Nicolas Poussin (1594–1665) and Salvator Rosa (1615 to 1673). The paintings of these artists were admired in England; they also fascinated Kent and gave him inspiration. During a study tour to Italy — from 1712 to 1719 — he devoted himself to painting and one of the results of his journey was a design for the title page of John Gay's *Poems on Several Occasions*; it incorporated the Temple of Sibyl at Tivoli. This building of Antiquity was frequently copied in landscape gardens and is also widely to be found outside England.

Kent was able to prove his all-round abilities at Stowe and Rousham. He worked at Stowe from 1730 until his death and was the link in a chain of architects and garden designers who planned, extended and re-fashioned Stowe in a period of nearly hundred years. His work is considered to be one of the most famous examples of "natural taste". Close contact with Kent was maintained by the royal gardener Charles Bridgeman; from him stemmed a previous plan for the transformation of Stowe, from a strictly formal to a landscape garden.

An engraving by Rigaud depicts the former appearance of the garden. While the overall impression is determined by the moving outline of free-growing wooded areas, nonetheless, strict symmetry is to be observed in individual sections. There is an open view into the distance; one gleans that the garden is an integral part of the surrounding landscape and is not shut off from it by a wall or an impenetrable hedge. The boundary of the estate is only marked by a masked ditch — the ha-ha. It is thought that Bridgeman introduced these effects to the English garden after getting the idea from Horace Walpole (1717 to 1797).

The Valley of the Elysian Fields and buildings in antique style

In 1730, Kent began the task of dissolving everything that was still symmetrical at Stowe and, together with Lancelot Brown, did away with all traces of the *allées* along the main axis in 1740 to be replaced by open areas of lawn. Around the lake they planted clumps of trees which developed quickly and satisfactorily and looked quite natural.

Kent's main work at Stowe was the Valley of the Elysian Fields. He developed it as a separate part east of a north-south axis. Later, the lake was extended right up to it. The long, gently winding valley ended in a sunken grotto, surrounded by yew trees. The river which sprang from it was dammed up in the middle to form a little woodland lake; where it again flowed out it was spanned by a bridge of bare masonry. A further interesting detail is the temple which Kent built in 1735; the busts of famous Englishmen are exhibited in its niches.

The Temple of Antique Virtue was a reminder of his tour to Italy. It was supposed to be a version of the Temple of Sibyl at Tivoli that was erected on the other side of the Styx. It stood over the valley, the whole scene being intended to give the impression of a Roman landscape. This aspect of the Elysian Fields resembled the landscape paintings of Lorrain.

Northwards, next to the Elysian Fields, there appeared a "natural" main axis: Hawkwell Field. An irregular "girdle" of trees bordered a lightly undulating lawn so that impressive views were also revealed. In the North the King's Temple was built and, in the South, the Temple of Friendship. At the highest point of Hawkwell Field — visible from all sides — a Gothic temple was built around 1741 by James Gibbs (1682–1754). The edifice is constructed of reddish ironstone and looks gnarled and uneven. It was originally called the Temple of Freedom and intended as a symbol of English liberty in contrast to the Absolutist rule in France.

The ideal of Lorrain's landscapes influenced the garden designers until about the sixties of the 18th century. The most impressive garden landscape based on this picturesque style was Castle Howard in Yorkshire. John Vanbrugh (1666–1726), a predecessor of Kent's at Stowe, worked here. Whole stretches of Castle Howard look quite empty because of the large open areas. Here and there interesting views open up and, according to Thacker, "the prospect of the Temple of the Four Winds [by Vanbrugh, built after his death in 1726 by Hawksmoor], the Roman Bridge [*c*. 1744] and Hawksmoor's mausoleum [begun in 1728, finished *c*. 1745] is the noblest of these ideal landscapes ever to be created". He continues: "No single photograph can do justice to this three-dimensional scene, where the visitor, though moving slowly through the garden and amongst these buildings, remains a spectator and not a participant in a recreation of an antique landscape."

Not as large as Castle Howard is Stourhead in Wiltshire, "one of the most picturesque landscape gardens in the world" (Walpole). Here it was landscape painters like Salvator Rosa, Maratti and Zuccarelli who served as models and whose idyls were to be created *in natura*. In 1714 the banker Henry Hoare Senior acquired the land. His son inherited the property in 1740 and began to design the garden. Its basic concept has survived to the present day, just as it was laid-out in 1783. The park lies in a flat valley and the upper edge of the steep slope forms its boundaries.

Building and park are separated from each other and, in this respect, Stourhead represents an exception, though in all other respects it may be seen as an exemplary model of an early English park. Between bright beeches with high trunks shines the Temple of Flora with a Doric portal. In front of the temple stands a vase depicting Flora with her attendants; in the temple, itself, there are a number of Roman busts. These stylistic elements, replicating those of Ancient classical times, also include a pantheon. Henry Hoare owned a copy of the famous painting "View of Delphi with a Procession" which has among its buildings an edifice based upon the Pantheon at Rome. Hoare had this building copied by Henry Flitcroft, and so arose "a pantheon incorporating some of Claude's features" (Thacker).

In addition to these buildings in antique style, there are others which are closer to the romantic style. Near the pantheon — more or less as a contrast — stands a cottage of Gothic appearance. Behind it there is an artificial grotto. These buildings are arranged around a remarkably shaped, three-pronged lake which is surrounded by wooded slopes. The visitor who contemplates the landscape — preferably looking out across the lake — is beset with variegated impressions.

It is not only these various buildings that make the park so worth visiting, but also the artistic arrangement of bushes and trees. The many rare specimens like araucaria, gingko, cedars, tulip-trees, swamp cypresses, magnolia and many different rhododendron species arouse a strange fascination in the visitor.

Another important example of this type of estate is Rousham. After Kent had done away with most of the symmetrical areas by many modifications, he laid-out meandering paths which imitated the bends of the river Cherwell. He retained only the dead straight *allée,* leading from the entrance to the statue of Apollo, and the large rectangular lawn in front of the house. He had a masterly understanding of how to design a variety of "pictures" on small sections of the park as he cleverly made use of the varying relief of the terrain and skilfully subdivided it by single trees or clumps of trees. In his *History of Modern Gardening,* Walpole remarked: "… the whole is as elegant and antique as if the Emperor Julian had selected the most pleasing solitude about Daphne to enjoy a philosophic retirement". Outside the garden, Kent created a structure to hold the attention — a tripartite arcade crowned with rough pinnacles.

Clumps and lakes

In the second half of the 18th century English gardens bore clear evidence of the influence of Lancelot Brown (1715–1783) — "Capability" Brown —, who can also be regarded as Kent's successor. In his early days he worked closely together with Kent and it was he who gave Stowe its final form. Few gardens were created in the first half of the 18th century, but Brown's period is marked by a rapid rise of the landscape garden. The old gardens almost without exception fell victim to the axe and for the new garden designer there was more than enough work. It is said that Brown was involved in the construction of 150 establishments. Originally a kitchen gardener, he quickly developed into an expert whose hand is unmistakable. Compact copses — clumps — on broad lawns, a wooded "girdle" of trees and bushes around the border of the garden, winding watercourses and lake shores with man-made bays were all his hallmarks.

With his composition of all these elements he achieved perfection to such a degree that critics believed he had "so completely placed the garden within the landscape that it was hardly to be recognized as a garden any more" (Thacker). By the interplay of light and shade he was able to stimulate the effect of perspective just as much as by the artistic use of form and colour. The skill lay in presenting the visitor with a variety of pictures from various positions, despite the wide dimensions of the gardens, without in any way boring him during his wanderings.

Lancelot Brown registered his greatest successes when he incorporated lakes as an important element in his designs. The most famous establishment is Blenheim. Here he called upon the services of the royal court gardener Wise, and the architect Vanbrugh, and they designed one of the most magnificent gardens in England. A mighty bridge that spanned the little river Glyme was the work of Vanbrugh.

When Brown was called to Blenheim, in 1765, to "improve" the landscape, he first did away with the formal garden. Then, between 1764 and 1774, he laid-out a "natural" landscape, incorporating Vanbrugh's bridge. In doing so, he also altered the proportion of the bridge to its surroundings, so that the structure stood out more effectively. By drastically damming up the Glyme, he raised the water level of the lakes, which were linked by the little river, by one to two metres. By thorough excavation, he also increased the surface area of the water, thus giving the impression that the bridge was spanning a great, broad river. In other respects Blenheim is characterized by its vast, open terrain with large numbers of free-standing trees, presenting us with artistic views on all sides. A special attraction at Blenheim is the kitchen garden, the only oustanding feature remaining from the time before Brown took the place in hand.

Pagodas and pavilions in Chinese style, flower gardens

In England it was William Chambers (1726–1796) who introduced elements from East Asia. He travelled through China and, in 1757, his *Designs for Chinese Buildings* was published. Chambers endeavoured to bring about a synthesis of the Chinese and the English garden. In this way he thought to enrich Brown's "empty and desolate" gardens. By citing the Chinese example, Chambers showed how entertaining and varied landscape gardens could be. But actually such gardens existed neither in China nor anywhere else. They were purely his own invention and simply originated from the many and variegated impressions he had gained from his travels. The idea was to arouse sustained enthusiasm to create, indeed, a new *style anglo-chinois;* in fact Chambers only introduced a few decorative Chinese features like pagodas and pavilions.

Chambers was able to create a Garden of Poetry — also known as the Poetic Garden — at Kew Gardens on the outskirts of London. The pagoda is one of the most famous buildings there; it was not only imitated in England but also in German gardens. Similar ones in Munich,

Oranienbaum near Dessau, as well as the Dragon House in Potsdam were all modelled on it. Taken as a whole, we can regard Chambers as having created a school of garden design, and gardeners outside England were glad to enrich their landscape gardens with those elements he had introduced.

This period, like preceding ones, was characterized by the search for foreign plants which, once introduced and acclimatized, could enrich landscape gardens. Some were cultivated in hothouses, and Kew Gardens gained great horticultural, botanical and scientific acclaim as one of the most famous plant collections in the world, a reputation it still retains. In 1761 Chambers designed the largest hothouse of his day.

A successor to Lancelot Brown was making a name for himself in the second half of the 18th century. This was Humphry Repton (1752–1818) who began his career as a garden designer around the year 1788. At first his gardens were similar to those of his predecessor but soon he developed a style of his own. He brought back the fountain, and his lawns no longer ended right in front of the building but terrace, path, balustrade or flower bed lay between them.

A remark of Repton's that "flower gardens on a small scale may, with propriety, be formal and artificial" was to achieve significance at a later time. Some examples of famous Repton gardens are Sussex, Sheringham Hall and Norfolk. He illustrated his designs and suggestions with pictures in two hundred *Red Books,* in this way making us acquainted with his intentions.

Some of his basic rules for the design of landscape gardens were "shedding light on the natural beauty of a landscape whilst, at the same time, concealing its natural blemishes; camouflaging the boundaries in order to give a landscape the 'feel' of unlimited space and freedom; the invisibility of all 'improving' techniques, as it should appear that nature had made the gardens as they were; and the hiding of all purely utilitarian installations which had not been 'improved' or which could be treated as a special area within the whole estate, without re-siting them in a place unsuitable for their use".

The "natural" garden in France

In France, the "natural" garden made its debut after 1763. The China craze was already widespread in France, and when the new garden style arrived from England it was perceived as an imitation of the Chinese. "When, in France, the curtain finally went up on a new garden play, both China and England stood together … on the stage; both experienced, both no longer timid debutantes. The English garden had long ago opted for the picturesque and, in order to increase the artistic effects as well as to satisfy the moods and need for entertainment of guests, had again integrated works of art; China was also represented here. In French gardens, the China craze had long since acquired a secure and habitual place as the most loved requirement" (Hoffmann).

Rousseau's ideas

That the new ideas were able so rapidly to take hold of the spiritual direction in which France was moving, was partly to be laid at the door of Rousseau who, as champion of the free, natural life with his "back to nature" demand, prepared the ground for the natural garden.

In his famous novel *La nouvelle Héloïse,* published in 1762, he describes a nature garden; his contemporaries were enthralled. He gave, it is true, no exact model for the design of gardens, but provided guidance and stimulated thought. The picture he painted was characterized by wild, untamed landscapes: "I demand rushing brooks, rocks, fir trees, dark woods, rough undulating paths and frightening abysses for my surroundings."

His ideas were to materialize in the area of Ermenonville, whose owner, the Marquis René Louis de Girardin (1735–1808), conceived a deep respect for Rousseau and gave him *carte blanche* in his garden. On a hill, with a view of the lake, stood the Temple of Philosophy, built in 1776. Although it was erected in imitation of the Temple of Sibyl at Tivoli, it was deliberately constructed as a ruin, to symbolize the incomplete works of the philosophers.

The six pillars of the temple are dedicated to Newton, Descartes, Voltaire, Penn, Montesquieu and Rousseau.

On the ground lies a pillar with the inscription: "Who will complete this?" There was also, in this most beautiful of all French landscape gardens, in addition to other centres of attraction, an Altar of Reverie and an archery stand, providing facilities for rural disport.

To help him in designing the garden, Girardin had invited artists like J.-M. Morel (1728–1810) and Hubert Robert (1733–1808), but he was also a garden designer on his own account. This landscape was created over a period of ten years, from 1766 to 1776. Rousseau spent the last six weeks of his life there and was laid to rest in the Île des Peupliers, an island south of the château bordered by poplars.

In this period many more gardens appeared in France, either new creations, or by extension or alteration of existing gardens. The attempt was made, in their construction, to achieve a certain grandeur but introducing a multiplicity of different features. Rousseau's intention of "uniting all epochs and every corner of the world in one single garden" stems from *La nouvelle Héloïse* where he, nonetheless, criticized the great abundance of detail at Stowe.

The painter and architect Louis Carrogis de Carmontelle (1717–1806), who designed the park of Monçeau near Paris, ventured to produce just such an effect. By the skilful planting of many different trees, he hoped to produce clearly separated scenes, each embodying a different stylistic tendency.

Monçeau was to present an abundance of surprises and novelties in a two-hour walk round the park. He filled it with Roman, Egyptian, Chinese, oriental, mediaeval — even pre-historic — figures that one might excusably regard as follies. There were artificial trees standing next to real ones; at night the whole could be illuminated.

"The main pavilion, in which the duke arranged courtly festivities and where he held his freemasons' meetings, stands in the middle of a symmetrically laid-out parterre and bosket. The ground of this artistic park, with its rippling, artificially constructed undulations, had all the variety on display that the period demanded; rural meadows side by side with vineyards, kiosks and hills; beside

Gothic ruins, the attraction in the northwest — the Naumachie; a great elliptical pool was encircled by artistically placed Greek ruins, towered by an obelisk. The most remarkable structures were the coloured gardens, little formal flower gardens right in the middle of the park that bordered a circular place with blue, red or yellow beds of flowers" (Gothein).

In the Petit Trianon, just as at Monçeau, the building is surrounded by formal parterres, complemented by an English section. Right next to this are the areas of the natural garden with winding walks and wild watercourses, full of bends and curves. Over the whole surface, single trees and clumps are very evenly spread, thus giving the feel of an artificial naturalness.

One more theory of garden design

In Germany, the new garden style entered the scene in the middle of the 18th century. As in England, it was the poets Addison and Pope who spread the new ideas, or, in France, Rousseau with his call for a natural way of life, in Germany it was poets and writers who described unspoiled nature in their literary work. This new outlook influenced garden design, too. Friedrich Gottlieb Klopstock (1724–1803) as a representative of the Enlightenment gave spiritual stimulation; the landscape descriptions of the Swiss painter and poet Salomon Gessner (1730 to 1788), who belonged to Klopstock's circle, should also be mentioned, or, for example, the poem "The Alps" by Albert Haller, written in 1729.

Earlier, some Rococo gardens had already shown a leaning towards the natural. This is not to say that they were the starting-point for the later English style of garden, but one did already find in them elements like grottoes, hermitages and ruins. In the Bayreuth Hermitage there were little wooden huts covered with bark, and in Moritzburg nature was no longer mere background. Formal gardens were also combined with English garden ideas like, for example, in the Deer Garden at Sanssouci, at Rheinsberg or Schwetzingen.

An early protagonist for the new art of gardening in Germany was Cajus Lorenz Hirschfeld (1742–1792). He was a pure theoretician; he wrote his *Theorie der Garten-kunst* (Theory of garden design) after a detailed study of English and French literature. In this work he laid down certain regulations and rules for the art of landscape gardening.

He denied the formal garden the right to be regarded as a work of art and thought "that the garden should be a landscape in miniature, separated from the great expanse of the countryside and, with the pleasing assistance of art,

presented in all its natural beauty". Harmony and unity had to be created "... to elevate the impression of nature by planting, by cultivation, by arrangement, by the use of contrast to improve the aspects of the natural area and by the harmonious coupling of nature with those features which properly belong to art".

For Hirschfeld, the building was also important and the bordering area had to be as regular as the building itself; in his view, there was no rivalry between architecture and garden. As architectonic element, the house was part of the whole, and works of sculpture were desirable in its immediate vicinity. In his theory of garden design he expressed his views on how the design of a garden

The Petit Trianon at Versailles. Ground-plan of 1774, designed by A. Richard.

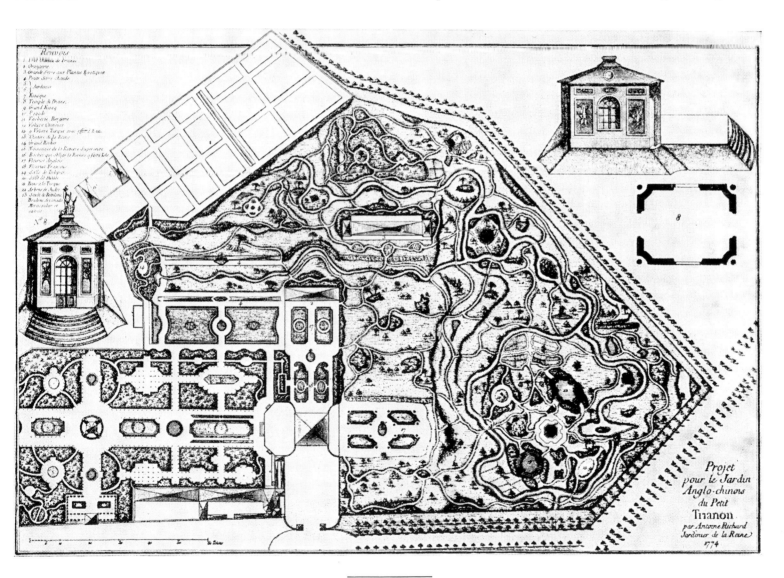

should, in general, be determined. They should be laid-out "so as to be a sojourn of pleasure", to offer "sweet enjoyment of freedom, meditation, walks, fresh air, coolness, pleasant aromas which advance the health of both body and spirit"; provide "favourable surroundings for the contemplation of nature; a refuge for philosophy" and "a temple for the worship of the highest wisdom". These are the characteristic features.

Title page of the most famous German work on the art of gardening, at a time when the English style of gardening began to gain ground in Germany, written by C. C. L. Hirschfeld.

Hirschfeld is also to be credited with having recognized the elements of the landscape outside the garden which could be used as a means of garden composition. Native trees interested him as much as foreign ones, all of which set the tone by their attractive growth, their multi-coloured foliage and the texture of their bark. Hirschfeld's works gradually gained highest acclaim in German-language garden literature and won wide recognition and an extensive readership.

He described in great detail the English Garden at Hohenheim near Stuttgart. These grounds of Duke Charles Eugene of Wurttemberg (1737–1793) can hardly be compared with any other German gardens; a rather closer association with French gardens — like Monçeau — is to be observed. The establishment is marked by its multiplicity of different elements, a variety of accessory ornamentation. The main idea was to erect new buildings in the middle of artificial ruins, as is so frequently to be seen in Italy, thus providing rich contrast. This was how the most significant complex of great ruins arose at the end of the garden; Cannstadt tufa was brought there for the purpose, "30,000 cart-loads", as Hirschfeld had it.

The interior of the ruins was decked out in magnificent style. In another place we read: "These ruins are the most marvellous that can be imagined in this kind of imitation. With their great, splendid and artistic waterfall they are a portrayal of the famous scenes at Tivoli ... On the pinnacle of these ruins stands a church in Gothic style with unusual windows made up completely of glass paintings ..."

While the church is a kind of bridge to the Middle Ages, the Temple of Sibyl at Tivoli is a link to Antiquity. Other buildings appeared, based on old models; there was, for example, a Carthusian monastery with a Gothic church, an old tower, a hermitage next to a chapel and the grave of the hermit. There were also an aqueduct, a column of Trajan, tombs, the Roman Prison or "The three pillars of thundering Jupiter".

Rural scenes like peasants' houses, Swiss houses, an alehouse, a dairy, a shepherd's hut etc. were also constructed. Special significance was attributed to the water arrangements; next to a brook with a waterfall there were ponds all of rectangular shape with the exception of a small lake. The Roman Prison surrounded by a moat was an imitation of an ancient Roman model. Hirschfeld paid special attention to the collection of foreign trees and bushes which he brought into the American Garden, and which he praised as follows: "The richest and most complete collection of foreign trees and bushes which we possess in Germany, categorized on the system of Linnaeus in a very lovely part of the garden." But the judgement of his contemporaries was contradictory. Goethe, for instance, was not enchanted by Hohenheim, as is brought to light in a letter he wrote to Duke Charles Augustus in 1796. Schiller, on the contrary, was touched by the poetic atmosphere.

German gardens
in the age of sensibility

The first establishment in Germany constructed according to these new conceptions is the park of Wörlitz near Dessau. Hirschfeld counted it "among the noblest gardens in Germany". It was built for Prince Frederick Francis of Dessau (1740–1817). At that time the Court of Saxe-Anhalt was regarded as a centre of Humanism, learning and the arts.

The new garden ideal quickly gained a foothold and spread out from here. Travel books about England made people acquainted with the English garden and thus con-

Sketch of a bridge of natural materials by C. C. L. Hirschfeld.

217

tributed substantially to an understanding of it. This was not only true for the prince, himself, but also for his companion, the architect Friedrich Wilhelm von Erdmannsdorff (1736–1800), for whom classical English architecture was to be the guideline for his future work. During his journeys to Italy he became acquainted with Johann Joachim Winckelmann (1717–1768). This led to an understanding of Antiquity, and the experience of the Italian landscape turned out to be of lasting effect. Despite this, England remained the most important point of reference. The Italian influence can be traced largely to the parts of the park of Wörlitz which were created between 1790 and 1798; the work proceeded in several phases.

A lake with many bays, surrounded by wide parklands, forms the core of this garden. This extensive stretch of water lends spaciousness to the park. Near the lake the palace is situated, the grounds around it are surrounded by

a semi-circle of water — a picturesque sight. This palace was built by Von Erdmannsdorff from 1769 to 1773 and established his reputation as representative of Early Classicism. A gently winding *allée* along the lake is the main approach to the palace and to the garden on this side of the lake.

The building is surrounded by rows of trees. The extensive lawns round the lake are only sparsely planted with individual trees, granting vistas in all directions. The Neumarkische Garden — also known as the island garden — lies between two arms of the lake in the eastern part of the park. It had previously been planted as a tree nursery serving, that is, purely utilitarian purposes. At the end of one arm of the lake is a small island, named after Rousseau. Another island bears the name of Herder. On the side of the park opposite the palace work was already begun in 1769. It was there that the Gothic House arose, in the middle of a great stretch of lawn with groups of deciduous trees, clumps of evergreen and scattered conifers. The Temple of Flora has stood within sight of this

A grotto designed by C. C. L. Hirschfeld for a landscape garden.

building since 1797. Rich flower decoration sets its seal on the building, dedicated as it is to the Goddess of Flowers and of Spring.

Crossing the chain bridge, built in 1781, the path leads to the Temple of Venus which stands in the middle of a wood of dark conifers. The Grotto of the Hermit and other romantic substructures were erected beneath the bridge. The Pantheon leads us on to further areas of the park. It is a replica of the Roman Pantheon and in former times housed a rich collection of antiques.

The Italian farmhouse looms out across wide cornfields. The path leads across the Sun Bridge to another part of the park. Here, to commemorate the Italian journey, a Vesuvius, a replica of the Blue Grotto of Capri, an imitation of the Villa Hamilton and an antique amphitheatre were built and additional grottoes. There is a wonderful view across the park from the Jewish Temple; the path winds along the shores of the lake and past the Egeria Grotto.

Wörlitz is a park for wandering through, not only on foot but also by boat on canals and lakes; this underlines its unique character. There are thirty objects in the park which arouse the visitor's inquisitiveness and lead him on from place to place. The idea is not only to stimulate the imagination but also, at the same time, to instruct. As its originator conceived it, the park should facilitate a rendezvous with history and literature, and evoke deep emotions.

Goethe's captivation is expressed in his letter of 14th May, 1778, to Charlotte von Stein: "Now it is beautiful here beyond description. It moved me deeply yesterday evening, as we glided through the lakes, canals and little woods, how the gods have granted the prince to create a dream world to surround him. Wandering about as I did, it's like a fairy tale unfolding, just like the Elysian Fields. In its oh so gentle manysidedness, all melts into one, no high point draws the eye or creates the longing for a particular spot; you wander around without even asking where you started from or where you are going to. The shrubbery is in its finest growth and the whole glows with the most perfect loveliness."

Wörlitz is one of the earliest landscape gardens in Germany. It was not only elements from English models that were incorporated; original ideas were also put into effect. According to Hoffmann, Wörlitz "already contains all the potentials for the further development of the natural garden style in Germany ... with its tranquility and its monumentality, however, it embodies the climax of all, in this development: the classical landscape garden".

In the 18th and 19th centuries, Weimar was the spiritual and cultural centre of Thuringia, and the Court of Anna Amalia (1739–1807) was its hub. Upon the image of the town and its surroundings lies the deep imprint of the fruitful co-operation of Goethe and Duke Charles Augustus. On the steep wooded slope on the left-hand bank of the river Ilm there developed the park on the Ilm. Goethe regarded the *Luisenfest*, which he directed in 1778, as the park's moment of birth. In 1776 he had moved into his famous garden house.

The development of the park took place in two main phases. The first phase was characterized by the tendencies of the age of sensibility. The death of a young lady called Christel von Lassberg, who was found dead in the river Ilm holding fast to a copy of Goethe's novel *The*

Design of a hermitage, made from tree trunks and bark, by C. C. L. Hirschfeld.

Sorrows of Werther caused Goethe to have stone steps cut out as a memorial, representing her "last path and place of death". Another expression of this sensibility is the Luisenkloster (Convent of Luise). This romantic edifice — it looks like a little bark-covered house — received its present appearance in 1784. The whole park may be seen as one large landscape garden, with the exception of the Stern (Star), a system of stellar walks constructed like the spokes of a wheel, surrounded by the Ilm and a channel running from it; this — like the Welscher Garten (Welsh Garden) — was also among the early structures. The sensibility expressing itself in garden design is evident, here, in a grotto with a sphinx, rocky towers and a waterfall as well as a spring and a brook. At the mouth of the brook stood a bas-relief — a Triton with bathing nymphs. While the Stern has remained the same to this very day, the Welscher Garten has been completely altered and is now permeated with numerous winding paths. The Schnecke (Snail) was retained right into the 19th century as a sentimental reminder of the past. Broken-up stones were used for a ruin to give it a genuine look. There are not many monuments to be found in this northern part of the park; but the Schlangenstein (Snake Stone) — a squat pillar with a snake coiled round it — and the Dessauer Stein, an unhewn rock, are worth mentioning.

The second phase in the development of the park is influenced by Classicism. The classical highlight in the park on the Ilm is the Roman House. It was intended to be the ducal country seat and is distinguished by its architectural precision. The building was erected at the slope and can be seen from the valley far and wide. It spreads widely over the steep slopes of the Ilm valley and thus takes on the character of a connecting link between the valley and the heights. The west side has a portico which opens out to a broad meadow above the valley.

About the lay-out of the park, Hoffmann says the following: "... anyhow, scenes that were graceful, melancholy, wild or of whatever other type, played the main role inside the oldest areas of the park. From this and from the fact that at first they proceeded bit by bit, a lay-out of the terrain in comparatively small and enclosed spaces seems to have appeared almost of its own accord. Such an arrangement with surprising changes of scenery touches the visitor's soul. But even in this area, the partition has been brought about less by conspicuous artificial intervention in the relief or by the way of planting than by utilizing and bringing out what nature had already fortuitously provided: rocks and woods on the slopes, shrubbery on the river banks, meadowland and copses in the valley and on the higher level of the terrain in the west. In the southern (i.e. the newer) part of the park, this kind of procedure was much more generously pursued and special consideration was given to the retention of distant views and to the creation of spacious images of the landscape."

The great botanical interests of the duke and his inclination for attractive tree shapes had a beneficial effect on the choice of species. In addition to many different native ones, foreign trees like Lombardy poplar, pencil cedars and North American species were planted in great number.

While the use of statuary was extremely moderate in the Weimar park, Tiefurt was worth a visit primarily because of it. Monuments and memorials were informally arranged along the paths. Tiefurt is, in the main, composed of a great valley meadow lying within a bend of the river Ilm; its trees are sparse but present an attractive picture. Winding paths lead through the park and effectively enclose a wooded mountain slope on one side. From there the Temple of the Muses can be seen, erected in 1803. The Duchess Anna Amalia, already mentioned, had considerable influence on the design of the park; in 1778 she occupied a small palace on the valley meadow which became her permanent residence.

The park of Belvedere, situated above Weimar, arose between 1724 and 1750 in the Baroque style; in 1806 it was re-designed as a landscape park. The remainder of this Baroque estate is, today, still recognizable in the area

Instructions on how best to arrange trees and shrubs according to the topographical criteria (after *Theorie der Gartenkunst* by C. C. L. Hirschfeld, 1780).

of the orangery. This hilly, 79-acre park terrain is subdivided by a series of terraces which lend it its special charm, enhanced still more by single trees and copses. The alterations were largely undertaken by the Russian Grand-Duchess Maria Pavlova, wife of the Hereditary Prince Charles Frederick (1783–1835). She received the greatest assistance from Johann Konrad Sckell (1768–1834), inspector of gardens at the Belvedere, and his son Louis (1796–1844). There is a small park theatre which is of special interest because of its design.

The park of Wilhelmshöhe near Kassel was originally created in Baroque style, though the penetration of English ideas is likewise evident. This phase lasted until 1785 and, when Elector William I (1743–1821) took over the reign in that year, he had the Baroque park re-modelled as a landscape garden.

There was a great leap forward in development here. William I had most of the statuary removed and the water below the palace dammed up, in order to create a lake. The plans for the alterations were put up by S. L. du Rys, who took charge of the work. The severe hedge screen was rooted out, too, and the formally laid-out gardens completely removed. The trees were arranged in clumps, groves or woods.

Soon, new structures arose like, for instance, the Löwenburg (Lion Castle), erected by Jussow between 1793 and 1800; an imitation of a mediaeval castle, it reflected the romantic leanings of the patron. In addition, there was a pheasantry and a zoo.

The park of Wilhelmshöhe is constructed on a hill; situated on different levels, the palace and the lake are divided by slopes without any terracing. There is a drop of 300 metres in a distance of two kilometres.

Evidence of the past is to be found in the great axis. The continuation of the axis — a cascade — is a glade which runs into a bowling-green, the carefully nurtured lawn in front of the palace. It appears to run through the great house, itself, and then continues into the Fürstenweg beside the lake and, further still, along the 5-kilometre-long *allée* of Wilhelmshöhe. It is frequently crossed by curved broad walks. A net of twisting and turning side paths through large meadows, surrounded by loosely aligned trees and copses of large individual trees, reveals a typical landscape park. Near the palace, isolated trees, spinneys or other tree arrangements break up the whole area. The mixture is composed of imported woods that enhance, even more, the effect created by the play of colour and form. Apart from the great cascade with the Neptune Pool, the other water arrangements are intended to have a natural character.

"All other water arrangements appear entirely 'à la nature', so concealed is its artificial construction, which cunningly uses the fall of the terrain. The water is collected in huge tanks at the highest points on the periphery of the park. While these tanks, as purely technical structures, were hidden in the Baroque gardens, the pool in the southwestern region, the 'Asch' — local dialect for pot — was dug out between 1796 and 1800 and treated as an element of composition: a picturesque lake amidst the woods on the hillside. The same technique is used for the little reservoir. The waterworks are supplied through pipes and open watercourses which form little dams that join up the springs on the various slopes. These waterworks display the water's artistic possibilities in numerous variations, whenever they are in motion" (Hoffmann).

In the early stages, the attempt to copy nature was not based on landscape models. The so-called Peneus Cascade (built between 1786 and 1790) was a "constructed form" and the aqueduct (1788–1792) was an imitation of an ancient aqueduct. The aim was to give the impression of age by the kind of materials which were chosen and the way they were used.

The Jussow Cascade, erected between 1791 and 1792, was the first structure to incorporate nature, exclusively in the sense of landscape. While the designers of this cascade were trying to present the visitor with the buoyant sound of rushing water, the waterfall at the Teufelsbrücke (Devil's Bridge; 1792–1793) was intended, rather, to convey an eerie impression. The Steinhöfer Waterfall, originating during the same period, is to be found in the middle of the woods; as it gushes through a cleft in the rocks it looks deceptively natural.

"This creative period at Wilhelmshöhe points, stylistically, to an elucidation of the decisive step away from the period marked mainly by figures and a plethora of sceneries in landscape garden design... The breakthrough to a maturity of style was achieved here after the decisive rejection of the fantastic and obligatory statuary which some critics — even in 1780 — had already demanded without, however, invoking an immediate response from the public. Wilhelmshöhe may also be regarded as the first park to introduce the new style, in that, already from 1785 onwards, the literary figures were unceremoniously cleared away from there ... The elements which breathe naturalness — and herein lies the great leap forward towards maturity in landsscape gardening — are the natural relief of the terrain, vegetation and water, light and shade, and these became the main components of this style of garden" (Hoffmann).

Famous landscape gardeners of the time

The artistic climax of the classical landscape garden in Germany was reached at the beginning of the 19th century. Gardens arose that are closely associated with the names of their creators. The most important garden designers of this epoch are Friedrich Ludwig von Sckell (1750–1823), Peter Joseph Lenné (1789–1866) and Hermann Ludwig Heinrich, Prince of Pückler-Muskau (1785–1871).

Sckell was still gaining his experience during the phase of French garden style and acquired solidly-based, practical skills from his work at Schwetzingen, Bruchsal, Zweibrücken and in France. While he was studying in England from 1773 to 1776, he came face to face with the conceptions of Brown and Chambers and directed his own ambitions as a garden designer towards a natural garden design. Hallbaum essayed an assessment of Sckell as follows:

"That his inspiration blazed new trails, that he was one of the first in Germany to devote himself to the English style of gardening and that he knew how to give this a specifically German stamp was a significant achievement but, historically speaking, it was to be expected. Change

was in the air. ... He brings about the most unusual harmony that spiritual life has ever known, the harmony of ideas and reality by means of a form which, from a multiplicity of natural elements and in order to imitate them, exploits exactly what corresponds to the innermost nature of phenomena, the style of natural form, in Goethe's sense. The difficulties of accomplishing a fusion of the natural landscape, the landscape ideal and the garden ideal into one landscape garden, were mastered by Sckell in a complete solution in the classical mould."

Sckell's main works were the English Garden in Munich and the re-fashioning of Nymphenburg Park in landscape style. In 1804 he was appointed Chief Superintendent of Gardens to the Court, where he completed the English Garden and began the transformation of the great formal Nymphenburg garden. His main object of attention in the English Garden was a restricted area bounded in the east by the meadowland along the river Isar and in the west by a higher-stepped terrain, the Hirschanger Wood, as nucleus, with its many complementary buildings like the Chinese Tower, the Rumford Hall and the Apollo Temple and a wide meadow.

The spacious partitioning of the grounds was maintained. Along the meadow paths, Sckell planted trees, singly or in groups, which called forth a lively effect by the play of light and shade. Along watercourses and folds in the terrain he had trees planted right round the meadow areas. They did not appear as screens, however, because he placed individual trees in front and, in other places, granted views into the distance. Trees and lawns were clearly and exactly separated; the wooded areas he drew together into cohesive creations. Few accessory structures were erected, apart from those of the first stage of construction in Hirschanger Wood. The artistic fulcrum was to be a circular temple, but this was only built after Sckell's death.

Water comes into the play mainly in the form of watercourses just as in the landscape of a fertile plain, or to add atmosphere to meadowland or woodland. The only exception are the shallow cascade made from broken slabs of rock, situated in the Schönefeld section and the enlarg-

Portrait of Peter Joseph Lenné.

In these woods, straight open glades are the main components of composition; they blend with the naturally formed borders of the lake as, for instance, in the open areas of meadow, which only have movement and depth through the occasional slight undulation of their surface, and in the spindle-like swelling out in the middle of the glade.

The great uniform wooded sections are more markedly striking here in Nymphenburg than in the English Garden at Munich. There is a special emphasis on achieving a monumental effect. Despite a uniformity in the overall impression, the picture is anything but boring because of the varied nature of the plant life. An example of this is the fact that the clumps of trees in the Pagodenburg half appear more compact than in the Badenburg section, where they seem to be much looser and thus lighter. Also, within the total conception, the design of the lake harmonizes with the plant life.

Lenné and Sanssouci

While Sckell was able to acquire his know-how in the country which originated the landscape garden, it was only by devious routes that Lenné learnt to appreciate the English garden which had, in the meanwhile, spread throughout the Continent. And because of this there is, on the one hand, a noticeable difference in Lennés conception and, on the other, he became acquainted with the widely recognized French garden designer Thouin (1747 to 1824).

After finishing his training in 1808, Lenné worked in the Rhineland, in southern Germany, in Austria and in Switzerland; from 1816, as a craftsman gardener in Potsdam. It was here that he developed a first plan for Sanssouci, which, however, never came into being. From 1824 he was joint Director of Gardens with Chief Building Surveyor Schulze, taking over sole responsibility in 1828.

Altogether, Lenné worked for fifty years in Potsdam and produced many designs, not only for gardens and parks but also for their environs, estates, town suburbs and so on. In addition to Potsdam, his work covered Berlin, its surrounding areas, Pomerania and Bavaria.

ed Kleinhesseloher Lake in the Schwabing section which, with its low-lying shores, is the very embodiment of restful vistas.

Sckell began the re-fashioning of Nymphenburg in 1801 and had completed it by the time he died. By retaining the great canal with its cascades, the parterre in front of the palace and the two *allées* on either side of the canal, Sckell was seeking to preserve the glowing majesty of the estate but to set the landscaped areas apart from these elements. Thus, the natural and the formal garden design exist side by side, however, they are separated from each other along their borders by dense screens. This makes it impossible to peep at the formal parts from a position in the natural ones, and vice versa. Likewise the woods on either side of the canal have no common features.

During his long working life, a change of style is to be noticed in his technique, which Hinz sets out as follows: 1. "the period of his earlier landscape designs", about 1816 to 1830, including designs for Sanssouci, Charlottenhof and the Berlin Tiergarten; 2. "the period of a more refined landscape style", about 1830 to 1840, "more finished in form and more brilliant in mastery of the material to hand, but no longer so original as his earlier creations"; "a slight leaning towards affectation" is evident; 3. "the period of his late landscape style" from 1840 till his death, "with varied expressions of style in his constructions". Thus, in the Marly garden at Sanssouci, he arrives at "an exceptional refinement of design", and in the Sicilian and Nordic gardens the formal style dominates, a reminder, it would seem, of his acquaintance with the French garden designer Thouin. He used this style, it is true, only where space was limited and only in the garden, not in the park or the surrounding landscape. If no general re-designing of the park along the lines of landscape architecture was actually carried out — as his plan of 1816 had foreseen — he did at least give the landscaped areas a new tone. Altogether, one can say that in the main Lenné created large areas of lawn, constructed groves and had trees planted, either singly or in clumps.

Lawn-mower. The signing of a contract in 1830 by Edwin B. Budding and John Ferrabee set the seal on the production of the first lawn-mower. This is one of the most important advances in garden techniques.

The network of paths was also re-arranged both from the practical and the aesthetic point of view. The alterations took place between 1819 and 1825.

Lenné soon demonstrated his diversity of talent again in creating the gardens of Charlottenhof and constructing the Roman Baths. The park of Charlottenhof was obtained by the crown prince, later to become King Frederick William IV of Prussia (1795–1861). He engaged Lenné to design the garden. Karl Friedrich Schinkel was invited to build a villa, who constructed the building in the style of an Italian villa, in accordance with the prince's wishes.

Charlottenhof was attached to the park of Sanssouci. It was done in landscape style with wide stretches of meadow, clumps of trees and winding paths. Long glades also appeared; they led to the Neue Palais (New Palace), to the main *allée* and to the Roman Baths. Most of Charlottenhof, itself, is of formal construction. There are flower gardens in front of the villa and, to the west, a chestnut grove with cast-iron fountains is situated.

North-east of Charlottenhof, the Roman Baths appeared, built by Schinkel and modelled on the Italian landscape style. The gardens were laid-out by Lenné in formal style; they are, however, not symmetrical.

He again took up the motif of the formal garden in the structure of the orangery. The building which housed it, whose centre section is orientated on the Villa Medici in Rome, was built between 1851 and 1860 by Stüler (1800 to 1865) and Hesse (1795–1876) after a design by Persius (1803–1845). In the same way, the designs of the Sicilian and Nordic gardens between the orangery and the Neue Kammer (New Chamber) also include these formal motifs. Both these gardens are similar and are noteworthy because of their richly decorative flowers. The Sicilian garden is rather more graceful and contains lawn parterres whose corners and edges are planted with summer flowers. A pool and plants set out in tubs enliven the picture.

The Nordic garden has evergreen conifers and deciduous trees as well as gay summer flowers which lend it its special character. Some twenty years after the construction of Charlottenhof, the Marly garden appeared. Here

Portrait of Hermann Ludwig Heinrich, Prince of Pückler-Muskau.

Lenné once more gave expression to the landscape style. Next to Persius' Friedenskirche a richly coloured flower garden was laid-out.

The most noticeable characteristic of Sanssouci is that, in this period of mature landscape gardening, formal landscape gardens are allowed to appear again, so that the garden and the park stand in visible contrast to each other.

The classical landscape garden at Muskau

There was also another creator of classical landscape gardens, contemporary with Sckell and Lenné — Prince of Pückler-Muskau. In his youth he travelled through Italy and France and stayed in England between 1826 and 1829, where he was especially inspired by the English style of gardening. Later he was able to put his ideas into practice on his own land. His first opportunity to do this was at Muskau, which he took over from his father in 1811; on 1st May, 1815, he informed the citizens of his intention to create a garden of extensive proportions around the town and the palace. The landscape itself was very picturesque. Hills alternated with valleys, there were lovely old trees in the Neisse lowlands — obviously the right place to create a park.

What he had in mind for Bad Muskau he later formulated in his work, entitled *Andeutungen über Landschaftsgärtnerei* (Some thoughts on landscape gardening), as follows: "… to mirror again that which has passed, in a comprehensive image, so to speak, whereby everything that was once in existence should be brought to the fore anew, improved as far as possible, rendered more attractive and combined with new ideas — to form a well-ordered unity."

Pückler, himself, was in charge of the construction for the first thirty years but he was able to rely on the assistance of numerous aides; first and foremost there was his head gardener (later Park Director) Jakob Heinrich Rehder (1790–1852) and Carl Eduard Petzold (1815 to 1891). The latter is regarded as Pückler's most important pupil and was responsible for completing the construction when Pückler, after thirty years, had to give up the park for financial reasons.

In this way, Bad Muskau obtained a classical landscape garden which represents the highest level of the German art of gardening. The park consists of several sections, its centre-piece being the 183-acre palace park, in which both the Old and the New Palace were situated. The New Palace is surrounded by a most picturesque countryside beyond Lake Luise, which borders it on three sides; it forms a great centre of attraction, today, with its row of unusual trees, like the cucumber tree, a Virginian bald cypress and a tulip tree. Pückler avoided tree combinations that produced an outlandish effect. In his opinion, idealized na-

This little bath-house is one of a series of illustrations in Prince of Pückler-Muskau's work *Andeutungen über Landschaftsgärtnerei*, published in Stuttgart in 1834.

ture should be at one with the natural local and climatic conditions of a garden or park. Despite this, he also grew foreign wood but, though it might set the tone, it did not interfere with the character of the landscape.

In contrast with Sckell who, in the main, only combined trees of the same species, Pückler combined trees of different species. There are few paths, only the carriageway to the palace and the meandering paths along the shores of the lake are of some importance.

Around the palace, Pückler laid-out a pleasure ground with three flower gardens. Also in this section of the park but at a certain distance from the palace, the orangery and the hot-houses were built beside extensive kitchen gardens which were surrounded by dense, man-made, small woods. About the flower gardens, Pückler wrote the following: "Everything here presents us with adornment, comfort, the most careful maintenance and as rich an array as the means permit. The lawn looks like a silken carpet embroidered with flowers; one finds … the most beautiful and strange foreign plants intermingling here, remarkable animals, prettily plumed species of birds, splendid resting seats, refreshing fountains, the cool shade of densely lined avenues … just like the different rooms and parlours inside a house, each decorated in a different style."

The path that traverses the side-arm of the river Neisse leads across several little bridges and past botanically interesting woody plants of the palace park. Further there are specimens of *Pieris japonica,* hemlock-spruce, many wonderful alpine roses and garden azaleas which are, however, all of a later date, as the original ones died off.

To the east of the Neisse lies the largest section of the park — an area that now belongs to Poland. It consists of large woodland and meadow areas, corresponding with the natural relief of the land. In this part of the park, it was planned to have a castle built and a small race-course, a temple and an English house, but Pückler was unable to put these ideas into practice.

Another part was the Bergpark (hill park), which was largely wooded and spread out over a hill, offering an excellent view of the palace park. The vineyard occupies the highest slope. The bathing park is reached via the beech-wood walk and links the palace park and the hill park. It gets its name from the Hermann Bath, opened in 1823.

This part of the terrain incorporates a series of contrasts; there is a rugged wooded area, a watering place and a mine with waste-tips and shafts. This is "certainly Pückler's most daring attempt to arrange aesthetically the great variety to be found in a locality, if not directly so as to interrelate extremes like dirty industry, a cultured watering place, wild nature and rustic idyls, than to place them side by side in such a way that those wandering through at least feel that the contrast is interesting and never unpleasant" (Hoffmann).

Around the pump-room, Pückler again constructed a pleasure ground with shady walks and colourful flowers which is greatly enhanced by a little flower garden to the right of the pump-room. Pückler conceived the plan to lay it out almost in the style of an oriental garden, with various colourful pavilions on the steep and rugged slopes.

In 1845, after Pückler was compelled to sell his Muskau property, he started to construct another landscape park at Branitz. This park is distinguished by its generous but simple design, which does not, however, tend towards the boundlessness to be found in the Muskau park. Even here, despite the sterile soil with only pines and heath growing, Pückler was able to create a first rate work of art.

A farm mansion of 1772 was reconstructed in 1850, a task for which the advice of Gottfried Semper was sought; the latter also designed the covered walks of the flower garden on the east side of the mansion. It stands on the shores of the lake and forms the centre-piece of the estate. Stretches of water are also an essential element of the design at Branitz and contribute to the effectiveness of the open spaces of the park. The palace is joined to the park by a broad outdoor stairway.

An outstanding feature of Branitz are three tumuli, which are reminiscent of Egyptian pyramids. With them the designer gave a special tone to the landscape with an amazing effect.

Arkadia, Wilanow and other imitations
of the English garden

Arkadia, a few kilometres south-east of Lowicz, is one of the most famous Polish landscape gardens, "Dellile places it among the most beautiful gardens of Europe, and Polish poets like Trembecki and Niemcewicz called Arkadia 'an Ariosto poem come to life', 'a fabulous wonder', 'the land of Sybilla and the sorcerer', 'land of fairies and charm'. Arcadian landscapes were painted by Bacciarelli, Lampi, Grassi, Vogel, Norblin, Orlowski and Plersch, among others" (Ciołek).

Arkadia grew, from its beginnings in 1778 to its completion in 1821; it was the life's work of Princess Helena Radziwill, who devoted forty years to the construction of this landscape park. She was able to count on the help of famous experts and architects like Szymon Zug (1733 to 1807), Henryk Ittar and others. The park lies in a river lowland; its centre-piece is formed by a great lake with an island. This position offered an excellent opportunity to design the garden in romantic style, which accorded with the princess' inclinations. The only exception to this lay in the southern part of the park, with the orangery, the stables and the circus. Here it was more purpose-built, and a straight *allée* with walks going off at right angles was created.

She pointed out the various features in a "Park Guide": "Arkadia may be seen as an ancient monument to antique Greece. One recognizes traces of a mythological veneration, previously to be found in art. Nature, yielding up its own, has created lonely and romantical out-of-the-way places, here, where the soul overflows with desire to deify existing feelings or those that were awakened in the tender heart by the mysterious charm of sanctified groves. There is a fountain at the entrance, and the fruit trees surrounding it with shade remind us of Palaemon's refreshing spring."

Several buildings are set into the picturesque landscape. The Temple of Diana stands right next to the lake; the princess explains how to get there: "Philemon's garden forms the passageway to the temple dedicated to Nature... Art has surrounded it with ever blossoming wreaths, as a place destined for the chosen. Those who want to belong to this charmed circle should direct their steps along the path shaded by conifers, the nearer they get to Sibylla's cavern" (by this she means the grotto of Sibylla).

Both the building and the park were richly adorned with art treasures like "Etruscan vases, precious statues, authentic Greek and Roman pillars, friezes, capitals and sculptures from Morca which were all used as part of artificial ruins" (Ciołek).

In the period from 1799 to 1892, the famous seat of Wilanow near Warsaw belonged to the Potocki family. The garden, which had originally been constructed in the Baroque style, between the village and the lake, was redesigned by Stanislaw Kosta Potocki (1752–1821) as an English landscape park. His life's work also included — apart from the construction of the Wilanow garden — three little summer seats in this district: Natolin, Gucin and Morysin. Potocki was also called "the Polish Winckelmann" because of his unusual knowledge of architecture, archaeology, art, history and garden-craft.

A container for transporting plants; it protected exotic plants on long journeys by land and water.

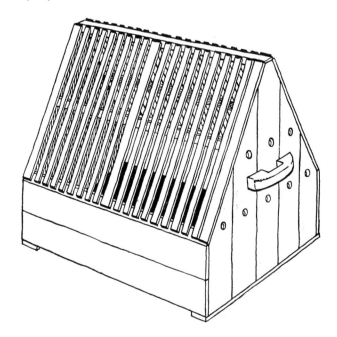

It was a great challenge for him to undertake the re-designing of Wiłanow in the English style, as the basic elements of the garden harmonized with the architecture of the palace and the other buildings. The approach ground to the palace was therefore left without any deep-seated alterations in its design. The main work related to the northern strip of the bank, which linked Wiłanow with the summer villa in Morysin. In 1799 Potocki began to erect an artificial island.

The years from 1806 to 1821 saw the emergence of very varied elements, e.g. a Chinese arbour, a Roman bridge and a memorial to the Battle of Raszyn. Many interesting answers were found to the problems involved, such as "perspectives" or vistas from the individual buildings. The buildings in the garden were created by Piotr Aigner with Wojciech Jaszczold as his co-designer (Ciołek).

On the southern shores of the Gulf of Finland lies the ensemble of palace and park of Oranienbaum (re-named Lomonossov in 1948). Its foundation goes back to Prince Alexandr Danilovich Menshikov (1673–1729), an in-fluential confidant of Czar Peter I. The construction of the park and the palace is closely connected with the foundation of St. Petersburg in 1703; both arose at the beginning of the 18th century and soon became the summer seat of Czarina Catherine II (1729–1796).

Before this, however, between 1710 and 1725, Prince Menshikov had the great palace — one of the most important Russian Baroque buildings — erected by M. Fontana (1701–1767) and G. Schedel (1680–1757); it was surrounded by formal gardens. As the successor to the throne — the later Czar Peter III (1728–1762) — took over the ensemble, he re-designed the park somewhat and had small buildings put up, like the stone hall, an enclosed tourney ground and an opera house. The last and most important structure was the palace itself, constructed between 1758 and 1762 under the guiding hand of A. Rinaldi.

It was only when Oranienbaum became the summer seat of the Russian czarina in 1762, that the park underwent an extension. The formally laid-out garden already showed signs of English taste. Now she had the upper park constructed. The most important erection in this part of the park is the Chinese Palace, created by A. Rinaldi between 1762 and 1768. It has been maintained in an exemplary condition and is of special significance because of its interior decoration.

One of the largest landscape gardens in the world is the park of Pavlovsk, situated near Leningrad. The construction was begun in 1782 when an obelisk was erected on the banks of the quiet little Slavyanka brook; it was designed by Charles Cameron, Catherine II's favourite architect. The obelisk carries the inscription: "The year 1777 started with the building of Pavlovskoye." It was in that year that Catherine presented this strip of land to her son, the later Czar Paul I (1754–1801).

The centre-piece of this 1,500-acre park is the Great Palace, a masterly construction that enthralls by its combination of monumentality and grace. Sixty-four white pillars support the flat dome of the building, whose centre section with a gallery is the work of Charles Cameron. The wings were added later by Vincenco Brenna.

This vessel, decorated with flowers and plants, served as a decorative element.

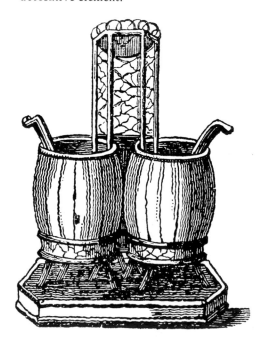

Pavlovsk impresses, above all, by its harmony and the great variety of impressions to be gained by a walk through the park grounds. In addition to the Great Palace there are a whole number of smaller structures, each a masterpiece, meriting detailed consideration.

According to Alpatov, "... the palace of Pavlovsk and the buildings in its park go back to the classical architecture of the 18th century". Further he states: "C. Cameron continued this latter tradition in the same way that the Greek tragic poets took up the ancient myths, or as the Italian masters of the Renaissance absorbed the idea of the iconographic Madonna types, which had arisen through the centuries. This creator of Pavlovsk saw it as his task to endow the classical elements with a new poetic sense, in a word — to transform the buildings thus to create a residential establishment on the banks of the Slavyanka, worthy of the age of Enlightenment."

Right next to the Great Palace lies the garden, divided into squares by its straight paths. The Pavilion of the Three Graces forms its main adornment; it was based on a design by Cameron and was erected after 1800, on the border of the estate. It is composed of sixteen white Ionic columns, which seem to form a frame for the group of the Three Graces. It differs from the Colonnade of Apollo, also to be found in the neighbourhood of the palace, "by the symmetry and porcelain-like delicacy of its forms" (Alpatov).

Drawing of the landscape park Arkadia in Poland from 1839.

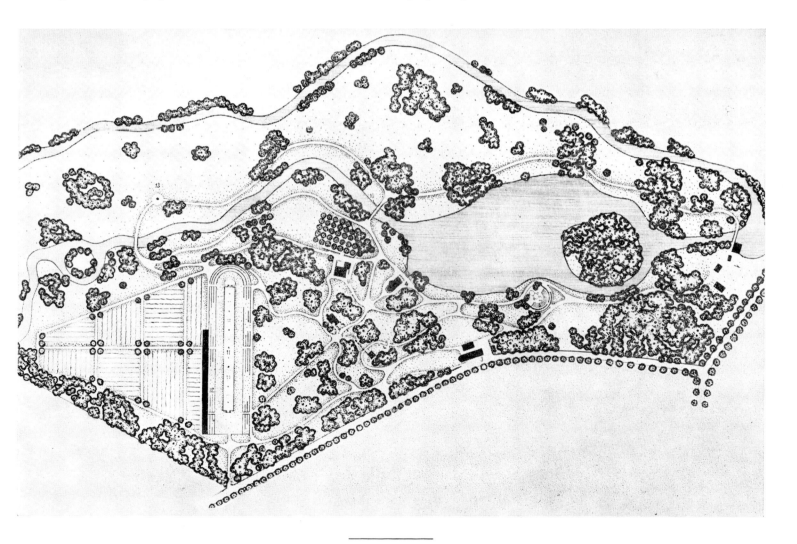

The colonnade appeared in 1783 on the hill above the Slavyanka brook, next to a tumbling cascade, and can be seen from afar. The waters of the Slavyanka reflect the Temple of Friendship, an attractive structure, built by Charles Cameron in 1782. This temple fits superbly into the surrounding landscape, and the trees around it are arranged in a way that it can easily be seen from quite distant places in the park. Apart from these structures with their joyous bright atmosphere there are others in the park that are memorials to the dead.

Although it was Cameron who initiated the lay-out of the park, in 1792 P. Gonzaga (1751–1831) took over the task of designing it, and his imprint is evident, above all, in the wooded areas. While architectural elements play a great role in Cameron's work and his park views are reminiscent of paintings by Claude Lorrain, it was Gonzaga who laid-out the great wooded tracts of land. He constructed walks, paths and glades through the woods, and had the faculty, through a masterly grasp of design, to produce the deceptive impression of depth. Unspoiled nature delighted him and he incorporated it in his design and thus enhanced its appeal. Indeed, it is often difficult to distinguish his park arrangements from their natural surroundings.

He grew trees in the valley of the Slavyanka and had paths laid-out; from those on the higher level south bank one can observe the north bank, beautifully lit up by the sun and looking most picturesque. It is precisely in autumn that Pavlovsk radiates its bewitching loveliness. The dark green of the conifers forms a wonderful contrast to the lively colours of the deciduous trees. It is the birch, oak, lime and aspen that stand out in this colourful display.

The park area containing the Rose Pavilion is given over, exclusively, to pine and birch. From here, the way leads in a straight line to the "White Birch", and it seems a coincidence that these two trees alternate to form the background scenery which opens out, here and there, to reveal the view of wide meadows, tree groups or woods. At the end of the path stands a big, luxuriant birch surrounded by twelve others of its kind.

There are also several parks in Czechoslovakia which, although they were originally laid-out in the formal style, were at a later date — in accordance with artistic tendencies — partly or completely re-fashioned as landscape parks. An outstanding example of this is the park of Lednice (known formerly by its German name, Eisgrub), whose buildings are strongly reminiscent of Antiquity.

The history of the castle park goes back to the 12th century. The castle stems from that time, to be rebuilt later as a Renaissance palace. After Prince Charles Eusebius had it once more rebuilt in 1666, it acquired a Baroque character. It was at this time, too, that the garden grounds were re-designed in the French style.

Radical modifications to the palace and park were completed in the 19th century, when Prince John I engaged the famous Viennese architect Josef Kornhäusel (1782 to 1860) to make alterations to the estate. It was at this time that the park was landscaped. Enormous sums were spent building a Roman aqueduct leading to a great pond, which was also an artificial creation. There was a river nearby offering obvious advantages, and this was drawn into the scheme. In the middle of the pond were sixteen islands of varying sizes.

The buildings had been constructed fairly rapidly, one after the other, and one of them, the Sun Temple — open on all sides — formed the centre-piece of the park. The 68-metre-high minaret, begun in an earlier period, was also completed by John I.

The baths were built in 1806; they incorporated a hall with sculpted figures and bathing cubicles. The Temple to the Muses, built for the prince in 1809, was decorated

Water machine on a roller for use on lawns and paths; it waters and rolls the ground at the same time.

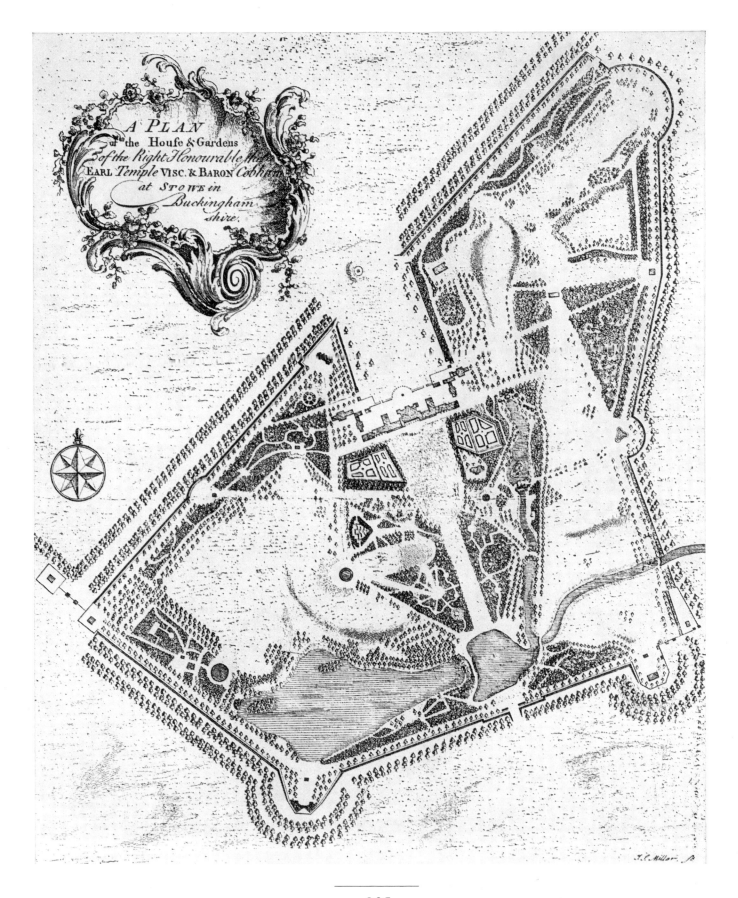

A PLAN of the House & Gardens of the Right Honourable the EARL Temple VISC. & BARON Cobham at STOWE in Buckinghamshire.

120   Stourhead in Wiltshire is one of the most beautiful
English landscape gardens, in which frequently changing
scenes offer new aspects to the viewer.

121   The park of castle Howard was originally laid-out in
formal style, but later partly re-arranged as landscape park.

122   The 2,500-acre Blenheim park contains this lake
constructed by Lancelot Brown as a setting for the Vanbrugh bridge.

123   Of all the oriental buildings by William Chambers,
the pagoda in Kew Gardens is still standing.

124   The hot-house in Kew Gardens,
designed by William Chambers in 1761.

125   In the 17th century Daniel Marot designed
the garden of Heemstede on level ground, which later was
to become a landscape garden.

126   Chinese Tower in the English Garden in Munich.

127   At Wilhelmshöhe, the buildings of the Löwenburg –
Lion Castle – are surrounded by an attractive landscape park.

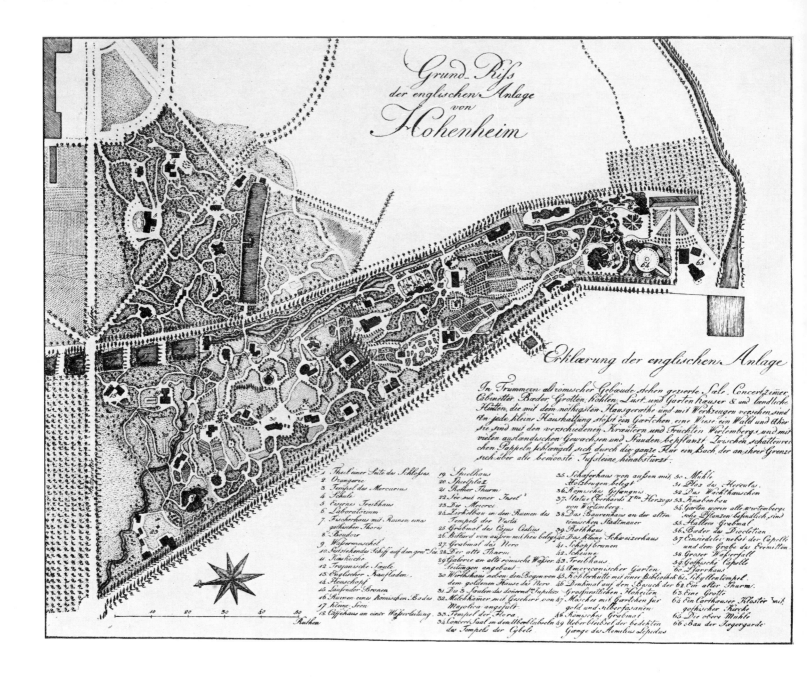

128   Plan of the 60- to 70-acre estate at Hohenheim
near Stuttgart (after Ruthen).

129   Grottoes and picturesque vistas are characteristic
of the widely spread grounds of the Wörlitz landscape park,
which covers an area of some 290 acres.

130   The lakes and canals in the park of Wörlitz
are crossed by little bridges.

243

131   In autumn, the Weimar park on the Ilm with its many
deciduous trees like maple, beech, oak, linden and chestnut
is turned into a sea of colours.

132   Prince Pückler-Muskau promised the citizens of Muskau
a park that would make the town a sight worth seeing
well into the distant future.

133   From the wooded slopes one has a wonderful view
of the temple, built in 1803, at Tiefurt park near Weimar.

134   The open-air theatre in the landscape park
at Schwetzingen near Heidelberg.

135   Aerial photograph of Sanssouci showing the Picture Gallery
with the formal garden embedded in landscaped wooded areas.

248

136 The landscape park at Pruhonice in Czechoslovakia
has an area of 765 acres and is divided in two by a road.
Stands of trees and great areas of lawn
are broken up by stretches of water.

137 A pergola obstructs the view of the raised garden
of the villa Charlottenhof in Sanssouci.

138 Harmonious interplay of architectural and garden elements
at the Roman Baths at Sanssouci.

140   This public park in Moscow with its numerous attractions
provides relaxation and recuperation.

141   The famous Central Park in New York provides distant views.

142   The Central Park offers sports possibilities
and meetings to followers of
American football, riders and ice-skaters.

143   The Italian terrace garden of the Villa Garzoni
in Collodi was laid-out in the second half of the 17th century
and inspired many garden designers and architects
to the present day.

Page 256:
144   The steps of natural stone at Tresco Abbey Gardens on the
Isle of Tresco (England) are bordered by decorative plants.

with statues by the Viennese sculptor Josef Klieber (1773 to 1850). This temple had to be dismantled when, in 1845, a new orangery (also called a palm house) took its place — part of the thorough-going reconstruction of the estate.

The plans for this were originated by the English architect P. H. Desvigues. Then, between 1870 and 1884, a parterre with a fountain and a rosarium were created in front of the palm house. Conifers were planted around it. Numerous other buildings attract the interest of the visitors to this extensive landscape park.

The radical social changes which took place in the course of the 19th century were accompanied by the constant growth of new demands in garden construction and their use. The ideas that lay behind the English landscape garden were later developed further in the establishment of public parks.

The demand for public parks

The rapid progress of industrialization in America and many countries of Europe, the pull of areas where industry was concentrated, the expanding cities with their worsening living conditions for a great number of their inhabitants placed new demands upon the art and practice of gardening.

Effect of the American example

The American example undoubtedly had a powerful effect on the creation of public parks. From the middle of the 19th century onwards, there was a growth of parks for the inhabitants of the great cities. It was precisely in such cities as New York, Washington, Philadelphia and Chicago that the problems of urban housing were already more urgent than in Europe. The fully developed iron and steel industries, the slaughter-houses and the meat canning factories of Chicago exerted a constant strain on the workers. New York with its skyscrapers and harbour facilities had to look for a compensation for the citizens. It was a question of "replacing" nature, as the negative effects of urbanization began to make themselves felt in a dangerous way.

Frederic Law Olmstedt

A leading planner and designer of these public parks was Frederic Law Olmstedt (1822–1903), an agronomist, social scientist and writer. He delved into the works of A. J. Dowing (1815–1852), published as early as 1840, concerning improvement of living conditions in urban areas, by the building of gardens and parks.

Olmstedt won a competition for designing the 650-acre Central Park in New York, jointly with the architect Vaux, and this laid the foundation-stone of modern town planning in America. He foresaw that Central Park — at that time on the outskirts of the city — would soon be surrounded by a great urban area, and laid down his planning principles with this in mind.

For him it was a question of creating opportunities for rest and relaxation, for sports and meetings and for instruction in a pleasant environment. So his plan contained a parade-ground, distant views, boating lakes which could also be used for ice-skating, flower gardens, promenades, an arboretum and paths for walking, riding and driving, whereby the crossing of the paths was avoided so that people did not get in each other's way.

In his other creations, Prospect Park in Brooklyn, the Riverside suburb in Chicago or Franklin Park in Boston, he applied the same principles, so that each of these later parks was to be but a single link in a chain of greenery that threaded its way through the whole urban area. It was in this connection that the idea of a so-called parkway was born; the individual parks were to be interconnected so that one could peacefully traverse the distance from one to the other along shady ways, without the noise and bustle of the city. His first opportunity to put this idea into practice was in the year 1896 when, together with his son, he was responsible for nineteen parks and parkways in Boston.

The suburb of Riverside in Chicago, covering an area of some 1,600 acres, became a garden city. Its purpose was not only to serve ecological and aesthetic ends but also to encourage communal and social intercourse. A river flowing through the whole area and its valley grounds became the connecting axis of a green belt.

Municipal parks in Europe

These American projects enticed emulation by the experts in Europe and formed the mainspring for new developments in Germany, too. One Wilhelm Benque, creator of the municipal park in Bremen, had worked on Central Park in New York under Olmstedt and his experiences now bore fruit in his own country. The design of the Bremen municipal park reveals elements like park buildings, arboured walks, a great pool — Lake Holler —, a landscaped lake, *allées,* playgrounds and the like, all typical of this kind of development.

While some garden designers of the 19th century copied the American model almost mechanically, a whole number of other designers rejected its basic principles vehemently.

One of these was Alfred Lichtwark (1852–1914) who, as director of the Hamburg Kunsthalle (Hall of Art), also played a lively part in architectural matters as well as those of contemporary garden design. A start was made with the Hamburg municipal park, in 1910, based on plans by Fritz Schumacher, but Lichtwark contributed ideas, too. This is the outstanding example of a municipal park arising on the threshold of the 20th century. Of this, Schumacher writes the following in his publication *Ein Volkspark — dargestellt am Hamburger Stadtpark* (Hamburg municipal park — a people's park): "It was now the task of the designers to put flesh on the bones and with the conception of how a people's park should come into being, the difference from other parks had to stand out clearly ... The aims lying behind the idea of such a park were not achieved if they were merely able to produce a terrain for a pleasant stroll; they were only achieved if, at the same time, they were able to design an area which was pleasant to inhabit, that is to say an area which could be occupied and was suitable for the most varied activities of life, that may be encompassed in the expression: recreation."

Ideas about public parks were not new in Germany. In 1780, Hirschfeld put forward the conception in his work *Theorie der Gartenkunst* (The theory of garden art) in the following way:

"According to the sensible opinion of the police, these people's gardens must be seen as an important necessity for the town dweller. Not only do they refresh his senses after a day's toil, with charming sights and agreeable sensations, they also imperceptibly entice him away both from the crude and the refined leisure pursuits of urban life by drawing him towards nature's showplace, and gradually accustom him to more worthwhile pleasures, to a gentler social intercourse, where he can become a communicative, social being ... Here everybody is able to claim his right to enjoy nature unhindered."

In this way, Hirschfeld made it clear that he thought all strata of society should use these parks. The first public park to appear in Germany was the English Garden in Munich. It was already in construction in 1729 but was only completed in 1804 by Von Sckell (see p. 223/24). Lenné, too, began to create public parks; in 1824 he planned the Klosterberge Garden in Magdeburg. This may be seen as setting the trend for the development of parks of this kind.

In the grounds of a former Benedictine monastery, there grew up a large park of 120 acres. The town was intentionally included in the design and there was a community house which was used as a restaurant and as a venue for meetings and festivities.

Around this building, which was designed by Schinkel, Lenné grouped trees in a kind of grove. Although most of the park was evidently of landscape design, here it acquired a formal section as a complement, and in this way Lenné laid a remarkable foundation-stone for a public park.

The demand for parks, for children's play-grounds, for allotments, in a word — for places of rest and recuperation for the citizens, was vociferous in Germany. A real people's park movement arose which resulted in a whole number of parks being built in Bremen, Hamburg, Cologne, Magdeburg, Berlin and Munich. This meant that the special privilege of the ruling strata — that only they had the right to construct and make use of gardens — was finally broken.

The combination of formal and informal elements

At the end of the seventies of the 19th century it was Gustav Meyer (1816–1877) who made an outstanding contribution to the development of the public park and gained great credit thereby. He worked for many years with Lenné in the latter's planning office and is regarded as his legitimate successor. In 1870 he was appointed Director of Gardens to the City of Berlin.

Now he began to put his theories, published in his *Lehrbuch der schönen Gartenkunst* (Textbook on the beautiful art of gardening), into practice. Humboldthain, Friedrichshain (*Hain* = grove) and Treptower Park appeared. Thus, in his short period of office (1870–1877), Gustav Meyer completed — or at least made a start on — parks covering an area of around 250 acres.

In Meyer's conception it was quite acceptable to have formal garden elements and free landscape forms next to each other. He only came down definitely on the side of formal arrangement when buildings were concerned. This was already a pointer to aspects of design that led to fierce arguments as to whether or not formal compositions should be introduced into landscape parks. Lenné, the outstanding exponent of garden culture in the 19th century, gave currency to both styles and gave impressive evidence of the aesthetic value of these forms, with his Roman Baths, at Charlottenhof and with the Sicilian and Nordic gardens at Sanssouci.

An interesting example of the use of formal elements in design is the hippodrome borrowed, as it were, from the gardens of Pliny (see p. 48). Lenné used it at Charlottenhof as an item of decoration. Meyer never failed to include it in his Berlin parks, not as a decorative way of presenting an open space, but as a mown meadow or lawn for activity or rest (Karg). This is not surprising, for in his above-mentioned book he propagated the idea that the people's garden must also provide the opportunity for outdoor activities. So he recommended places for playing ball, racing tracks and provision for gymnastics. For recreation and social intercourse, meadows or lawns had to be provided.

He desired everything to be situated in pleasant surroundings; this was to give an inviting over-all impression to be achieved by planting artificial groves. He warned against the erection of restaurants for serving refreshments "so as not to reduce the recreational area to a romping ground".

Villa gardens augment the public parks

In addition to the public parks, there appeared a ring of house and villa gardens in the ever expanding cities, which was the outcome of economic development. It was here, above all, that the *nouveau riche* bourgeoisie settled and created a world of their own. They used the municipal parks but little, and surrounded their villas with large gardens and grounds which formed a kind of green belt around the towns. These villa gardens reflect the taste of their owners, who took the great aristocratic gardens as their model and kept its design in their mind's eye; the result was a wide variation of styles. Some gardens were orientated on the classical world; other owners preferred Baroque or Renaissance motifs or took the English landscape garden as their model. They seldom reproduced exactly any specific style in the art of gardening *en miniature,* so to speak; instead, they took up certain elements only. Curved stairways, baroque vases and waterworks were introduced; there was no lack of plaster, concrete or sandstone statues of the gods, either. This often arbitrary choice of individual garden elements has meant that villa gardens from the turn of the century to the present day are frequently eclectic in nature. These gardens have a pleasing effect, thanks to the profusion of flowers. We find an abundance of colours and plant varieties there which give these villa gardens an unmistakable note. In the 20th century, the public park movement created open spaces that would correspond to the citizens' desires, not only for rest and recreation but also for sports facilities and playgrounds. Social needs, the present state of urban public hygiene, the demand for anti-pollution measures must all be taken into account and tackled jointly by landscape planners and garden architects.

Bibliography

Selection of the literary sources used.

Alberti, B.: *Opere volgari, della famiglia ed. Bonucci*. Florence, 1845–1849.

"Alcuini... carmina", in: *Monumenta germaniae historica etc. (Poetorum Latinorum medii aeri)*. 1877.

Allinger, G.: *Das Hohelied von Gartenkunst und Gartenbau*. Berlin (West), Hamburg, 1963.

Alpatow, M. W.: "Über die westeuropäische und russische Kunst. Beiträge zur Geschichte", in: *Fundus-Bücher* 80/81. Dresden, 1982.

Argenville, A. J. D. d': *La théorie et la pratique du jardinage*. Paris, 1709.

Attiret, J.-D.: *Lettres Edifiantes*. Vol. XXVII, p. 749, 1749.

Aurenhammer, H.: *Ikonographie und Ikonologie des Wiener Belvederegartens. Wiener Jahrbuch für Kunstgeschichte* 17, pp. 86 ff., 1956.

Bābar, Emperor of Hindostan: The Bābarnāma in English. London, 1922.

Bacon, F.: *Bacon's Essays*. London, 1877.

Behling, L.: *Die Pflanze in der mittelalterlichen Tafelmalerei*. Weimar, 1957.

Berckenhagen, E.: "Bildnis und Lebensabriss berühmter Gärtner", in: *Das Gartenamt* 11, 1962.

Bernoulli, J.: "Edler v. Rothenstein, Reise nach Bayern im Jahre 1781", in: *Archiv für neuere Geschichte* 3, p. 271, 1786.

Berrall, J. S.: *Die schönsten Gärten*. Vienna, 1969.

Bertram, M.: *Die Technik der Gartenkunst*. Berlin, 1902.

Biesalski, E.: "Urblumen der Menschheit", in: *Antike und Abendland* 11, p. 63, 1962.

Black, D., and C. Loreless: *Woven Gardens,* London, 1979.

Bleibtreu, E.: *Die Flora der neuassyrischen Reliefs*. Vienna, 1980.

Boeck, W.: *Alte Gartenkunst. Eine Kulturgeschichte in Beispielen*. Leipzig, 1939.

Böttger, l. G.: *Triumph der schönsten Gartenkunst*. Leipzig, 1800.

Boyceau, J.: *Traité du jardinage*. Paris, 1638.

Brachvogel, A. E.: *Aus drei Jahrhunderten. Historische Novellen*. Schwerin, 1870.

Capelle, W.: *Der Garten des Theophrast. Festschrift für Friedrich Zucker*. Berlin (West), 1954.

Caus, I. de: *Hortus Pembrochianus*. No place, 1615.

Caus, S. de: *Hortus Palatinus*. Frankfurt, 1620.

Chambers, W.: *Über die orientalische Gartenkunst*. Gotha, 1775.

Ciołek, G.: *Gärten in Polen*. 1st Part: *Inhalts- und Gestaltsentwicklung*. Warsaw, 1954.

Clifford, D.: *Geschichte der Gartenkunst*. Munich, 1966.

Coats, P.: *Great Gardens*. Frankfurt/Main, 1964.

Cowell, F. R.: *Gartenkunst. Von der Antike bis zur Gegenwart*. Stuttgart, 1979.

Davies, N. M.: *Ancient Egyptian Painting*. Chicago, 1936.

Dehio, G.: *Handbuch der deutschen Kunstdenkmäler*. Vol. 1, 3rd edition, Berlin, 1924.

Dickie, J.: "The Hispano-Arab Gardens, its Philosophy and Function", in: *Bulletin of the School of Oriental Studies,* XXXI, 1968.

Dubjago, T. B.: *Russki reguljarnye i parki*. Leningrad, 1963.

Eberle, W.: *Schöne alte Gärten*. Bayreuth, 1979.

Erasmus von Rotterdam: *Convivium religiosum*. No place, 1518.

Etienne, R.: *Das Leben in Pompeji*. Stuttgart, 1974.

Evans, A.: *The Palace of Minos*. London, 1921–1936.

Fabos, G., and G. T. Milde: *Frederic Law Olmstedt, Founder of Landscape Architecture in America*. University of Massachusetts, 1968.

Fischer, H.: *Mittelalterliche Pflanzenkunde*. Munich, 1929.

Fitch, J. M.: *Treasury of American Gardens*. New York, 1956.

Fox, H. M.: *André le Nôtre. Garden Architect to Kings*. London, 1962.

Friedell, E.: *Aufklärung und Revolution. Kulturgeschichte der Neuzeit*. Munich, 1961.

Furttenbach, J.: *Architectura civilis*. Ulm, 1628.

Furttenbach, J.: *Furttenbach Mannhafter Kunstspiegel*. Augsburg, 1633.

Ganzenmüller, W.: *Das Naturgefühl im Mittelalter*. Berlin, Leipzig, 1914.

Gielen, P., and E. Levy: *Muster-Album der modernen Teppichgärtnerei*. Leipzig, 1896.

Das Gilgamesch-Epos. Translated by A. Ungnad, with a commentary by H. Gressmann, Göttingen, 1911. In: *Forschungen zur Religion und Literatur des alten und neuen Testaments*. No. 19.

Glinka, J.: *Choroszsz — letnia rezydencja hetmánska w XVIII wieku. Biuletyn Historii Sztuki i Kultury*, VI. Warsaw, 1938.

Gollwitzer, G.: *Gartenlust. Zeugnisse aus 2 Jahrtausenden*. Munich, 1956.

Gothein, M. L.: *Geschichte der Gartenkunst*. 2 vols., Jena, 1914.

Gothein, M. L.: *Indische Gärten*. Munich, 1928.

Günther, H.: "Peter J. Lennés Arbeiten am Volksgarten in Magdeburg", in: *Deutsche Gartenarchitektur*, 6, No. 2, 1965.

Hager, L.: *Nymphenburg*. Munich, no date.

Hager, L.: "Nymphenburg, Schloss, Park und Burgen", in: *Amtl. Führer*, Munich, 1961.

Hallbaum, F.: *Der Landschaftsgarten*. Munich, 1927.

Harado, J.: *Japanese Gardens*. Boston, 1956.

Hennebo, D., and A. Hoffmann: *Geschichte der deutschen Gartenkunst*. Vols. 1–3, Hamburg, 1962/63.

Heyne, M.: *Fünf Bücher deutscher Hausaltertümer*. Vols. 1–3, Leipzig, 1899.

Hinz, F.: "Peter Joseph Lenné und seine bedeutendsten Schöpfungen in Berlin und Potsdam", in: *Kunstwiss. Studien*, XXII, Berlin, 1937.

Hirschfeld, C. C. L.: *Theorie der Gartenkunst*. Vols. I–V, Leipzig, 1777–1782.

Hohnholz, J.: *Der englische Park als landschaftliche Erscheinung*. Tübingen, 1964.

Hokky-Sallay, M.: *Das Schloss Eszterházy in Fertöd*. Budapest, 1979.

Holzhauer, H.: *Gärten und Parks in Weimar*. Weimar, 1971.

Homer: *Ilias und Odyssee*. Translated by Johann Heinrich Voss. Munich, 1957.

Hrdlička, Z., Hrdličková, V., and Z. Thoma: *Japanische Gartenkunst*. Prague, 1981.

Ismail, I. M.: *Die Gärten der alten Ägypter und die Entwicklung der Bewässerung bis zum Hochdamm bei Assuan*. University Thesis, Munich, 1960.

Ito, T.: *The Japanese Gardens*. New Haven, 1972.

Jäger, H.: *Gartenkunst und Gärten sonst und jetzt*. Berlin, 1888.

Johnson, H.: *Das grosse Buch der Gartenkunst*. Stuttgart, 1980.

Josephson, R.: *L'architecte du Charles XII, Nicodemus Tessin, à la Court de Louis XIV*. Stockholm, 1930.

Jünger, F. H.: *Gärten im Abend- und Morgenland*. Munich, 1960.

Justi, C.: *Diego Velásquez und sein Jahrhundert*. Bonn, 1888.

Kann, P.: *Die Umgebung Leningrads. Reiseführer*. Moscow, 1981.

Karg, D.: *Der Schlosspark von Rheinsberg*. Rheinsberg, 1981.

Kaufmann, A.: *Der Gartenbau im Mittelalter und während der Renaissance*. Berlin, 1892.

Keller, H.: *Kleine Geschichte der Gartenkunst*. Berlin (West), Hamburg, 1976.

Kirchner, G. F.: "Das Karlsruher Schloss als Residenz und Musensitz", in: *Veröff. d. Kommission für Geschichte und Landeskunde Baden-Württemberg*, Series B, 8, 1959.

Kirschen, F.: *Weltwunder der Baukunst in Babylonien und Ionien*. Tübingen, 1956.

Kisky, H.: "Die Baugeschichte des Brühler Schlosses", in: *Kurfürst Clemens August, Landesherr und Mäzen des 18. Jh.* Cologne, 1961.

Klebs, L.: *Die Reliefs und Malereien des mittleren Reiches, VII.–XVII. Dynastie*. Heidelberg, 1934.

Koldewey, R.: "Die Königsburgen von Babylon", in: *54. Wiss. Veröff. d. deutschen Orient-Gesellschaft*. Leipzig, 1934.

Kreisel, H.: *Der Rokokogarten zu Veitshöchheim*. Munich, 1953.

Křiž, Z.: *Berühmte Parks Nordböhmens*. Ostrava, 1971.

Kuča, O.: *Zur Entwicklung der europäischen Park- und Gartenlandschaft*. Berlin, 1974.

Kühn, M.: *Schloss Charlottenburg*. Berlin, 1955.

Landau, P.: "Der Gartenbaumeister des Wiederaufbaus (J. Furttenbach)", in: *Gartenschönheit*, 9, p. 449, 1928.

Lauter-Bufe, H.: "Zur architektonischen Gartengestaltung in Pompeji und Herculaneum", in: *Sonderdruck aus Neue Forschungen in Pompeji*. Recklinghausen, edited by Deutsches Archäologisches Institut, Vienna, pp. 169 ff.

Law, E.: *The History of Hampton Court Palace in Tudor Time*. London, 1883.

Lenné, P. J.: *Über die Anlage eines Volksgartens bei der Stadt Magdeburg*. Berlin, 1825.

Lenoir, A.: *Architecture monastique*. Paris, 1852.

Leontev, P. V.: *Die Parks der Moldau*. Kisinev, 1967.

Leppmann, W.: *Pompeji*. Munich, 1966.

Le Liber Pontificalis. Edited by L. Duchesne. Athens, 1886.

Lohmeyer, K.: *Südwestdeutsche Gärten des Barock und der Romantik mit ihren in- und ausländischen Vorbildern*. Saarbrücken, 1937.

Lorris, G. de: *Der Roman von der Rose (Roman de la rose)*. Vienna, Prague, Leipzig, 1921.

Magnus, A.: *De vegetabilibus*. Edited by E. Meyer and C. Jessen. Berlin, 1867.

Mánkowski, T.: *O poglądach na sztukę w czasach Stanisława Augusts*. Lwów, 1929.

Martin, F.: "Schloss Hellbrunn bei Salzburg", in: *Österr. Kunstbücher* 28, Vienna, Augsburg, 1927.

Masson, G.: *Italienische Gärten*. Munich, Zurich, 1962.

Meister, G.: *Der Orientalisch-indiani-sche Kunst- und Lustgärtner.* Weimar, 1973.

Meyer, F. S., and F. Ries: *Die Garten-kunst in Wort und Bild.* Leipzig, 1904.

Meyer, R.: *Hecken- und Gartentheater in Deutschland im 17. und 18. Jahr-hundert.* Emstetten, 1934.

Migge, L.: *Die Gartenkultur des 20. Jahrhunderts.* Jena, 1913.

Möbius, M.: "Pflanzenbilder der Mi-noischen Kunst in botanischer Be-trachtung", in: *Jahrbuch des Deut-schen Archäologischen Instituts* 49, 1933.

Mollet, A.: *Le jardin de plaisir.* Stock-holm, 1651.

Neubauer, E.: *Die Lustgärten des Ba-rocks.* Salzburg, 1966.

Newson, S.: *A Thousand Years of Japanese Gardens.* Tokyo, 1957.

Oehmischen, F.: "Ein Park — Beginn der modernen amerikanischen Stadtpla-nung", in: *Garten und Landschaft,* 12, Munich, 1973.

Oertel, F.: *Schloss Nymphenburg.* Mu-nich, 1899.

Orthmann, W.: *Der Alte Orient.* Berlin, Frankfurt/Main, Vienna, 1975.

Osten, H. von: *Der niederländische Gar-ten.* Hanover, 1706.

Patterson, G.: *The Gardens of the Great Moghuls.* London, 1972.

Plinius, C. S. G.: "Epistularum libri de-cem", in: *Lat.-dt. Briefe,* translated by H. Kasten, Munich, 1968.

Pope, A. U.: *A Survey of Persian Art.* Oxford, 1938–1939.

Pückler-Muskau, H. von: *Andeutungen über Landschaftsgärtnerei.* Stuttgart, 1834.

Rachum, I.: *Illustrierte Enzyklopädie der Renaissance.* Königstein/Taunus, 1980.

Repton, H.: *Observations on the Theory and Practice of Landscape Gardening.* London, 1803.

Repton, H.: *Sketches and Hints on Landscape Gardening.* London, 1794.

Rohlfs, G., and A. Rohlfs von Wittich: *Die schönsten Gärten in Deutschland.* Stuttgart, 1967.

Rommel, A.: *Die Entstehung des klassi-schen französischen Gartens im Spiegel der Sprache.* Berlin, 1954.

Rüthy, A. E.: *Die Pflanzen und ihre Teile in biblisch-hebräischem Sprach-gebrauch.* Bern, 1942.

Sanssouci. Schlösser, Gärten, Kunst-werke. Edited by Generaldirektion der Staatlichen Schlösser und Gärten Potsdam-Sanssouci with a team of authors directed by H.-I. Giersberg, Potsdam, 1975.

Schnack, F.: *Der glückselige Gärtner.* Düsseldorf, 1952.

Schöchle, A.: *Pflanzenleben und -pflege in der Wilhelma (Stuttgart).* Stuttgart, 1937.

Schöchle, A.: *Blühendes Barock in Lud-wigsburg.* Stuttgart, 1956.

Schüttauf, H.: *Parks und Gärten in der DDR.* Leipzig, 1969.

Sckell, L. von: *Beiträge zur bildenden Gartenkunst.* Munich, 1825.

Semler, C. A.: *Ideen zu einer Garten-logik.* 2nd edition, Leipzig, 1803.

Shen, F.: *Six Chapters of a Floating Life. Tien Hsia Monthly,* 1935.

Sierp, H.: "Walahfrid Strabos Gedicht über den Gartenbau", in: *Die Kultur der Abtei Reichenau. Erinnerungs-schrift zur 1200. Wiederkehr des Gründungsjahres des Insel-Klosters, 724–1924.* Munich, 1925.

Sirén, O.: *Gardens of China.* New York, 1949.

Słowenik Geograficzny Królestwa. Polskiego i innych krajów słowiańs-kich … pod redakeya F. Sulimierskiego, B. Chlebowskiego i W. Walewaskiego. Vols. I–XIV, 2 Supplements, Warsaw, 1880–1902.

Sörensen, W.: "Gärten und Pflanzen im Klosterplan", in: *Studien zum St. Gal-lener Klosterplan.* St. Gallen, 1962.

Stadler, H.: *Dioscorides Langobardus,* II, III, IV, V. Erlangen, 1897.

Strabo, W.: *Des Walahfrid von der Rei-chenau Hortulus.* Munich, 1926.

Sühnel, R.: *Der Park als Gesamtkunst-werk des englischen Klassizismus.* Heidelberg, 1977.

Sulze, H.: "Die Dresdner Barockgärten an der Elbe", in: *Jahrbuch zur Pflege der Künste,* 2nd Series, pp. 173 ff., 1954.

Thacker, C.: *Die Geschichte der Gärten.* Zurich, 1979.

The Tuzuk-i-Jahangiri. Memoirs of Ja-hangir. Delhi, 1968.

Tuckermann, W. P.: *Die Gartenkunst der italienischen Renaissance-Zeit.* Berlin, 1884.

Ungnad, A., Ranke, H., and H. Gress-mann: *Altorientalische Texte und Bil-der.* Tübingen, 1909.

Verzillin, N. M.: *Po sadam i parkam mira.* Leningrad, 1961.

Vitruvius, P.: *Zehn Bücher über Archi-tektur.* Translated and supplemented with notes by Curt Fensterbusch. Ber-lin, 1964.

Wagner, E.: "Das Neue Palais in Pots-dam-Sanssouci", in: *Urania,* No. 8, pp. 25–29, 1981.

Walpole, H.: *On Modern Gardening.* London, 1789.

Winogradowa, N., and N. Nikolajewa: *Kunst des Fernen Ostens.* Dresden, Moscow, 1980.

Woenig, F.: *Die Pflanzen im alten Aegyp-ten.* Leipzig, 1886.

Wolffhardt, E.: *Beiträge zur Pflanzen-symbolik. Zeitschrift für Kunstwissen-schaft* 8, No. 3/4, 1954.

Wundram, M.: *Renaissance. Belser Stil-geschichte.* Herrsching, 1981.

Yoshida Tetsuro: *Der Japanische Garten.* Tübingen, 1963.

Sources of Illustrations

ADN, Zentralbild 103, 140
Aerofilms, London 118
Alinari, Florence 12, 14, 21, 22
Amtliches Französisches Verkehrsbüro,
    Frankfurt/Main 45, 59
Artothek Hinrichs, Planegg 24
Ashmolean Museum, Oxford 17
Bavaria Verlag, Munich 47, 51, 143, 144
Bergmann, Klaus, Potsdam 92, 93, 137,
    138, 139
Bildarchiv Preussischer Kulturbesitz,
    Berlin (West) 8
Breitenborn, Dieter, Berlin 2, 3
British Library, London 31, 33
British Museum, London 1, 6, 114
Brockhaus Verlag, Leipzig p. 139
BTA, London 48, 56, 116, 120–124
Deutsche Fotothek, Dresden 16, 25, 43, 73
    75, 76, 81, 82, 86, 94, 99, 134, pp. 113,
    147
Deutsche Staatsbibliothek, Berlin
    pp. 216, 217, 219, 227
Deutsches Museum, Munich 60
ENIT, Frankfurt/Main 36–39, 41, 71
Fabri, Milan 35
flora-Bild, Offenburg 58, 95, 96
Grambow, Axel, Berlin pp. 59, 118, 224,
    226
Hänse, Ingrid, Leipzig 98, 101, pp. 49,
    91, 111, 112, 120, 123, 135, 188, 225,
    232
Herzog August Bibliothek, Wolfenbüttel 32
Interfoto, Budapest 78
Japanische Fremdenverkehrszentrale,
    Frankfurt/Main p. 205

Jürgens, Karl-Heinz, Cologne 50, 83,
    84, 88, 90, 91, 126, 128
Lavaud, J. A., Paris 57
MAS, Barcelona 29, 30, 44, 69
Matt, Leonhard von, Bouchs 11
Museum für Geschichte der Stadt Leipzig
    p. 218
National Portrait Gallery, London 117
Nerlich, Günter, Berlin 104–112, 115
Östasiatiska Museet, Stockholm 100
Österreichische Fremdenverkehrswer-
    bung, Vienna 72, 74
Petri, Joachim, Leipzig 26, 27, 62, p. 28
Plessing, Carin, Leipzig 102
Portugiesisches Touristik-Amt, Frank-
    furt/Main 42, 70
Publisher's archives 18, 28, pp. 12, 26,
    55, 58, 72, 79, 85, 119, 125, 126, 127,
    145, 215
Reinhold, Gerhard, Mölkau 34
Rössing-Winkler, Leipzig 52, 55, 66, 68,
    80, 89, 129, 130, 132, 133, ill. on half-
    title
Scala, Antella, Florence 10, 15, 19, 20
Sembritzki, Christa, Leipzig p. 69
Sickert, Anton, Innsbruck 49
Staatliche Museen zu Berlin 4, 5, 7, 9, 23,
    113
Watz, Jørgen, Lyngby 63, 65
Wengel, Tassilo, Berlin 13, 53, 54, 67,
    77, 79, 131, 136
Willmann, Lothar, Berlin 85, 97, 135
ZEFA, Düsseldorf 141, 142

The other illustrations were taken from
the books mentioned in the following:

Bleibtreu, E.: *Die Flora der neuassyri-
    schen Reliefs.* Vienna, 1980, pp. 16, 25
Böttger, I. G.: *Triumph der schönsten
    Gartenkunst.* Leipzig, 1800, p. 227
Garies Davies, N. de: *Two Ramesside
    Tombs at Thebes.* New York, 1927, ill. 2, 3
Gielen, P., and E. Levy: *Muster-Album
    der modernen Teppichgärtnerei.* Leip-
    zig, 1896, p. 121
Gothein, M. L.: *Geschichte der Garten-
    kunst.* Vols. 1/2, Jena, 1914, pp. 13, 56,
    79, 80, 88, 89, 111, 112, 117, 122, 129,
    132, 143
Hirth, G.: *Kulturgeschichtliches Bilder-
    buch aus vier Jahrhunderten.* Vol. 1,
    Leipzig, 1923, p. 91
Jäger, H.: *Gartenkunst und Gärten sonst
    und jetzt.* Berlin, 1888, ill. 119, 128
Loudon, J. C.: *An Encyclopaedia of
    Gardening.* Parts I and II, London,
    no date, pp. 29, 49, 135, 188, 225, 230, 232
Meyer, F. S., and F. Ries: *Die Gartenkunst
    in Wort und Bild.* Leipzig, 1904, p. 46
Sirén, O.: *Gardens of China.* New York,
    1949, ill. 101, p. 202
Slowenik Geograficzny Królestwa. War-
    saw, 1880–1902, p. 231
Tuckermann, W. P.: *Die Gartenkunst der
    italienischen Renaissance-Zeit.* Berlin,
    1884, p. 48
Woenig, F.: *Die Pflanzen im alten
    Ägypten.* Leipzig, 1886, pp. 10, 13, 14, 15

Index